MATHILDE FAST...
ØYSTEIN SØRENSEN

The Norwegian Exception?

Norway's Liberal Democracy Since 1814

HURST & COMPANY, LONDON

First published in the United Kingdom in 2021 by
C. Hurst & Co. (Publishers) Ltd.,
83 Torbay Road, London, NW6 7DT
© Mathilde Fasting and Øystein Sørensen, 2021
All rights reserved.

Printed and bound in Great Britain by Bell & Bain Ltd, Glasgow

The right of Mathilde Fasting and Øystein Sørensen to be identified as
the authors of this publication is asserted by them in accordance with the
Copyright, Designs and Patents Act, 1988.

Distributed in the United States, Canada and Latin America by
Oxford University Press, 198 Madison Avenue, New York, NY 10016,
United States of America.

A Cataloguing-in-Publication data record for this book
is available from the British Library.

This book is printed using paper from registered sustainable
and managed sources.

ISBN: 9781787385603

www.hurstpublishers.com

CONTENTS

CONTENTS

INTRODUCTION

Norway is among the richest, happiest and best functioning liberal democracies in the world. Is there anything exceptional in Norway's development through the last 200 years or so, compared to other relatively small Western European democratic countries? Has Norway been blessed with exceptional luck? Have Norwegians done something extraordinary that other Western democracies have not been able to do, and if so, what? In this book we explore how Norwegian society developed from a province in a large, composite multi-ethnic state, governed from Copenhagen—a small underdog—to an independent and economically strong nation.

The traditional explanation for the name Norway (*Norge*) has been 'the road towards north', or 'the Northern land'. However, recent explanations contest this, suggesting instead that *nor* means a 'strait, inlet or a waterway or fjord,' also found in the English 'narrow', which then means that Norway is the road along narrow inlets. Geographically, the borders of Norway have been relatively stable throughout history, and the idea of a unified Norway has existed since the early Middle Ages. Certainly, Norwegians have always thought of themselves as a *folk* excluding the land's Sami people, Swedes and Danes.

THE NORWEGIAN EXCEPTION?

In the Viking Age—from the arrival of Norwegian Vikings at Lindisfarne in 793 CE, until the failed Norwegian invasion of England in 1066—Norwegians expanded mostly westwards across the North Sea and Northern Atlantic. In the eighth and ninth centuries, there were several regional Viking kingdoms in Norway. The story goes that in around 870 CE the first King Harald promised his future wife that he would not cut his hair until Norway was unified, even if this unification likely wouldn't include the whole of Norway. He cut his hair and became known as King Harald 'Fairhair', and throughout the late Middle Ages Norway became an important Northern European power, with several strong kings and North Sea colonies including Iceland, Greenland, Shetland and the Faroe Islands. King Magnus Lagabøter—'the lawmaker'—institutionalized a strong rule of law and private property in the 1270s, building on the oldest Nordic law from the *Gulating* legislative assembly in Western Norway. In the Viking Age and medieval times, free Norwegian men regularly met at the *ting*: bargaining, compromising, solving conflicts and making laws.

From the early fourteenth century, Norway became involved in dynastic and political unions with her neighbours Sweden and Denmark. Especially after the Black Death in the mid-fourteenth century, the Norwegian economy, aristocracy and political institutions declined rapidly. Thought to have wiped out around a third of the population, the plague drastically reduced Norway's political and religious capacity; one bishop and two *lagmenn* (judges) remained, while the chancellor was the only surviving member of his council. This left Norway vulnerable politically, and from the 1530s Norway was both de facto and de jure ruled by Denmark.

Our story begins with the end of the absolutist dual kingdom of Denmark-Norway and Norway's emergence as a separate polity. Since the Danish-dominated monarchy had become involved in the Napoleonic Wars on the side of the vanquished French, Denmark was forced to cede Norway to Sweden in January 1814. A Norwegian insurrection against this treaty after the Napoleonic Wars, led by Christian Frederik—the Danish heir to the throne and Governor-General in Norway—ended in the proclamation of a new Norwegian state with a liberal, monarchical constitution. The new Norwegian kingdom was forced later in 1814 to accept a union with Sweden, but this was a loose alliance and Norway kept its own Constitution and political autonomy. The political system established in 1814 was not strictly a democracy, as it is not possible to talk about democracy in a modern sense before universal suffrage was introduced in 1898 for men and in 1913 for women. Yet Norway's journey to liberal democracy began in 1814, and as this book will show, these roots are still evident in Norwegian culture, society, politics and economics. The union was dissolved peacefully in 1905, and by this time Norway had transformed into an industrialized, capitalist society with a parliamentary democracy; during the twentieth century, the welfare state became substantial. Norway was neutral under the First World War and occupied during the Second World War, and oil was first discovered in the North Sea in 1969, making the country one of the richest in the world. At the time of writing, Norway is the only Scandinavian country that is not a member of the European Union. In 200 years, Norway went from being a country dominated first by Denmark, and then by Sweden, to becoming the richest of the three.

The national myth and anthem

The national myth is that Norwegians were few and poor, heroically fighting their way to independence, democracy and prosperity. Foreign countries wished to dominate the Norwegians and strong forces had to be defeated. First, our ancestors man-

aged to free themselves from Denmark and secure a liberal constitution, then Norway seceded from the union with Sweden
almost 100 years later. The country was occupied by the Nazis
during the Second World War but endured this as well.

All in all, Norwegians have struggled and succeeded. The
Norwegian national anthem builds heavily on this myth, as is
clear from the last two verses:

> Norwegian man in house and cabin,
> thank your great God!
> The country he wanted to protect,
> although things looked dark.
> All the fights fathers have fought,
> and the mothers have wept,
> the Lord has quietly moved
> so we won our rights.
>
> Yes, we love this country
> as it rises forth,
> rugged, weathered, above the sea,
> with those thousand homes.
> And as the fathers' struggle has raised
> it from need to victory,
> even we, when it is demanded,
> for its peace will encamp (for defence).[1]

The anthem remains important and is often sung all over
Norway, especially on the national Constitution Day (17 May).
The Norwegian self-image is that of a humanitarian power, a
peace negotiator, an advocate for global climate change, and a
role model for democracy and social justice worldwide. Norway
is the host of the Nobel Peace Prize, and covets foreigners who
praise the country, immediately branding them *Norgesvenner* or
'friends of Norway'.

Although it contains some truths, this national trope is still a
myth. Norway was poor but not as poor as the story goes. The

INTRODUCTION

union with Sweden wasn't damaging, and foreign domination after 1814 was always fought off with words rather than bloodshed, with the 'intruders' retreating gracefully and peacefully. Contrary to popular belief, Norway was largely independent throughout the nineteenth century. At the time of writing, over seventy after the war, historians and journalists are increasingly digging into the Norwegian heroic efforts during the Second World War, discovering that not everything during the German occupation was righteous and heroic. Yet in many ways, Norwegian identity has been connected to the fact that the country has never been a large, important power in Europe or even Scandinavia—at least not since the thirteenth century. It is therefore useful to analyse what happened to the Norwegian identity over the last fifty years, after Norway became a rich, oil-producing power.

Who are the Norwegians?

Norwegians are no longer widely religious, nor are they peasants or poor, but the notion of a Lutheran, peasant and relatively poor society still prevails. Norwegians like to think of themselves as modest, feeling a hint of shame if life is too good, and often talk about duty. There are a set of meanings and values, tied to Norway's past, which are vital for understanding modern Norwegian society.

Firstly, Norwegian identity is closely connected with nature. There are about fifteen Norwegians per square kilometre, and no large cities. The capital, Oslo, has almost 700,000 inhabitants, and the entire Oslo region is home to about 1.5 million out of a total population of over five million. To the ordinary tourist, Norway doesn't have many man-made places or buildings of interest, but it does have nature: fjords, mountains, waterfalls, lakes, small islands along the long coastline, the

5

THE NORWEGIAN EXCEPTION?

Northern lights, the midnight sun and snowy winters. Tourism started with British mountaineers coming to Norway to climb and to fish salmon, and nature is still what any Norwegian will tell you to visit first.

Nature, not culture, has long been the symbol of the nation. The dichotomy between the polluted urban cities and beautifully pure natural world became even stronger at the turn of the twentieth century. This is still a potent metaphor, painting towns as something Norwegians escape when they can.

The national myth claims that Norwegians are born with skis, and both historical and contemporary heroes are skiers. Fridtjof Nansen nearly reached the North Pole and crossed Greenland, Roald Amundsen was the first man on the South Pole, and Norwegians dominate ski sports. When Norwegian identity was being formed during the nineteenth century, poets, artists and writers all emphasised nature. Nature appeared in folklore with Trolls and the Huldra, in *Peer Gynt* by Ibsen, and in the music of Edvard Grieg. It was also a prominent theme in Knut Hamsun's *Markens Grøde*, a depiction of rural life for which he won the Nobel Prize for Literature in 1920. Hamsun later became a controversial national figure, visiting Adolf Hitler and openly supporting Nazism during the Second World War.

Connected to nature is the *hytte*. A saying goes that in Norway you find houses and *hytter*, but no castles or palaces. There are 437,833 *hytter* in Norway, and half of all Norwegians say that they have access to one. *Hytte* comes from the Low German dialect *hütte* which meant a simple, rural shelter or a cabin. Today, having expanded with economic growth, a *hytte* can easily be larger and better equipped than houses, and for many it is a second home. During the outbreak of the COVID-19 pandemic in 2020, access to these dwellings was denied because of the dangers of infection, making it the first time in living memory that Norwegians did not celebrate Easter at their *hytte*; many thought this denial constituted a real violation of their rights. The *hytte* is closely connected to *koselig*, a concept similar to the more famous Danish *hygge*. Due to the cold climate and long winter nights, staying indoors and keeping warm and cosy is epitomized by *koselig*. Importantly, *hytte* also means freedom, leaving civilization and life in the town and returning to nature.

Norwegians often see themselves as frugal and industrious, coming from the country's Lutheran Protestant heritage. Lutheran Protestantism has contributed strongly to Norwegian identity, even if, at the time of writing, it is one of the most secular countries in the world. Norway became Protestant after the Reformation in 1536–37. One practical consequence was that church officials became government bureaucrats in the initial state and local administration, forerunners to the bureaucratic secular state. The Reformation led to the foundation of a strong state governed by the King of Denmark, for 150 years also an absolutist king. The state derived legitimacy and the king received riches from the church's properties. Particularly towards the eighteenth century, literacy became widespread so that people were able to read the catechism. Schooling became obligatory, including for girls, in order to read the catechism and be confirmed. As we shall see, Lutheran entrepreneurial and puritan values, combined with little or no acceptance for luxury or excess, were ideals followed by many.

The Norwegian *bonde*—a farmer—needs a special introduction. *Bonde* is closely connected to Norwegian identity, even if only a few can say that they are farmers today. Norwegians are perceived to be egalitarian as most Norwegians are descended from peasants and farmers. However, our ancestors were not subjugated peasants, but free and proud; they had a better life than peasants in most countries. The Norwegian *bonde* was historically a freeholder; Norway never developed feudalism, despite the existence of quite a few wealthy farmers. Due to geographical circumstances, deep mountainous valleys and fjords far north, only certain parts of the country could be successfully farmed, so the size of farms was limited. The Norwegian odal right ensured that farms were kept in the family, not only by primogeniture but by a right for anyone in the family to buy a farm back within a certain timeframe if it was sold to a stranger.

One important element here is what we may call the peasant myth in Norway: that liberty and equality were achieved not through violent revolution, fighting and bloodshed at the barricades, but through peaceful bargaining and healthy compromises. At the core of a peacefully, pragmatic and gradual development were bargaining peasants. In Norway, so the myth goes, the peasant has always been a free man.

During the Danish rule over Norway—from around the fifteenth century until 1814—Norwegian freeholders continued being free men. The priest Erik Pontoppidan wrote in 1752 that the Norwegian farmers were remarkably sharp and informed. It has been said that 'the freedom the [Norwegian] farmer has is really greater than in most other European countries, and it contributes to his courage and delight, and spurs him to conduct his affairs to his own choice and his best knowledge.' The Norwegian Constitution was written at a farmhouse at Eidsvoll, about 70 kilometres north of Oslo, in 1814. Thirty-seven of the 112 delegates were farmers, and the odal rights were secured in the Constitution.

The farmer was—at least ideologically and (perhaps) emotionally—connected to the king. When Norway was under Denmark's rule, farmers had access to the Danish king through the so-called *Supplikk* right, a right to appeal directly to the king. During the nineteenth century, Romanticism in literature and arts played an important part in the forming of a Norwegian identity. Folk tales described the king as a big farmer and he was likewise depicted in drawings as a farmer rather than a knight or nobleman. *Folk* is probably the term that epitomises being Norwegian: it means people, as in the German *Volk*, but in Norwegian it captures a sense of commonality, something for everyone, a solidarity and togetherness.

The characteristics of Norwegian politics

There has always been a political basis for collaboration and compromise between different interest groups and movements, as well as political parties, despite periods of deep conflicts. In 1814, Norwegians managed to write a constitution in just a few months and avoid armed conflict with the Swedes. When parliamentarism was introduced in 1884, overthrowing the civil servants' regime, two political parties were founded: the conservatives, Høyre, and the radical-liberals Venstre, meaning right and left after the model of the French revolution. Thus the Norwegian parliamentary democracy was born, and over the next century a significant number of political parties were established, often resulting in coalition or minority governments.

From the start of the parliamentary period in the early nineteenth century, there was a division between towns—which broadly speaking had been few and small in size before that time—and countryside. This was because the two key political forces were essentially wealthy farmers running local government, and university-educated bureaucrats running national government, a pattern still present in Norwegian politics at the time of writing.

With rising industrialization and urbanization, the working class became a political force. The Labour Party was founded in 1887, and around fifty years later, before the Second World War, it became a leading political force as a *folk*-party. Over the course of the twentieth century and particularly after the war, a more recognisable political spectrum developed with Socialists,

Centrists, Greens and right-wing populists, some of them even founded before the war. True to Norway's roots, farmers have remained a significant political force, continuing to advocate for strong local government just as they did in the 1830s.

The Norwegian Model

We often refer to the Norwegian Model when describing Norwegian society. The Norwegian Model is based on several, equally important pillars. Norway is a strong liberal democracy and one of the world's most globalized countries; it is open to international trade, with capital flows on all goods except agricultural products. At the same time, Norway's is a socioeconomic model, based on universal free health care, free education and affordable housing with a considerable degree of self-ownership.

Secondly, Norway has a well-established working relationship between labour organizations, employers and the government, securing rights for workers as well as stability and cooperation for employers. Strikes in Norway never escalate. A combination of flexibility and security can describe the labour markets, meaning that employers may lay off workers to some degree and hire them with some flexibility, and that employees are secured through unemployment benefits and rights. This builds on a long history of trust between employers and employees, who by and large have a positive, constructive relationship.

The Norwegian Model is also known for quite high levels of tax and contribution, a large public sector, universal benefits and a regulated labour market. Each of these traits can be found elsewhere, but the constancy and comprehensiveness of this picture in Norway is fairly unique. It may have the same origins as many other welfare states, but it survives in an extraordinary form partly due to Norwegian political culture and partly due to the money generated by oil. Importantly, the Norwegian Model is also flexible and open to change; it is becoming less distinct within the frame of increased collaboration and benchmarking in the EU and the OECD. The dynamic element of the model is surely important, as it has demonstrated the ability to change when needed.

However, the main point is this: all of these pillars are mutually dependent on each other. A large welfare state and a large public sector could not be sustained without a thriving private sector and a well-functioning democracy. Redistribution would be much more difficult without strong liberal rights such as private ownership. Without an open, liberal, market economy, combined with strong, liberal, individual rights, it would have been impossible to bear such a large welfare state.

There is a lot of interest in the Norwegian Model. Many researchers are engaged in understanding and explaining it, and politicians discuss who deserves praise for developing this successful model. According to Stein Kuhnle, currently Professor of Comparative Politics at the University of Bergen, if any of the Norwegian political parties were to apply for a patent on the Norwegian Model, none of them would get it. The success of the model is more feasibly explained by overall consensus on its main principles.

How is this possible? How is it possible to combine high growth, high productivity and a large welfare state? Several explanations have been proposed. Some argue that high and equal wages enforce efficiency. High taxes drive less productive businesses out of business and thus create, on average, stronger companies. Small differences in wages also make for cheap high-level competence, removing the least productive from the labour force. Another explanation is that the welfare state itself makes workers more productive and willing to take risks, because they know they have free education, a health care system for all, and benefits if they cannot work. A third explanation is that—except for the wealth tax which is a Norwegian exception—taxes on business, investment and capital are below average, while taxes on consumption are high compared to many other countries.

The tripartite system is a model for cooperation in the labour market. The role of unions and employers' organizations drives willingness to necessitate change and to moderate claims. There is also a principle called *arbeidslinjen*, policies of the labour market, which first and foremost states that working should be beneficial and more attractive than living on welfare benefits.

Everybody has the right to three years of schooling after a ten-year obligatory education; most Norwegians finish high school and many continue to universities or colleges. Consequently Norway has highly skilled workers, and they receive continual training or upgrade their education through different initiatives by companies and universities. This creates more flexibility for the workforce in general, and when people get laid off, they generally find employment fairly quickly. The labour market organizations continuously work together to ensure possibilities for everyone to improve their skills and find new employment.

To summarize, the Norwegian Model has some essential traits: a welfare state, a distinct labour model, and open markets. Markets and capitalism remain, but not without government involvement or the welfare state. Thus, the most important aspect of the Norwegian Model is balance: you cannot adopt the welfare state without having a vibrant, free market economy.

The presence of the state

The presence of the state is not limited to welfare. Norway has the largest share of employees in the public sector, both if measured by total employment as a percentage of mainland GDP in OECD countries, and also by public expenses. The state is involved in commercial business, and we find a similar concord around state ownership of domestic commercial enterprises outside the oil fund. The state is a major owner in five of the seven largest companies on the Oslo Stock Exchange, which includes oil, fertilizers, aluminium, telecoms and finance. Their management and boards are recruited on the same professional basis as in other parts of the business sector, and there is a broad consensus that they should operate on ordinary commercial terms. The role of the state shares is mainly to preserve long-term national ownership. Although different from the structure and scope of the oil fund, we find a similar pragmatic consensus in trusting state institutions with huge values on which future welfare depends. Moreover, the high legitimacy of the state is partly rooted in a long-standing perception of it being competent and honest.

Norway's Scandinavian neighbours have moved further away from strong government control. Norway has a long tradition of imitating Swedish welfare reforms, such as their 'modern welfare capitalist model', and the Swedes have been the Scandinavian leaders in reforming public administration. They have also regularly been used for scaremongering, including Swedish district policies resulting in centralization and a desertion of the Swedish countryside, and today's less generous labour and social policies. Danish reforms have also been contested, such as local government reforms and productivity initiatives, but in Norway the public sector is still prominent.

As well as valuing central government control within domestic society, it is fascinating that the national imperative to keep major industry headquarters in Norway, in order to maintain control, is deeply rooted in a fear of being politically or economically controlled by others. A deep desire to be autonomous has its origins in the 400 years of Danish rule, the short and more lenient Swedish rule, and the independence felt by someone from a valley or district. Resistance to governance from Brussels and by large foreign oil companies is rooted in the same fear of external control. On the other hand, however, Norway is not an inward-looking economy; it has long been a seafaring nation engaged in global exports, and today it is one of the largest investors in the world through the sovereign oil fund.

The outlier—a lucky exception?

Ideas about equality are deeply ingrained in society, in its culture, history and politics. This has manifested itself in many different statistics and studies.

In addition to ranking among the most equal countries in the world, with a Gini coefficient of 26.8 in 2019, Norway is also considered to have one of the highest indicators of gender equality. The World Economic Forum's Global Gender Gap index rates Norway as second in the world in 2020, only beaten by Iceland.[2] The UNDP's Gender Inequality Index ranks Norway as number one in 2020.[3]

The World Happiness report for 2020 ranks Norway as number five of 156 countries, only beaten by its Nordic neighbours and Switzerland.[4] A CNN report asked, 'Why are Norwegians so happy? In a word: "*koselig*"', referring to the concept of cosiness and warmth. That is one reason, living in this Northern corner of the world, but it is not enough of an explanation.

If we look at the rankings of GDP per capita, Norway is number four (behind Luxembourg, Ireland and Switzerland) on the IMF index for 2021.[5] Life expectancy is high, ranking number twenty of all countries. Norway also scores highly in valuing freedom and self-expression, as stated in the World Values Survey.[6]

According to the World Economic Forum's most recent Global Competitiveness Report, Norway is one of the most open and competitive economies in the world. The International Institute for Management Development lists Denmark, Sweden, Norway, and Finland among the world's top fifteen most open and competitive economies. Importantly, the social trust level is among the highest in the world. In the Transparency International Corruption Index for 2020, Norway has the seventh 'cleanest' public sector according to experts and business leaders, just beaten by its Nordic neighbours, Switzerland, Singapore and New Zealand.[7]

Likewise, if we measure the quality of rule of law, Norway is number two on the World Justice Project Rule of Law Index.[8] We can continue; the 2020 Corruption Index added that education levels and living standards are high. It is clear that Norway, together with its Nordic neighbours, is a positive outlier in almost all indexes measuring different aspects of society.

Norway is seen as a success in the so-called resource curse literature, because Norwegians have been able to establish a successful oil and gas industry together with petroleum extraction. The theoretical explanation is that Norway has both a stable and well-functioning democracy and a capable state bureaucracy, one with very low levels of corruption and a high level of involvement in the oil sector. The authors of 'The Resource Curse Revisited' state that, 'Norway, arguably, is a special case—the only way its experience can be replicated is to start with 4.5 million Norwegians.'[9]

We may conclude that Norway has been lucky, apart from dark nights and long, cold winters; yet luck is not the only explanation. To achieve stability and prosperity as Norway has done takes wise decisions and an ability to build unity, and for these two conditions to sustain across history. It requires not just the occasional coincidence of an individual leader making the right move, but a certain national political culture.

Can politics, culture and luck explain the Norwegian exception?

The above question is the main one we have posed, and we will attempt to answer it throughout this book. Our hypothesis is that politics and culture together explain Norwegian society today, but also that throughout history we have had considerable luck, such as having kind neighbours and discovering oil and gas in the Norwegian continental shelf.

Our history begins in 1814. This year is chosen because it was arguably the most pivotal year in Norwegian history. This is the year when Denmark had to give up Norwegian dominion and when a rebellion secured a constitution, the most liberal and modern to appear in Europe at the time. Later that year Norway was forced into a new union with Sweden, albeit a lenient one with autonomy to govern internal affairs. The following century was used to build institutions and modernize the state, aided by an already functioning, Danish-educated bureaucracy.

Chapter 1 tells the story of 1814. It could have had many other outcomes, but by New Year's Eve 1814 Norway had avoided war, managed to produce the Constitution on 17 May, and could in many ways start out as a young nation.

The nineteenth century was the era of building a nation and an identity, and we explore how Norwegian identity was formed in Chapter 2. Norwegians looked back to former centuries of glory such as the Viking Age, and even when Norway was in a union with Sweden, liberation encompassed the surviving Danish culture. By and large, this cultural nationalism grew without any Swedish attempts at interference.

In Chapter 3 we turn to Norway's economic, institutional and political development in the nineteenth century. As we will argue, a period of almost seven decades can be described as 'the civil servants' state', implying that civil servants and bureaucrats were not simply servants of the state. Instead they were its rulers, at the forefront of modernizing and liberalizing Norwegian society.

The last milestone of the nineteenth century was political nationalism. In Chapter 4, we describe the introduction of parliamentarism and the peaceful dissolution of the civil servants' state.

INTRODUCTION

We explain how socialism, liberalism and conservatism found their ways though *folk* movements and later political parties. Towards the end of the century, tensions between Sweden and Norway rose due to protectionism and disagreements over international policies and trade. In Chapter 5 we tell the story of what happened in 1905, when Norway finally became independent.

Chapter 6 takes a closer look at industrialization, especially at how hydroelectric power dominated the first decades of the twentieth century, as well as discussions about a variety of social policies and the radicalization of the Labour Party. Norwegian political culture was partly able to continue developing in this period because Norway remained a 'neutral ally' to the Triple Entente during the First World War. In Chapter 7 we describe the interwar years, one of the most turbulent political periods in Norwegian history. Norway managed to calm the political situation by agreeing to a crisis settlement in 1935, but just a few years later it was taken by surprise when the Germans invaded on 9 April 1940.

Chapter 8 explores the traumatic German occupation of Norway during the Second World War. A Norwegian politician, Vidkun Quisling, and his political movement collaborated with the Germans during the war, and his surname became a universally recognised synonym for 'traitor'. He had numerous followers, but most Norwegians stayed true to King Haakon, who played an important role in encouraging and inspiring Norwegians throughout the war from his exile in London.

Chapter 9 recounts the Norwegian version of what is known as *Les Trente Glorieuses*—the roughly thirty-year post-war period of European recovery—characterised by rapidly improving living standards and the arrival of consumer capitalism. Social democracy was prevalent; a strong sense of togetherness was formed during the war, and the Labour Party capitalized on this. The social democrats' ambitions led the large nation-building project of the post-war decade. Economic growth was high, education was booming and welfare increased. In a certain sense, this is also the paradox of social democracy. When social democratic struggles succeeded in creating increased wealth and education for all, voters no longer wanted social democratic policies. The 'mental revolution' of the 1970s was a transition from equality and unity to freedom and diversity.

In Chapter 10, we describe the development during the 1970s and 1980s, starting with two pivotal moments around 1970: the discovery of oil and gas in 1969 and the turbulent EEC vote in 1972. The 1970s changed Norway, and these changes continued throughout the 1980s with a marked turn in government from the Labour Party to the Conservatives in 1981. Modern Norway was emerging.

In Chapter 11 we concentrate on the two things that stand out in comparison with Norway's European neighbours in the last couple of decades: firstly, the Norwegian solution to the EU— remaining outside and yet inside, without a vote—and secondly, the discovery of oil and gas and how Norway has handled its extremely valuable natural resources.

In Chapter 12 we turn to modern identity discussion and immigration. We will try to explain why Norway experienced violent terror on 22 July 2011, when seventy-seven people were killed by Anders Behring Breivik. We also discuss the implications of increased immigration.

We are historians and not soothsayers, but in our concluding chapter we will also attempt to discuss what will happen to Norwegians in the years to come. Will Norway still be an exception in many spheres, or are we aligning with other similar Western countries when it comes to economic and political development? As always, the outcome will depend on wise policies but also on luck and opportunities. On the other hand, Norway may also risk a downturn, as we are not immune to international affairs.

INTRODUCTION

There is no way to predict whether history will continue to be lucky for Norway, but this book hopes to show where society and culture have played a role in its success to date; these foundations should stand Norwegians in good stead as they forge a path through the twenty-first century.

PART ONE

FORMING A NATION, 1814–1905

1

THE 1814 EXPERIENCE

For Norway, 1814 was an establishment year par excellence, pro-claiming the creation of a new state with a new political system. The ideas of 1814 became the frame of reference for all Norwegian political life, for Norwegian nation-building, and for all strands of Norwegian nationalism. These notions became the core of modern Norwegian political culture and identity.

1814 was coined Norway's 'miracle year'—*annus mirabilis*—by some contemporary observers. One of them noted in his diary on 31 December 1814: 'I don't believe any other nation's history can show anything like this.'[1]

Indeed, the transformation of Norway during that year did seem quite miraculous. Consider for instance that the indepen-dent Norwegian state—quasi-independent if one may—was established without any previous demands for independence before 1814. During the prior thirty to forty years there were numerous indications of an increased awareness and interest in the small sections of the elite classes in Norway. Yet there is virtually no concept of (certainly no calls for) an independent Norwegian state. Nationalist historians have searched in vain for evidence of such demands for nearly 200 years.

THE NORWEGIAN EXCEPTION?

If someone were to argue that the Danish absolutist regime allowed no room for public demands of this sort, there are no traces of a desire for a separate Norwegian polity in private letters or journals either. Furthermore, the ideological climate was rather unusually liberal and open in the late eighteenth-century Danish monarchy, particularly during the years 1784–99. A number of opposing and even explicitly revolutionary ideas were quite freely expressed. Thus, during the Jacobin dictatorship in 1793–94, the most radical phase of the French Revolution, a periodical was published in Copenhagen which supported the French Republic fully, and which freely reprinted the great and militant speeches of Robespierre in the National Convent.

Of course, the experience of 1814 did not take place in a vacuum, and the ideas proclaimed were not uniquely Norwegian. The events in Norway were part of a larger movement through the late eighteenth and early nineteenth centuries, with revolutionary thinking based on Enlightenment philosophy and political theory which produced the spectacular events of the North American and French revolutions. But even in this big picture, there were some distinctly Norwegian strands. The Norwegian ideas of 1814 were the result of a meeting, an amalgamation or clash, between certain international impulses and domestic traditions.

A treaty and a revolt—historical background

The French Revolution generated wars which had raged almost continuously for over twenty years. In 1814, however, the Napoleonic Wars were drawing to a close, and a broad alliance of states was on the point of defeating the French Emperor.

The kingdom of Denmark, which we Norwegians like to call the dual kingdom of Denmark-Norway, found itself on the losing side. In 1807, afraid that Napoleon might conquer the kingdom's large fleet, the British navy had captured it instead. Since then, Denmark had been an ally of Napoleon; the Swedes, however, were members of the victorious alliance.

In fact, the main Swedish protagonist in this Scandinavian drama was Crown Prince Carl Johan (1763–1844). The Swedish king was old, ailing and without heirs, and Carl Johan had been chosen as crown prince in 1810. In many ways he was an odd choice. Christened Jean-Baptiste Bernadotte, he was a lawyer's son from the south of France who had risen quickly through the French revolutionary army, being an exceptionally proficient soldier. In 1804 he had been appointed to the highest rank, Marshal of France.

When the Swedes selected this French Marshal to succeed their throne, it was because they wanted to ally themselves with Napoleon's French Empire against Russia. Russia had seized Finland from Sweden in 1809, and the hope was that a Swedish-French alliance would bring about the return of Finland.

Yet Carl Johan—the 'Swedified' name the new crown princ had given himself—did not do what the Swedish elite expected, instead turning against his old friend Napoleon and bringing Sweden into the war against France. In treaties with Great Britain and Russia he had been promised a new reward: Norway, a prize Sweden had coveted for a long time.

During the autumn of 1813, Swedish troops attacked Denmark from the south and threatened to overrun the whole of Jutland. King Frederik VI of Denmark appealed for peace, signing a treaty on 14 January 1814 at Kiel. Dominion over Norway was transferred from the King of Denmark to the King of Sweden, but its old dependencies—Greenland, Iceland and the Faroe Islands—were not included in the transfer, instead continuing to belong to Denmark. In Norway there had been some dissatisfaction with the government during the Napoleonic Wars; many businessmen had close contacts with England and disliked being dragged into the war on Napoleon's side. Nevertheless, the Treaty of Kiel came as a great shock to Norwegians.

THE NORWEGIAN EXCEPTION?

The single most important figure in the story of the Norwegian Experience in 1814 was the Danish Prince Christian Frederik (1786–1848). He was a member of the Oldenburg dynasty, who had ruled Denmark and Norway for nearly 400 years, but to be more precise he was the king's cousin and heir to the throne. In May 1813, the war situation was critical, and the twenty-six-year-old crown prince was sent to Norway as Governor. Christian Frederik was charming, eager and easily fired with enthusiasm; as Governor he soon became popular in Norway. For a time he had had Norwegian friends and advisers, and once he was situated in Norway he immediately set about developing new friendships and connections.

Prince Christian Frederik refused to accept the Treaty of Kiel and tried to foment resistance in Norway. The Norwegian elite responded enthusiastically and he won adherents among the military. In the spring of 1814, it appeared that there was hardly a soul in Norway who did not support the insurrection. So far, the revolt was a peaceful one.

The timing of the revolt was auspicious. The Swedish military forces were preoccupied with the war against Napoleon in continental Europe, so the Swedish king was not ready to collect his prize from the Treaty of Kiel. Christian Frederik's revolt was against the Treaty of Kiel and against the Swedes. However, he did not intend to return to the dual monarchy of Denmark-Norway, instead raising the banner of Norwegian independence.

In a broader, historical sense this revolution may seem unique and perhaps a little confusing; one would have thought that after 400 years of Danish rule, a separatist insurrection in Norway would be directed against the Danes. However, thanks to a historical coincidence like the Treaty of Kiel, this was not the case.

Originally, Christian Frederik had intended to have himself proclaimed king and absolute ruler of Norway considering his right to the throne, but this idea received little support among his Norwegian advisers. On 16 February, the Danish prince and a select group of influential Norwegians held a private meeting which became known as the 1814 Assembly of Notables. There, Christian Frederik agreed to let himself be elected King of Norway. It was resolved that a national assembly should be summoned, one which would elect the king and decide on a new constitution for Norway.

After this meeting, Christian Frederik revealed himself to be a brilliant political tactician. He issued a decree to the effect that, on an extraordinary day of worship, all Norwegian men were to congregate in the churches and elect delegates to the national assembly. Immediately before the election they were obliged to swear an oath, promising to 'assert Norway's independence and to venture life and blood for the beloved country.' It was difficult to refuse to take such an oath, and so even if a few quietly grumbled about the Prince's ulterior motives, Christian Frederik was able to claim the entire people's support for his insurrection. The Oath may be called both clever politics and the principle of popular sovereignty in action. A parallel here, and a possible role model, is Napoleon's love of referendums as a means of claiming legitimacy.

On 11 April, 112 men came together as a constituent national assembly. They met at Eidsvoll, sixty kilometres north of the capital Christiania (today Oslo), at a manor house belonging to one of Christian Frederik's closest advisers. By European standards the manor house was not particularly large or luxurious, and many of the delegates had to make do with cramped and basic accommodation.

The National Council that met at Eidsvoll in April 1814 was elected by local parishes and military bases. Of the 112 members of the National Assembly, thirty-three were specially elected from the military, while the rest represented the rural districts and the towns. More than half of the assembly were holders of civil and military public office; a handful of delegates were owners of large estates; and thirteen were merchants. Christian Frederik's election rules ensured that farmers should be well represented, making up nearly a third of the group. Many of the men at Eidsvoll were also very young, with an average age of 42.8 years.

A national assembly of this nature would have been unthinkable in any other country, with the possible exception, perhaps, of France at certain times during the Revolution. However, if we disregard the numerical strength of the various groups, the constituent assembly accurately reflected Norwegian society in 1814: no aristocracy to speak of, many small farmers, and an elite dominated by civil servants.

The leading faction at Eidsvoll was made up of Christian Frederik's supporters, who were wholeheartedly in favour of the revolution against the Swedes. They called themselves the Independence Party but were dubbed the Prince's Party by their opponents. The most prominent member of this party was a magistrate, Christian Magnus Falsen (1782–1830). He had participated in preparing an important draft constitution for Norway, one which gave the monarch a fairly powerful role. Falsen and his associates were fierce opponents both of absolute monarchy and of a Swedish union, though a number of them did not totally reject the possibility of restoring the union with Denmark.

The other main faction at Eidsvoll had a more conciliatory attitude towards Sweden and was sceptical of Christian Frederik. Their opponents called them the Swedish Party and they later became known as the Unionist Party. The natural leader of the unionists was Count Herman Wedel Jarlsberg (1779–1840), one of very few noblemen in Norway. Wedel Jarlsberg probably had more political experience and insight than any other representative at Eidsvoll, having been in touch with Swedish circles since 1809 and having worked to achieve a union of Norway and Sweden. However, there is much evidence to suggest that such a union was first and foremost a means for Wedel to rid Norway of the system of absolute monarchy.

When Christian Frederik raised the banner of revolution against the Treaty of Kiel, Wedel and his supporters had to adopt a low profile, but at Eidsvoll they made their mark. In their view, a union with Sweden was unavoidable and the only realistic solution. They suspected Christian Frederik and his supporters of having as their ultimate goal the reunification of Norway and Denmark. Thus the stage was set for a showdown between two different visions of Norway's future.

The 1814 Constitution

At the Eidsvoll Assembly there were many opinions as to the type of Constitution Norway should have. Yet absolute monarchy had few, if any, direct advocates; likewise, there were no supporters for republicanism. The adopted Constitution represented a drastic break with the past. The elite at Eidsvoll had been educated in Copenhagen, which in the 1790s was a place where intellectuals discussed new and foreign concepts. Many of the men at Eidsvoll were captivated by these ideas.

Wedel and his followers were defeated in some important votes at Eidsvoll regarding Norway's relations with Sweden, but they accepted the defeat and rallied behind Christian Frederik and the sovereign Norwegian state.

On 17 May 1814, all the representatives at Eidsvoll signed a new constitution for an independent Norway and elected Christian Frederik king. The new monarchy was to be hereditary, and the king's son Frederik became crown prince of Norway. The most important notions expressed in the Constitution were the radical beliefs that had triumphed in the American War of Independence and the French Revolution.

At the root of these ideas was the sovereignty of the people, stating that ultimately power should rest with them. The

Eidsvoll Assembly saw itself as an embodiment of this principle: as the representatives of the people, they were to provide Norway with a new political system. In this system power in the political community should be shared between the new king and a popularly elected assembly. The king's power was executive, while the elected assembly would primarily legislate, impose taxes and grant funds. The king in person would appoint his ministers, who were to be appointed and dismissed individually.

Another important idea was freedom of the individual. From this point all Norwegian citizens were guaranteed certain rights, the most important being freedom of expression. They were also assured the rule of law.

Compared with most constitutions at that time, the Norwegian 1814 Constitution was highly democratic, especially concerning the right to vote. It was mostly conditional on property ownership, but the qualifying limit was set very low. Nearly forty per cent of the adult male population was enfranchised; there were no movements to liberate women in 1814.

On the other hand, the power of the new national assembly was somewhat limited. It was to meet for a few months every three years. In the meantime, Norway would be ruled by the king and his ministers. The king could make provisional laws when the assembly was not in session, and he also had suspensory veto to the assembly's legislation. In this arrangement, the king and his advisers would be a strong force. The Constitution was designed for Christian Frederik by his friends and followers, who made up the majority at Eidsvoll.

The Eidsvoll Assembly considered several proposed constitutions for which there were various foreign prototypes. The model that in the event was the most influential was the French Constitution of 1791. However, the new Constitution was not solely the sum of its foreign influences. Among the Eidsvoll Assembly members, the Norwegian elite and many writers pre-1814, there existed a strong awareness of Norway's historical traditions and of the Norwegian national character. In some ways this was expressed in the Constitution itself.

The new national assembly was named the Storting, a name which had associations with the old Norse word *ting*, meaning a deliberative assembly which was an important institution in the Viking Age and Medieval Norway.

The strong position of the civil servants was revealed in two ways in the 1814 Constitution. They all received the right to vote—being the sole exception from the property ownership rule—and it was determined that an official could be dismissed only after a trial in a court of law. In 1814, there were around 1,800 civil servants in Norway. The country's total population was around 900,000, and the overwhelming majority of them were members of farming communities.

The interests of the farmers were safeguarded in that the odal rights, the principle of pre-emption and redemption of family land, was written into the Constitution. This system of owner-ship and inheritance was considered specifically Norwegian, the cornerstone of the free peasant society of Norway. The reformist absolutist regime, with its liberal ideas on economy, had been preparing to abolish the odal rights before 1814, so this particu-lar reform was reversed in the 1814 rebellion.

A shameful feature of the Constitution was its article two, which denied Jews the right to enter the realm, and stated that Jesuits and monastic orders would not be tolerated. The article became particularly discreditable because it was initially supposed to contain a passage about religious freedom, but this part was forgotten during the deliberations. Only the planned exceptions remained in the Constitution, and to make things worse, at the prominent place of article two.

One may also add in this context that the Constitution didn't change the strict pre-1814 legislation regarding religious gather-ings. Such gatherings without permission were banned, and this ban continued until 1842.

The Constitution was signed in May, but just a couple of months later independent Norway was obliged to fight a war against Sweden. Carl Johan and his troops had returned from the war against Napoleon, determined to take possession of Norway, and Swedish troops invaded Norway in late July 1814.

The war was conducted half-heartedly by the Norwegians and ended within a few weeks. The outcome may be called a swift victory for the Swedes but not a crushing one. Christian Frederik received an offer of armistice and negotiations in early August, and accepted after some deliberations with his government and military advisors. In certain quarters he was considered a coward, there being quite a few Norwegians who wanted to fight to the last man—or at least who said they would.

Yet in the spring and summer of 1814, events were in fact decided by the Great Powers of Europe. Christian Frederik's envoys received no real encouragement for their revolution. The Great Powers had given firm guarantees to the Swedes and Carl Johan, even in the case of Great Britain, where there was considerable sympathy expressed for the Norwegian insurrection both in government and in the press.

Free, but in a new union

On 14 August at the city of Moss, Norway and Sweden signed a ceasefire agreement. This agreement has become known as the Moss Convention, and it is one of the most important documents in modern Norwegian history. The main conditions for Carl Johan laying down arms were as follows: Norway had to accept a new union with Sweden; Christian Frederik had to renounce all claims to the Norwegian throne; and last, but not least, Norway was to keep its new Eidsvoll Constitution, with some amendments made necessary because of the new union. The Treaty of Kiel was not mentioned.

Christian Frederik's enthusiasm for the Norwegian revolt faded fast. He became ill and depressed, and on 10 October 1814 he formally renounced the Norwegian throne. In due course he inherited the Danish throne and reigned from 1839–48 as King Christian VIII, an absolute monarch seemingly uninterested in reforming the Danish political system.

In the autumn of 1814, an extraordinary session of the Norwegian national assembly—some historians have called it another constituent assembly—was convened. It had to negotiate the conditions for a union with the Swedes.

A vehement tug-of-war took place, characterized by some deft manoeuvring on the part of the Norwegians, and producing a result we may call very satisfactory from a Norwegian point of view. The Swedes gave up trying to impose the provisions of the Treaty of Kiel by force. There may be several reasons why Norway got such a good deal when Sweden seemed to hold all the cards. Certainly, one reason is that the Swedes wanted to avoid a military occupation and any scenario involving a hostile population and possible armed insurrections in remote parts of Norway. Instead, Carl Johan was eager to present a peaceful solution on the Scandinavian peninsula at the upcoming Vienna Congress. He may have thought that he could always impose tighter Swedish control in the union later, when things were settled. It is important to remember here that the main reason Sweden coveted Norway was strategic. The Swedes wanted to avoid a two-front war and a hostile Norway in possible future conflicts with their traditional rivals Russia and Denmark.

The new union between Norway and Sweden was a loose one: the two realms would share a king, but Norway would have full internal self-government and its own political institutions. The new king had his own Norwegian government and had to rule together with a sovereign Norwegian parliament in accordance with a sovereign Norwegian constitution. The new Norway had its own institutions, its own judiciary and its own military force.

In short, the only common institution was the foreign office and the foreign minister.

On 4 November a new Norwegian constitution was approved, a very slightly revised version of the Constitution of 17 May. Some changes were necessitated by the new union, yet their main effect was to weaken the power of the monarchy. Since the king was going to reside in the Swedish capital of Stockholm most of the time, he would not, for instance, be able to keep his government in the Norwegian capital of Christiania under constant scrutiny.

Carl Johan became King of Sweden and Norway in 1818. He made several attempts to alter the Constitution, but the Norwegian national assembly, the Storting, refused point blank. Among the Norwegian elite, there was full agreement that the Constitution had to be preserved. The king tried several strategies to expand the executive power in the Constitution, among them threats and bribery, although he never used brute force. Even in unionist-friendly circles, the king's moves were perceived as inappropriate pressure exerted by the monarchy and by Sweden. It did not take long for constitutional conservatism to become a political and cultural principle in Norway: in short, the Constitution was not to be tampered with. Another result of this power struggle was that it strengthened the civil servants' legitimacy as a ruling elite.

Admittedly, a few amendments to the Constitution have been made over the years. The infamous article excluding Jews was removed in 1851. Nevertheless, conservatism regarding the Constitution has become a national attitude in Norway.

The 1814 experience and Norwegian political culture

What was the significance of these historical events to Norway's political culture?

THE 1814 EXPERIENCE

There are several interconnected themes here: (1) The elevation of the 1814 Constitution to a prime national symbol and the relationship between national sovereignty and liberal-democratic ideas; (2) the two different strands, cultural and political, of Norwegian nationalism; (3) the Norwegian (Nordic) peasant myth and the triumph of the compromise strategy; and (4) Norway's historical luck, especially her benevolent neighbours. Let us take a closer look at each of these themes.

(1) There were basically two separate revolutionary changes regarding Norway in 1814. On the one hand, Norway went from being part of a Danish-ruled state to an independent political entity. Of course, one must qualify this by saying that Norway was not a completely sovereign state after 1814. She was forced into a new union with Sweden, but the new union was a very loose one.

On the other hand, Norway went from being ruled by an absolutist regime to getting a political constitution based on modern Enlightenment thinking, including the sovereignty of the people, separation of powers and freedom of the individual. The new Norwegian Constitution was as of 1814 the most democratic in Europe.

There was and is no logical necessary connection between national sovereignty and a liberal constitution. An independent Norway could have gone on having an absolutist ruler, and a liberal constitution might have been introduced in the Danish monarchy. Yet these elements were already considered to be two sides of the same coin. Often they were entangled into the concept of freedom, be it national, political or individual.

As a result of this entanglement, the main strands of Norwegian nationalism have been liberal and democratic. This was most certainly the case in 1905 when Norway split from Sweden. It was the case in 1945, when a democratic, sovereign Norway was restored after five years of rule by Nazi Germany. It was also arguably the case in the public debates about Norwegian membership in the European Community/Union in 1972 and 1994.

Further on, the dominant popular concept of the Norwegian nation has been heavily civic, based on Enlightenment values and symbols of 1814 including the Constitution and the Storting. Essentially, all national concepts are a mix of civic and cultural elements, and of course there are also significant folk and romantic ideas in the Norwegian concept of nation. However, in comparison with several other small European countries (like Ireland, Scotland, Wales and Finland), the post-1814 Norwegian national concept is one of the most civic-oriented ones.

(2) Another result of the events in 1814 was that Norwegian nationalism was split in two, with politics and culture parting ways. Politically, Norway's former ruler Denmark was no longer considered a threat or a problem; the potential enemy for Norwegian nationalism was its new union partner, Sweden. Culturally, the picture was quite different. In 1814 Norway's elite culture was more or less Danish, especially regarding the written language, and the events of this year had no effect on this sphere. Most significantly, perhaps, Sweden did not in any way try to 'Swedify' Norwegian culture: there was no effort, for instance, to make Swedish a common language, nor to get Norwegian pupils to learn Swedish in school. In short, Sweden left the Norwegians alone in a cultural sense. As a result of this, nineteenth-century cultural nationalism in Norway had Denmark, or rather 'Danishness', as its sole enemy. This anti-Danish cultural sentiment will be explored in detail in the next chapter. Thanks to the events of 1814, political nationalism was anti-Swedish while cultural nationalism was anti-Dan-

ish. The picture would be quite different had history developed as expected. If Norwegian separatism had been able to develop inside the Danish monarchy, both political and cultural nationalism would have been anti-Danish. Norwegian nationalism would have become a more coherent political and cultural force.

(3) Norway could have had a long, bloody, heroic war with Sweden in 1814. Swedish forces could have occupied Norway; Norwegian armed anti-Swedish resistance could have gone on for many years in faraway mountains and rural areas; there could have been brutality on both sides, a harsh Swedish rule and a reciprocal relationship based on violence and hatred. To cut the throat of a Swede could have been considered a noble and patriotic act in Norwegian rural areas and townships. But this was not the case. The Swedish-Norwegian war of 1814 ended before it really began, and resulted in a peaceful compromise. The consequences were great for Norway: the union of 1814–1905 was a period of peace and prosperity in which Norwegian society was modernized and its political system was democratized. The compromise also defined a standard that was to be repeated during several critical moments. In 1884, when a large crisis dominated the whole political system in Norway, it might have ended in a coup d'état or even a bloody civil war, yet it did not. Instead the result was another compromise, after which the losers accepted the defeat and found their place in a new political order, and the winners were cautious and moderate in their victory. Later, in 1905, the political and military situation between Norway and Sweden was very tense. A war threatened and both sides began mobilizing their military forces. This situation might have escalated out of control, with Great Britain supporting Norway and Germany supporting Sweden, the Great Powers might have

been involved, and in the worst case a Great War might have been unleashed on Europe as a result of conflicts in Scandinavia—rather than in the Balkans nine years later. Nevertheless, this was also not to be the case. The result in 1905 was that the union between Sweden and Norway was abolished after successful negotiations and a peaceful compromise, without a single bullet fired.

Some might call this peaceful development a demonstration of the Norwegian peasant myth. In short, the narrative of this myth is that liberty and equality during the Middle Ages and even under Danish rule were achieved not through violent revolutions but through peaceful bargaining and healthy compromises. This myth was an important cultural precondition for the main ideas of 1814 and for Norwegian political culture after that point. We will elaborate on this point further in the next chapter.

Further on, what we have called the Norwegian peasant myth is only the Norwegian brand of a common Nordic peasant myth, as one may also find strong concepts of free peasants and peaceful compromises in Sweden and Denmark. There are interesting variations, however, and in the next chapter we will have a closer look at some specific traits in Norwegian nationalism and national identity compared with Sweden.

(4) Of course, these triumphs of the compromise strategy would not have been possible with more aggressive, less understanding and less practical adversaries and neighbours. If Sweden, or anyone else, had wanted to invade and conquer Norway, it wouldn't have mattered much how peaceful and reasonable Norway's peasants were.

2

CREATING A NATION

The 1814 rebellion and the compromise with Sweden created a semi-independent Norwegian state. From this point, the Norwegians had to build a nation. We can identify three main processes of nation-building in Norway during the nineteenth century: practical, political, and identity-forming. We will look at the first, the institutional nation-building, in the next chapter, and at the second, the development of political nationalism, in Chapters 4 and 5.

In this chapter we will have a closer look at the third process of nation-building: the search for a Norwegian national identity, or cultural nationalism; even, to use a more academic phrase, the cultural construction of the Norwegian nation.

The search for a Norwegian identity

The most striking part of Norwegian nineteenth-century cultural nationalism is national Romanticism. In Norway, this phenomenon was widely evident from the 1840s onwards. It was known, with a characteristic formulation, as 'the national breakthrough'.

This was part of a typical European pattern, but one uniquely Norwegian aspect was its late development in the country; another interesting aspect is its relationship to Enlightenment ideas.

The central features of Norwegian national Romanticism are typical. A Norwegian national culture was fostered and shaped across all areas, largely a process of discovering and developing raw cultural material. This material was already present in Norwegian peasant culture on local and regional levels, in fairy-tales, legends, songs and dances. Some, but not all, were slightly altered and proclaimed common national heritage by a national-ist elite. Furthermore, an important topic was Norway's ancient history. Artists and composers made rural culture their starting point, while writers based themselves both on contemporary popular culture and on Norwegian history.

This 'national breakthrough' was of course closely connected to the nation-building process of modernization. National con-sciousness could be spread through a developed school system, increasing public life, as well as a completed communication system which included harbours and railways.

The political preconditions are also significant. As mentioned briefly above, political symbols of the flag and 17 May caused strife, but in context these are exceptions from the rule, which was that Norwegian cultural nationalism grew without any Swedish attempt at interference. The conflicts and battles in this wide field were left to Norwegians alone, and to a great extent these struggles dealt with the Danish elements of our culture.

The emergence of national awareness

We can identify two most important, albeit very controversial, areas in Norwegian nineteenth-century cultural nationalism.

The first area was that of history. Norway was, according to the nationalist terminology of the nineteenth century, a historical nation. It had been a developed, independent kingdom for several hundred years in the Middle Ages. The territory was smaller in 1814 than at its largest in the thirteenth and fourteenth centuries, as some of it had gone to Sweden, some to Denmark, and the North Sea islands like Shetland and the Orkneys to Scotland. Yet the core areas were mostly the same, and the Norwegian elite, mostly public servants and professors, had been aware of the basics of this history all along.

Late in the eighteenth century there had been a strong flowering of interest among the elite in Norway's ancient history. Snorri's royal sagas—a thirteenth-century history of Norwegian Viking and medieval kings—had been both translated into Danish and republished in the original Norse language. At the same time the translator and publisher, Gerhard Schøning, had written his own large work of Norwegian history.

An awareness of the old Norwegian medieval kingdom, and the concept of continuity from the old to the new state, was strong among the 1814 elite. A main view held by the Eidsvoll rebellious constituent assembly was that the Norwegian kingdom had been restored.

Personal freedom, social equality and justice

One person who, more than anyone else, placed the connection between ancient and modern Norway on the national cultural agenda was the poet Henrik Wergeland, son of one of the Eidsvoll men. In a speech at Eidsvoll in 1834, entitled 'In Memory of the Ancestors', he developed the strong and attractive metaphor of the twin half-rings of Norwegian history: the old medieval state and the new Norwegian state fitted together as 'two broken parts of the same ring'. The intervening period, when Norway was governed from Denmark, was an 'impure soldering' that should be excised.

In other words, the job at hand was to join the twin, genuine halves again. Wergeland expressed in very strong terms the importance of Norwegian medieval history for modern national awareness. He said that the history of no other people may show such a succession of great and noble kings, 'and from this we surely may conclude that the people was likewise'. Snorri's royal sagas were 'The Norwegian Patent of Nobility among the Nations'. Wergeland maintained that the book should be in every Norwegian home and, along with the Bible, it was to be 'The idol of the High Seat, as were Odin and Thor of old'.[1]

We may call this an ideological program for national rebirth, or a creation of a Norwegian Golden Age myth. Yet Wergeland's program was of a particular kind, based on core values he found in his interpretation of Norwegian medieval society. These values were not belligerent and heroic; instead, Wergeland proposed that the ancient society was characterised by personal freedom, a wide-ranging social equality, justice, compromise and coopera- tion. Moreover, these values had to be rediscovered, reinterpreted and utilized in modern nineteenth-century society.

In medieval Norwegian society Wergeland looked for some core values and specific virtues. Most peasants were free men, and at a very important institution, the *Ting*, free and equal men could meet, discuss problems and make binding laws. This legal institution meant that medieval society had, to some extent, a rule of law.

For Wergeland, freedom and liberty were the core Norwegian virtues. With Norway's recently acquired liberty—the new Constitution and the abolishment of Danish rule—the people's virtues had been 'recalled to life'. All the specifically Norwegian virtues, such as sense of education, enlightenment and respect for the law, flowed from liberty. Furthermore, this freedom was 'bound by law', based on 'reason and moral understanding'. It stimulated 'right before might' and shaped 'the spiritual forces of the people'.

This view had some basis in actual history, with emphasis on 'some'. For instance, contemporary research of social trust and values in Norwegian society shows that the introduction of Protestantism in the sixteenth century, with its promotion of non-hierarchical structures, had an important influence on trust levels and values like freedom and equality.

Nevertheless, Wergeland's view of Norwegian medieval history was first and foremost a cultural construction and myth. 'Myth' is not used here in the pejorative sense of fabrication, but in the sense that all social coherence is created through symbols and myths. Furthermore, this myth was partly based on projection. Wergeland took contemporary values and ideas, heavily inspired by Enlightenment ideas, projected them back onto medieval society and declared them old Norwegian values, which in turn had to be re-discovered and put to use in the present. This cultural construct was a powerful narrative which helped to shape Norwegian nationalism in the nineteenth century.

From the end of the 1830s onwards, academic historians worked more systematically in order to create a national science of history and historical writing. University professors Rudolf Keyser and P.A. Munch founded the so-called 'Norwegian historical school', and they and their successors were of immense importance to the later development of Norwegian national consciousness. Broadly speaking, they extended and systematized the perspectives of Schøning and Wergeland, interested mostly in the Middle Ages. Norway's history was the story of a remote Golden Age, several hundred years of eclipse, and a possible new Golden Age.

Firstly, Keyser and Munch formulated a theory of the ethnic origins of the Norwegian people, which we could call a Norwegian origin myth. According to this theory, the ancestors of the Norwegians had mostly immigrated to the northernmost parts of the country from the east. This indicated that Norwegians had different lineage from related peoples, as the Swedes were supposed to have arrived mostly from the south. Munch in particular insinuated that Norwegians were therefore 'purer' and, ethnically speaking, more noble than their Nordic and Germanic neighbours.

This theory of immigration was speculative and untenable; it faced criticism, fell apart and was abandoned as early as 1870. But this did not happen until its originators had died, and by this point the theory had left a strong imprint on Norwegian national development in the two crucial middle decades of the nineteenth century.

Ownership and medieval history

The other theme was likewise characteristic, concerning the cultural and spiritual ownership of ancient Norse cultural material and the language in which it was written. This was an extensive and important cultural conflict. The cultural material—in literature, history and mythology—was incredibly rich. Among the most important relics of the Middle Ages were the Eddaic poems and other verse works, as well as saga literature written in prose. Munch, leading a great many Norwegian historians and other scholars, was the champion of the view that both the written language and the cultural material were exclusively Norwegian. He and his peers brought forward many subtle historical and philological arguments to strengthen this position. A central part of the argument was that Iceland, having been colonized and a subject of the Norwegian state from the middle of the thirteenth century, was therefore Norwegian. This was a necessary part of the argument, not least because Snorri Sturlason, the author of the Norwegian royal sagas and most other important medieval literature, was demonstrably a native of Iceland.

Munch made it clear that this was not merely an academic discussion establishing truths and untruths; rather the conflict was of vital importance to the Norwegian nation:

No property rights among the Nations should therefore be more respected than the ones that each Nation has to its own historical Memorials. To deprive a Nation of these, is almost as unjust as to conquer a piece of its Territory. And doubly unjust is such Deprivation, when it affects a Nation like the Norwegian, with so few historical Memorials, that the loss of a single one, however humble, is intolerable, not to mention that of the most precious the Nation owns.[2]

For example, Munch promoted the view that Leif Eriksson—the Iceland-born Viking who around the year 1000 discovered the continent later known as North America—was Norwegian.

As one may imagine, such positions were controversial. Danish historians absolutely and vehemently rejected Munch's attempt to make large parts of Norse cultural heritage exclusively Norwegian. Munch's view that medieval Iceland and its inhabitants were basically Norwegian did not gain much acceptance among Icelandic historians either (nor, presumably, among other Icelanders).

Today there are few if any who would accept Munch's position. Yet in our context his views, and more generally the interest in Norwegian medieval history and Norse medieval culture, were of immense importance to the development of Norwegian national identity. One of Munch's prominent successors, the nationalistic and democratic historian Halvdan Koht, who was also foreign minister in a Social Democratic government 1935–41, described in vivid phrasing how 'we' had to 'struggle against the Danes for the ancient Norse literature and for our own history'. To Koht it really was 'our historians' who 'won back our own past'; they had 'connected us to our ancestors and shown us the continuous line of the people's development'.

This influence may be seen most directly among Norwegian writers and in schoolbooks. Major Norwegian authors like Bjørnstjerne Bjørnson and Henrik Ibsen wrote a series of dramas using themes from the Norwegian Middle Ages—so-called 'saga plays'—during the 1850s and 1860s. They were very much influenced by the activities of the Norwegian historical school. Bjørnson even had a close personal relationship with Munch and labelled himself as a 'Munchian'. Furthermore, he found in Norwegian medieval history not only dramatic material; the saga plays were to contribute to the creation of a national consciousness.

Henrik Ibsen is an interesting case in this regard. His early dramatic plays were clearly influenced by national Romanticism, but he soon distanced himself from full-scale Norwegian nationalism. In 1867 he published his play *Peer Gynt*, widely perceived as a satire on what one may call Norwegian national character traits, but also containing strong roots in national folklore. Later, Ibsen's literary output would develop in other directions, towards his famous sociological-psychological plays.

From the early 1830s onwards, much space in schoolbooks was taken up by medieval history, at first mostly influenced by Snorri's sagas, and later by the work of the Norwegian historical school. Later in the century, this interest in Norwegian medieval history and its culture reached a wide section of contemporary arts, music and architecture.

As already hinted, Norwegian nationalist writing on history falls into a well-known pattern. However, we could argue that this area was probably more significant to Norway than to many other national identities being formulated and developed. Ancient Norwegian history, as interpreted by historians, teachers and writers, was unusually rich and dramatic. It could offer heroic and conquering Vikings. It could offer great feats of exploration, asserting that America was not discovered by Columbus but by the Norwegian Viking Leif Eriksson. It could offer kings who were both great personalities and great statesmen. It could offer a developed and functional Norwegian state and a Norwegian North Sea Empire. It could offer a cultural and social life with an extensive code of law, an expressive religion, a well-developed moral code; and it could offer impressive poetry, both epic and lyrical.

At the time, the contrast between this impressive remote past and the unhappy recent past—the so-called Danish Era—was especially notable. In the centuries before 1814, Norway had been reduced merely to part of the Danish realm. It is reasonable to believe that this contrast made the discovery, reconstruction and dissemination of Norwegian medieval history seem all the more impressive. To put it another way, the need to find a continuity between medieval Norway and the new Norway was even stronger.

In addition, an element of pure competition in Scandinavia should not be underestimated here. To Norwegians, their medieval history appeared more spectacular and glorious than that of Sweden and, to a lesser extent, of Denmark.

The interconnectedness between ancient and recent Norwegian history reached a kind of conclusion at the very end of the century, when a luxury edition of Snorri's royal sagas was issued, lavishly illustrated by leading Norwegian artists. The artist's model for one of the great Viking kings, Olav Tryggvason, was the new national hero of the 1890s, the explorer and scientist Fridtjof Nansen.

These constructivist uses of ancient history to create a new national identity could have resulted in a heroic and aggressive Norwegian nationalism, inspired by Viking conquests, brutality and heroic deeds. The new Norwegian national identity could have been hell-bent on righting ancient wrongs: getting old Norwegian territories back from Sweden, for instance, or restoring the ancient North Sea Empire. There were certainly nationalist cries at this time, especially anti-Danish voices who felt that Iceland, Greenland and the Faroe Islands were legitimately and legally still Norwegian colonies. But these assertions were sur-

prisingly few. The main strands of Norwegian cultural nationalism in the nineteenth century followed Henrik Wergeland's lead
and, in picking and choosing from the Golden Age, peaceful
deliberations were chosen over heroic action.

In the twentieth century, the connection to ancient Norwegian
history has been of lesser importance. Of course, various
strands of right-wing nationalism have been influenced by
efforts in the preceding century to foster a specifically Norwegian
sense of identity. The Nazi party Nasjonal Samling (NS), under
its leader Vidkun Quisling, tried to recreate and redevelop the
close connection with Norwegian medieval traditions in the
1930s and during the Second World War. However, Quisling
and his followers did not exactly follow in Wergeland's path,
instead playing up Norway's aggressive and heroic Viking past
in a rather absurd manner. After 1945, many medieval symbols
were loosely associated with the NS and thereby brought into
disrepute in Norway.

How we ended up with two languages

The second important area—the literary language—was problematic in the development of a national identity during the nineteenth century, and has still not been satisfactorily resolved at the
time of writing. If one had to nominate a candidate for The Great
Norwegian Culture War of the last 200 years, the clear frontrun-
ner is the conflict over Norway's written language.

After 1814, the problem was simply this: the written, literary
language of Norway was Danish. The old Norwegian, or Norse,
literary language had been abandoned during the Danish Era. So,
what to do?

The Norwegian elite in 1814 tried a quick fix, attempting what
one might call a linguistic coup. The revised Norwegian
Constitution of 4 November 1814 quite simply used the term 'the

Norwegian language' for the existing written language. An explanation for this may be sought in pure power politics. The revision was a compromise with the new union partner Sweden, and said that 'all presentation of Norwegian matters' was to take place 'in the Norwegian language'. This should be read as a conscious attempt to counter cultural Swedification from the outset, since the new Norwegian king was Swedish and thus Sweden, regardless of formal equality, would be the stronger partner in the union.

This Norwegian attempt to take over the Danish language and call it 'Norwegian' received support from quite a few Norwegian intellectuals, who argued that the common language in the Danish kingdom was Norwegian just as much as it was Danish. Yet Danish linguists and other intellectuals protested vehemently against this interpretation, and the Norwegian elite were not all satisfied with this linguistic coup attempt. Around 1830, concerned Norwegian nationalists started exploring other solutions.

The problem with the written language could only be considered as part of a larger one: the culture of the Norwegian elite was, as might be expected, strongly influenced by Denmark and Danish culture. During the second half of the century nationalist historians and others formulated a theory that there were actually two separate cultures in Norway after 1814: a Danish-dominated elite culture, mainly belonging to the towns and urban areas, and a Norwegian popular culture in rural areas. This view obviously served the nationalist myth-making agenda, and was a simplification of a complex linguistic and cultural reality. However, it is true that many members of the urban and bureaucratic elite spoke a more or less Norwegianized Danish, and quite a few civil servants were of Danish stock. On the other hand, very few Danish farmers had migrated to Norway and intermarried with Norwegians.

The written language was viewed as a key to this problem. To many nationalists, it was evident that one could not create a real Norwegian nation without having a separate Norwegian language.

Originally, the Norwegian written language was Danish, whereas spoken Norwegian deviated considerably; Norway is said to have had a dialect for each town or village. Ideas of constructing a written language that was more coherent with the oral language gradually became stronger and branched into two directions: the first to make Danish-Norwegian gradually more Norwegian, and the second to use dialects to create a new language.

Various solutions to this problem were proposed. A radical thought was to start with Old Norse, which incidentally had been well-preserved in Iceland, both in the written and spoken language. One might assume that the nationalist historian P.A. Munch would have been a supporter of this solution. Instead he argued that the Old Norse language was a thing of the past, and that the written Danish language was appropriate and expedient for modern Norwegians, even if it was Danish. His main point was that every attempt to replace the official language with purer Norwegian alternatives was reactionary in a cultural sense. It would mean Norwegians abandoning their participation in 'the common European course of development'. Munch allied the official written language not only to general cultural development but also to the modernization of society.

Instead, Munch wanted history to be the central marker of cultural nationalism. In his view it was Norway's ancient history, with its rich cultural heritage (and, indeed, its ancient language) which would separate the nation from its Nordic neighbours. However, most of the intellectual class clearly felt that the 'Danish problem' needed addressing if Norway was to build its own identity.

The alternative Norwegian literary language was developed in a different fashion in the 1830s and 1840s. The self-taught philologist Ivar Aasen assembled samples of the spoken language from the areas of the Norwegian countryside which, in his opinion, were the least influenced by Danish. From this he constructed a new Norwegian written standard, inspired by the work of the German Brothers Grimm and others.

To adherents of Aasen, a purely Norwegian written language was a necessary condition for creating a fully developed Norwegian nation. As the author and publicist Arne Garborg put it:

> The language boundary is the boundary of nationality, the people are recognized and judged according to their language, their spiritual independence, their originality, their moral power, in other words: Their right to exist.[3]

The Aasen standard (or *Landsmål*) won strong acceptance in nationalist circles from the 1860s onwards, but it was and remained very controversial. The struggle to introduce a new literary language met a lot of resistance, particularly towards the end of the nineteenth century. To the chief resistor, Bjørnstjerne Bjørnson, the striving towards *Landsmål* represented an attempt to force an artificial language, imprinted with an inferior, provincial peasant culture, on a high and flourishing national culture. Bjørnson was also concerned about cultural ties to the rest of Scandinavia and to other parts of the world. Earlier, Munch had expressed a similar view, writing in the 1850s that *Landsmål* was nothing but an expression of a stage in the development of a civilization which had been left behind—the pre-modern, agrarian society. In addition, according to Munch, attempts to Norwegianize the language were philologically unsound.

An alternative method of development was to Norwegianize the Danish written language by degrees. This solution was rejected by adherents of *Landsmål* on nationalist and philological grounds, but the strong parallel movement developed, resulting in a written language from the early 1930s officially named *Bokmål* (book language).

THE NORWEGIAN EXCEPTION?

When Ivar Aasen created his *Landsmål*, he did not assemble any spoken language samples from the cities. In his opinion, the urban language was hopelessly infected by Danish. In this way he tapped into an important conflict in Norwegian social and cultural life: town versus countryside. If anything, this conflict was actually strengthened by Aasen's solution to the language issue.

In 1885 the Storting decided that *Landsmål* was to be considered equal to what was then called 'the common literary language'. This decision meant, broadly speaking, that it was left to the people themselves to select which literary language they wanted to use. Essentially, the decision to enshrine *Landsmål* as an official written standard meant that the problem of language remained unresolved.

From the early twentieth century, the political majority in the Storting continued attempts to impose a solution to Norway's written language problem. The official policy was to gradually merge the two written languages in order to create a unified Norwegian identity, and several language reforms were implemented to begin this process. Alas, there were fierce reactions from both sides of the language barrier against the merged language policy. The backlash became especially fierce after the Second World War, primarily from conservative adherents of *Bokmål*; a protest movement gathered more than 400,000 signatures. This was a cultural struggle but also a social struggle. On the one hand, it was a protest against the state meddling and dictating how Norwegians should speak and write. On the other hand, it reinforced the conflict between urban and the rural parts of the country. The bitter struggle didn't calm down until 1981, when this merger policy was definitively abolished.

With such conflicting views it is no wonder that the language question has been extremely emotional and controversial, even at the time of writing. Despite all political efforts, *Landsmål*—later known as *Nynorsk* (New Norwegian)—has never been anything but a minority language in Norway. In Norwegian schools, everyone must learn both *Bokmål* and *Nynorsk*, but only one is emphasized. It is up to each municipality to decide which language is to be the main language in its local schools, though the majority has preferred *Bokmål*.

Danish and Norwegian remain relatively similar in their written form; even *Nynorsk* is not very remote from written Danish. For example, in his well-known 1913 article 'Marxism and the National Question', Joseph Stalin, who was the Russian Bolsheviks' designated expert on nationalities, quite naively stated that Danish and Norwegian were the same language. This drastically differentiates the case of Norway from those of countries like Ireland or Finland, where the written languages in question— English versus Irish Gaelic and Swedish versus Finnish, respectively—are perceptibly different. Such similarities, however, have made the matter no less controversial.

Modern Norwegians thus live with two official written languages, a wide selection of spellings, and still a plethora of dialects. Language remains highly connected to where you come from, but more so for oral than written language, since *Bokmål*— the Norwegianized version of written Danish—continues to dominate written Norwegian.

For Arne Garborg, the Norwegian nation could not be completely developed before all Danish traces were gone, and before the sole official language became a pure literary Norwegian. From this perspective, the development of a fully Norwegian national identity has still not been accomplished at the time of writing. In other words, the Norwegians are still not completely Norwegian.

3

LIBERAL BUREAUCRACY, MODERN SOCIETY

The period 1814–84 has been labelled *embetsmannsstaten* or 'the civil servants' state'. For seventy years Norway was governed by educated bureaucrats, often professors, as an 'executive' elite in government. In modern times this would be called a technocracy or expert regime, and would in some ways be considered non-democratic and even authoritarian. The main reasoning behind this system was that those who shall govern are those who are capable.

At this time, Norway was a country almost without elites of any kind. The few bourgeois elites had lost most of their economic means after the Napoleonic wars at the beginning of the nineteenth century. Nobility was abolished in 1814, and Norway counted just a handful of families that could be said to constitute an elite. The only small group of people who could administer and govern the newly founded state were the educated bureaucrats. They were Norwegians who had mostly received an education in Copenhagen, since the University of Oslo was founded as late as 1811. Their common educational background was jurisprudence, theology and, in later years, economy.

THE NORWEGIAN EXCEPTION?

In 1814, the parliament consisted of seventy-nine representatives, of whom fifty were civil servants, nineteen were farmers and ten were businessmen. They met every three years. We have mentioned that the farmers constituted an important group, but they were underrepresented in the administration of the civil servants' state until much later. Indeed, they were one of the main forces that finally overthrew the civil servants' state in 1884 and established the parliamentary system that still exists at time of writing. The most extraordinary aspect of the civil servants' state was that it lasted as long as it did, without losing legitimacy until its final decades. Up to that point people accepted being governed by so-called professor-politicians.

The legitimacy of this regime was based on several factors. The civil servants had led the successful rebellion in 1814, and in both the Storting and the government they defended the Constitution in the 1820s and 1830s against King Carl Johan's attempts to strengthen his power. In a strictly formal sense, this was a power struggle between the Norwegian king and the Norwegian parliament. Yet since Carl Johan was also King of Sweden, it was widely perceived as a struggle on behalf of all Norwegians against the Swedes.

Furthermore, the civil servants showed some clever political manoeuvring in their fight against special interest groups. As mentioned, they managed to stay in power for seventy years; they were present in all key functions of government and gradually also in the institutions built during the century; and, of course, they were professors. How could this be? The main reason was that the civil servants proved themselves able to manoeuvre politically and ensure support from different groups including farmers (see Chapter 4), while also making sure that other groups with privileges were abolished. For instance, operating sawmills had become a special privilege for certain individuals, and this was reversed without resistance. They were also able to keep various forces in Norwegian society in a state of balance. Over the decades, the civil servants managed to govern with a broad consensus and support from landholding farmers and other property holders. The source of their legitimacy ultimately came from the founding ideas of the 1814 Constitution, especially the idea that the best-suited should govern. Lastly, they defended the rights and interests of property owners against possible threats from below.

It could be argued that we were lucky to have liberally-minded, progressive bureaucrats whose intention was to modernize Norwegian society. However, was a homogeneous and equal society perhaps less inclined to quarrel? And could the absence of deep divisions have made it easier to accept benevolent bureaucrats?

The civil servants' state

The civil servants' state has been perceived differently by Norwegian historians. Some say it was a bureaucratic coup, while others claimed it established the modern rule of law, defining the limits to power and the scope of the state, but admitting that politics was not the important issue. A modernizing, administrative and technocratic management was conducted, with emphasis from the liberally inclined bureaucrats and their wish to rule according to the law. Some even argued that the civil servants wished to use the state to modernize society, calling the leading officials 'activist ideologues'. These bureaucrats were liberals, but they were not afraid of state interference where it was seen as necessary for Norway's modernization. The two main issues were nation-building and economic development.

The civil servants, *embetsmenn*, were the political elite who had gained their position through education and superior knowledge. In the early decades, they had little competition in ruling the country, either from the farmers or from virtually non-existent other elites. They knew each other as friends, through marriage and professional activities, forming a small but nationwide network that did not only include the capital, but smaller cities, towns and rural places around Norway. They generally communicated through correspondence, but also met if possible. During the 1830s, a small, informal circle was formed called *intelligenskretsen* or 'group of intellectuals'. The protagonist of this circle was Anton Martin Schweigaard (1808–70), who came from the small southern town of Kragerø and had been educated at the University of Oslo, graduating as the best student in jurisprudence in 1832. Many of his ideas about the development of Norwegian society began in this circle, which included several jurists. The group saw communications and infrastructure in the widest sense, as well as a general liberalization of trade, as key to the modernization of society. A universal education was also part of their vision; in their view, an educated population would enhance economic development. The main ideas from the Enlightenment, including a belief in progress, were embedded in their concept of a developed society. The Norwegian nation-building project was founded on reforming and ameliorating institutions to create a modern rule of law and to improve economic development.

The eagerness of the Norwegian professors to engage in practical institution-building, both private and public, was greater than in many other European countries. Given the scarce possibilities of raising an economic elite, the state was a natural vehicle to implement reforms. The ideas of this circle formed the early beginnings of modern economic, political and social thought in Norway.

It is also worth mentioning that the building blocks of a capable state were quite solid even before 1814. Norway was not starting from scratch, and a peaceful nineteenth century gave space and time to develop a sound government and bureaucracy, as well as modernizing the economy.

LIBERAL BUREAUCRACY, MODERN SOCIETY

Building state capacity and liberal institutions the Norwegian way

The role of the state as promoted by the *embetsmenn* in the nineteenth century can be summarized as follows: to fight against corruption and develop a trustworthy bureaucracy; develop a stable and functioning monetary system; facilitate construction of communications and infrastructure; develop medical services and increase the emphasis on education; and, finally, to liberalize the economy and abolish any remaining economic privileges.

The civil servants' state was the era of institution-building and bureaucracy in a Weberian sense: it was meritocratic, transparent and impartial. Many Norwegian institutions were founded in this period, including the Office of the Auditor General as early as 1816.

A trustworthy and corruption-free bureaucracy is a crucial pillar of all liberal democracies. Historically it is interesting and important to note that the Danish-Norwegian bureaucracy was relatively honourable and efficient compared to other state administrations. However, the division between the Danish and the Norwegian bureaucracy that followed from 1814 established a greater transparency and more stringent control routines. Recent historical analyses show that the governmental administration was 'clean' from 1814 but regional administrations, especially the local customs administration, were the source of trouble.[1] Large-scale corruption was discovered in 1817, and resulted in better control of state finances and local government, as well as a less corrupt bureaucracy. These economic irregularities were reduced to a minimum by the 1850s. The story of the two ink pots originated in the nineteenth-century civil servants' state: the civil servant was said to have two ink pots, one for his duties as a civil servant and one for his private correspondences, keeping them separate and therefore non-corrupt.

Of interest here is the political organization of the economy, which was centrally planned at the beginning of the century. It was characterized by privileges and political sanctions, especially when it came to the exploitation of raw materials such as mining and lumber industries. These privileges also included crafts and different trades.

The kingdom of Denmark and Norway had a mercantilist economic system during the eighteenth century, which meant that political measures were taken to enforce the comparative advantages of Norwegian mining and lumber trade. The measures were built on a small but sustainable milieu of an entrepreneurial bourgeoisie, where companies were given favourable terms for trade and production. After the Napoleonic Wars, Norway established its Constitution, which provided a political and democratic boost but led to a phase of low growth and deep economic crises for many businesses. Politically, Norway was close to starting afresh, combining liberal ideas, modern political institutions and new general conditions for economic activities based on equality of treatment, protection of property and a stable monetary system. This indicates a staged strategy, quite quickly resulting in a growing middle class of traders, producers and entrepreneurs. It must be emphasized that this bourgeoisie comprised smaller businesses and industries, therefore closely tied to their operations and employees, and included many small freeholders. Jacob Aall, a politician and representative at Eidsvoll, noted during the 1840s that 'everything in our country is in some sense middle class'.[2]

By the turn of the century almost all restrictions were abolished, which meant that Norway had a more open economy than both Sweden and Denmark. This should not imply a withdrawal of the state; on the contrary, public investments were crucial for facilitating economic activities and trade. In the first decades of the twentieth century, the state was once again an active investor and policy maker, especially when it came to industrialization of energy and raw materials.

LIBERAL BUREAUCRACY, MODERN SOCIETY

One of the most important characteristics of Norwegian social development from the early 1800s was the combination of a strong state and an active vision of a modern, liberal society. Even before the turn of the century, there was generally great political recognition of the significance of public responsibilities. Existing alongside this were the fundamental ideas of liberalism, as the conservative economist Bredo Morgenstierne pointed out in 1889:

> The limits of the state's responsibilities in this domain are decided just out of the considerations for individual freedom. But where these limits are drawn in each case, cannot normally be given. Some states are going in a more socialist direction, whereas others in a more liberal direction. A contemporary example of the first one is Germany, and the last one is England, while our country might be described as being somewhere in between.[3]

The Norwegians were well acquainted with European sociological and economic ideas mainly coming from German, French and British thought. The empirical tradition was prominent, and law and economics were closely connected for many decades. A national expert was needed, and the first step was to establish a chair in economics. The second step was to develop appropriate Norwegian theoretical literature, but the principal civil servant Schweigaard quickly became absorbed in politics and did not have time for this extensive scientific work. One remark can be made, however: Schweigaard clearly saw Norway as a unique entity with its own history, culture and sociological structure, and therefore wanted to make sure that theories were adaptable to that structure.

One of the clear ambitions was to establish a sound basis for statistical information about society and economics. From the 1830s, this development of statistics can be seen in discussions of what to measure and especially in valid comparisons over time to trace progress. Schweigaard claimed that statistics should be relevant, concrete and realistic in order for economics to be interesting and applicable: 'economics, in a Norwegian context, should provide correct guidelines about what to rectify and what to develop...something that included a thorough insight to the national institutions which were a condition for the development of the productive forces.' He aspired to conduct economic, scientific and theoretical work adapted to Norwegian circumstances and experiences. He writes,

> If it were only a matter of translating the main international literature in political economy, it would have been easy. But in this case an independent, Norwegian discipline, that may justly serve Norwegian needs, is necessary. Guidance on improvements, to an understanding of our own economic and financial affairs and institutions, can only be obtained through a thorough scientific analysis and development of our economic institutions, their aims and their workings.[4]

Statistics would become an important auxiliary discipline in the development of Norwegian economic thought, and the 'Statistical Office', later to become the Central Statistical Bureau, was founded in 1851.

In 1869, a politician remarked that 'it was not right to have such a tight connection between law and economics... [the weakness of Norwegian economics] was the lack of disciplinary development, especially adapted to Norwegian conditions that might lead to a better comprehension of our Norwegian context.'[5] But this can also be reversed: the focus on law, economics and the emphasis on Norwegian conditions may have contributed to a more pragmatic building of institutions. The discussion of law and economics had its background in the different impulses and development in economic thought, underlining both the proper Norwegian ideas of economics as well as the different theories coming out of Europe. The empirical tradition, underlining an understanding of context and history, came from English empiricism but also from the German historical school. It was important for Norwegian intellectuals to build their own professional basis in law and economics.

Institutional readiness and the luck of the Navigation Act

How did Norway become a capitalist, industrial country? Was it through a shift in dynamics from a market-demand perspective to a supply-technological perspective?

The market-demand perspective can be described as export-driven growth, which in the case of Norway came from lumber, fisheries and shipping. The main point is that entrepreneurs use market possibilities; if a market grows it will be satisfied by suppliers, who are responding to demand. This did not occur in other peripheral countries, and the difference between them lies in Norway's institutional and structural conditions. The question is whether institutions should exist before such growth, or be built as a result of it.

The institutional, political and cultural readiness of Scandinavian countries took them from poverty to plenty within a short period of time. Even though the industrialization lagged at first, the catch-up was quick. The estimated GNP per capita shows that the Scandinavian countries climbed from US$219 in 1830 to US$682 in 1913, closing the gap between themselves and the industrial core of continental Europe, including France and Germany. Thus, Schweigaard's modernization strategy of building institutions and infrastructure can be called a success. As David Landes recently put it,

> ... getting lucky isn't about culture, but staying lucky often is. When a society, or the controlling parts of a society, is sitting on wealth-making resources, a country can be pretty rich as long as the resources remain. But when the resources are used up and any investments from them exhausted, that country often reverts.[6]

THE NORWEGIAN EXCEPTION?

Norway avoided getting stuck in this way by innovating and adapting throughout the nineteenth century. First came export capacity, then strong capital, then entrepreneurship, technological reform and specialization. In all these, Norway took approaches from already-industrialized European nations and altered them for its own context. Generally, Norway seems to have taken advantage of being a latecomer—not inventing but adapting quickly to new measures—which is also underlined by Landes. Norway was open to world trade at a time when its dynamics and conditions were shifting. In this way it was the lucky, small imitator in Western Europe.

Norway's economy thrived successfully thanks to deliberate strategy and also luck, when the UK removed the lumber tariff and agreed on the Navigation Act. Free or freer trade was a credo from the Enlightenment and these ideas were gradually influencing politics. In 1842 the British Prime Minister Robert Peel presented a state budget, which included the abolishment of customs for more than 750 goods and the reduction of many tariffs. For Norway, the reduction on customs for lumber was of great importance.

For Norway, as a small economy and greatly dependent on exports, these changes had extensive consequences both for the shipping and lumber trade. In 1849, the UK repealed a series of Navigation Acts that had been passed over the seventeenth and eighteenth centuries. The 1849 repeal essentially instituted the philosophy and practice of free trade, by doing away with former customs and tariffs and thus opening a large market for Norway. Before this point, Norwegian ships could not sail between foreign ports, but afterwards could find business internationally without always having to return to Norwegian ports. According to Schweigaard, this was the greatest event in Norway's history since 1814, as Norwegian shipping entered the world market. This remark also shows the international, outward-facing Norwegian mentality. The country certainly had natural resources, but had constantly depended on imports to secure the supply of those things that were impossible to grow or produce in a cold and northerly country. The importance to Norway of trade and shipping cannot be understated; along with fisheries and local trade is the fact that the coastline, islands and fjords total 100,915 km, the second largest area in the world after Canada. Along with farming, shipping and seafaring have also been deeply ingrained in the Norwegian sense of self. Oftentimes, farmers were also seafarers in order to generate several sources of income.

The repeal of the Navigation Acts resulted in Norway becoming the world's third largest shipping nation, only surpassed by Great Britain and the United States, which was a great achievement for a small nation. Explanations for its ability to build a large and important fleet are mainly the structure of insurance. It was comparatively cheap to insure in the Norwegian market, and there was often cooperation between shipowners based on trust and transparency. These shipowners formed companies which fostered mutual dependence; each owner had a quota, thus efficiently sharing possible risks. Local bourgeoisie based in the smaller towns, together with egalitarian-oriented and free farmers in the countryside, made smaller businesses more successful. Also important was the widespread use of partnership—*partsredere*—in shipping, which was often a side business in order to conduct trade.

On the other hand, for a long time the main Norwegian exporting industries, including shipping, were astonishingly technologically conservative. Technology worked as long as growth could be sustained. Around 1870, the same year of Schweigaard's death, waves of international crises started which gradually created a need for technological innovation and change. For shipping this meant a move from sailing to steam. The eventual spread of technology did not happen because of a well-

65

educated population, which Norway had at least on a primary school level; it was not necessarily a prerequisite for the adaptation of advanced technology. It sufficed that key clusters had either the knowledge that was needed or the opportunity to acquire it. It appears that education was well-adapted where it was needed, and therefore also efficiently applied. The political and institutional conditions were already in place, as was a functioning credit and monetary system. As we are about to see, this financial readiness for industrialization had been set up from the start of Norway's independence.

Industrializing based on natural resources

Before the Napoleonic Wars, Norway was a peripheral country in Europe. Apart from fisheries, mining and the lumber industry, which had an international market, its primary agrarian activities were local. Industrialization and modernization processes in the nineteenth century were commonly Western-European, but the Norwegians had two differentiating factors: the lack of both military and colonial interests on other continents, resulting in greater emphasis on internal Norwegian affairs and a lack of investment capacity. In 1814 the financial foundation of the Norwegian state was weak. Historically, Norwegians had an aversion to paying taxes, and the main source of the budget was customs and tariffs, mostly on alcohol.

The period 1814–90 can be described as the transition from an agrarian society to a private-capitalist industrial society, especially prominent after 1840. Norway had eleven commercial banks in 1875; twenty-five years later the number was almost ten times higher, and the banks played an important role in providing capital. Typically, there were many smaller banks which decentralized this structure, and almost all Norwegian towns had their own commercial bank which served the local market. This suggests that the country lacked larger credit institutions, able to finance bigger companies and projects. Loans from the existing banks were typically short-term operational credits rather than long-term investment loans.

By 1875, the standard of living in Norway equalled the average level of Western European countries. Because of the egalitarian profile of the population, this implied that the average Norwegian had a slightly better living standard than many contemporary Europeans.

Only around ten per cent of the Norwegian population lived in urban areas before 1800. The rest occupied rural areas and mainly lived off farming, often combined with other activities such as forestry or fishing, as well as crafts, shipping, mining and trade.

The last part of the nineteenth century witnessed large changes to this structure. In short, the main reasons were an increased international demand for Norwegian goods, a higher level of education among the population, technological development and huge investments in infrastructure. The first railway was opened in 1854, and infrastructure—including railways, roads, rivers and ports—became a high priority after 1850, as in many European countries, realized through state budgets in cooperation with local capital. The amelioration of transportation was important for trade and communications between different parts of the country. This included not only shipping but railways, roads, bridges, canals and harbours. The growing population, together with a better transportation system, created a home market for many consumer goods. Aided by a growing export market, the home market developed as well. Economic growth was volatile but strong, and resulted in steadily increasing living standards. Compulsory schooling led to a better-educated population. In the course of 100 years, Norway moved from a nation of peasants and fishermen to a modern, industrialized nation.

THE NORWEGIAN EXCEPTION?

Norwegian industrialization has been discussed in relation to Schweigaard, and many historians claim to find less enthusiasm for industry than for trade, communications and institutional building in his views. Schweigaard had said in the 1840s that '[a]ll that can be expected from the future is that the country, using its own factories, will be capable of supplying itself with simple woven fabrics of mediocre quality but will have to import higher quality fabrics.' He thereby underlined the general impression from the Ministry of Finance, which stated in 1842 that '[t]he difficulties with competition from foreign factories mean that Norway will never be industrialized on a large scale.'[7] The last statement was proven to be wrong by the turn of the century, but it demonstrates reluctance towards industrialization on a large scale. There was a widespread view that Norway had simply arrived too late to the game. Nevertheless, a couple of economic crises, as well as the development and change in shipping and the emerging industrialization, changed the country.

The social changes of the nineteenth century were accompanied by the emergence of a new culture of entrepreneurship. An important figure that may illustrate the Norwegian entrepreneurial tradition was Hans Nielsen Hauge (1771–1824), a farmer's son who became one of Norway's most famous entrepreneurs. He was greatly influenced by Northern European puritanism, arguing for individual, political, religious and economic freedom. Initially he founded a religious movement—*Haugianere*—named after himself, which was a bottom-up protest for more freedom. Because religious gatherings without permission were banned until 1842, Hauge was imprisoned on several occasions. His religious views can be compared to what Max Weber described in *The Protestant Ethic and the Spirit of Capitalism*. Hauge combined his entrepreneurial activities with Norwegian puritan values, hard work and creating value for society. Soon Hauge was followed by many *Haugianerne*, and their work and beliefs became influential, especially the idea that poverty could be reduced by giving people the means to support themselves through labour. Many of his followers became important contributors to society, leading to the perception that employers and entrepreneurs had a social responsibility. Later followers argued for religious freedom, for freedom of trade and running of businesses, as well as for workers' welfare and general public education. They also put these ideas into practice by starting their own businesses.

By the turn of the twentieth century, Norway was relatively industrialized by European standards. However, it had a raw material-based profile and compared to other countries such as Sweden, it lacked technically advanced industries, machineries and chemicals.

Since new methods were adopted in small steps, industries slowly gained confidence to risk larger projects and investments. In the lumber industry, the development from lumber to pulp, to cellulose, and finally to paper was a great improvement. Norway was successful in one aspect, namely, in its ability to adapt and circulate new production methods in order to develop key cluster industries. It is important to note that this adjustment was more than just imitation. As economic theory came to Norway from the Continent and from England, it was discussed and reshaped to fit Norwegian political and economic circumstances. One might say that the Norwegians were quick learners when they saw an opportunity.

Machinery was important, and much of it was imported from England. Many Norwegians, commonly technicians, mechanics and business managers, travelled to England in the late 1840s. When it came to technical know-how, German expertise also played a significant role, especially in the wood-processing industry. Once again the Norwegians were quick adapters and soon learned to make the machinery themselves, later doing the same with electrical equipment out of Germany. For industrialization and economic theory, Norway turned both to the Continent, especially Germany, and to England.

As we've seen, transport links and other infrastructure were rapidly developed in the second half of the nineteenth century, but Norway was not at the forefront when measured by infrastructure investments per capita. The building processes were mainly administered by publicly employed engineers, but many of the local railways were organized as private shareholding companies. As with the shipping industry, this private sector in Norway was characterized by partnership and cooperation; arguably, this cultural and social tradition contributed to Norway's swift economic growth and industrialization.

Several initiatives throughout the nineteenth century demonstrate a high level of trust and cooperation in society. Mutual insurance companies, cooperatives and savings banks all had low thresholds of participation, and were used by servants and peasants. Norway never developed strong investment banks; the majority were small, local savings banks and this continued long after the turn of the century. The management of these banks was often identical to that of local municipality politicians, thus playing a crucial role in local industrialization and development.

In the last decades of the nineteenth century, leading politicians advocated liberal policies combined with a strong and active state. Free trade did not come under pressure until the 1905 dissolution of the union with Sweden. Consequently, different laws were passed, aiming to prevent foreign companies from buying and controlling Norwegian natural resources (see Chapters 6 and 11).

However, according to another nineteenth-century economist, Einar Einarsen:

> If one goes back in time a hundred years or so, back to the 'good old days' [...] and thereafter traces the movements of the views on economic policies that have been advocated, we may compare these movements with a pendulum that swings back and forth.[8]

Though the trend would be reversed at the other end of the century, it is clear that the intense period of modernization after 1814 took place in a context of liberalization and deregulation, with a less comprehensive state and significant reliance on private initiatives to fund and organize economic development. During the nineteenth century, local taxes were mostly connected to property and there were no direct taxes to the state in 1836–92. The state generated its income from customs and tariffs.

Demographic development during the nineteenth century

From 1815–75 the Norwegian population increased from 900,000 to 1.8 million, which was the highest proportional increase in Europe.[9] This was due to a sharp decrease in child mortality thanks to better vaccination, health measures and information, especially in the second half of the nineteenth century. When it came to increased life expectancy Norway was more advanced than her neighbours, Sweden, Denmark and the UK. The increase in population was too large and too rapid to be sustained by adequate employment growth.

As we have mentioned, Norway was a traditional peasant society in the beginning of the nineteenth century, but did not have a usual continental structure. Norway never produced many wealthy farmers simply because climatic and geographical circumstances made it impossible to farm on a grand scale, except perhaps in the south-eastern parts of the country. The Norwegian farmers, or smallholders, were independent and wanted to govern local affairs, supported by the egalitarian and liberal ideas in the 1814 Constitution. In addition, many of them could read and write and owned their own property. During the first part of the nineteenth century, Norwegians coped with the population increase by letting second and third sons become smallholders on their fathers' or eldest brothers' farms. They could farm small pieces of land for their own use and they could work on the main farm. So long as it was possible to sustain the smallholders, this system worked. In the Northern parts of the country, the smallholders could add to their income by participating in fisheries. This structure was far more egalitarian than in any other European country, and Norwegian farmers had another great advantage, which was that around eighty per cent were freeholders in 1850. They owned their farms, although many of these were small, and this ownership provided personal freedom and a basis for income. This also meant that buildings and land were well looked after.

Yet by around 1840–50, the pressure on land was too big to be handled by the smallholder regime. Increases in population and in industrialization gradually led to a labouring class of second and third sons and daughters, who started seeking paid work in urban areas if they could not stay on their parents' farm. Towns increased in size and rural areas in the eastern parts of Norway witnessed the highest emigration rates to the United States. The social and economic distance between the farmers and the smallholders had been relatively small in many regions, but this changed with industrialization and the opportunity to obtain paid work.

Until the 1850s, Norway had been an exception when it came to settlement patterns. There were no typical villages like in the rest of Europe, and the few towns were generally very small. Instead, people lived together on a few farms clustered together in what we call *bygd*, but with none of the usual activities one could find in a European village. Everything happened on the farms, and they were owned by the farmer himself. This unusual pattern might explain the lasting homogeneity and sense of equality between Norwegians. Social and economic differences did exist, but not to the same extent as other European countries, not even Scandinavia. There were of course churches, and the farms had a local church, but the vicar was often a farmer him-self. We might say that there were no estates in a European sense, and the clergy were part of society rather than existing in a separate sphere. This dissolved amidst increasing urbanization and industrialization which made classes relevant: first and fore-most, the labour class.

The age of marriage was historically high because men could not marry before they had finished military service; many also waited to marry until they could take over the farm or the small-holding. The latter explanation is probably the most plausible, as it was a way of gaining economic security for oneself and one's family. The average marrying age was 28 years old for men and 25–26 for women, relatively late compared to other Western countries. This also meant that the birth rate was lower than one might expect. From 1801–1900 the average household decreased from 5.36 people to 4.33. However, the overall trend was still one of enormous population growth; though the birth rate declined slightly over the century, the death rate dropped much more sharply.

Norway has historically been a far more egalitarian country than any of its neighbours, or countries like France and England. According to a civil servant in 1859, Norway could be described as 'an even waterline',[10] meaning that there were no large differ-ences between people. With trade and industrialization, this picture changed. It is true that social mobility was high, and income was still relatively evenly distributed, as earning money was open to many. Yet with the new industrial-capitalist econ-omy, fortunes became larger and more concentrated. In 1875 the top ten per cent wealthiest Norwegians living in the two largest cities, Oslo and Bergen, owned sixty per cent of the total private wealth due to prosperity coming from trade. Alongside this, inequality also rose because of the aforementioned increase in population, particularly in rural areas.

THE NORWEGIAN EXCEPTION?

Population growth also increased the awareness of social problems, and several initiatives were taken to support Norwegians economically. An international comparison in the mid-1850s indicated that Norwegian social security support was high, but not sufficient for all. One result of this was the high emigration rate in the following decades, in which quite capable people moved to the United States and started sending large amounts of money home. Even though Norway gradually became more industrialized, possible means of income were threatened by the population increase, especially lack of farmlands. In some parts of the country one son inherited the farm, keeping the size intact, whereas in other parts land was divided between sons, resulting in smaller farms. The second solution was usually chosen in the western and northern parts of the country, where fisheries often compensated for the smaller sizes of farmland. In the eastern parts, many people found themselves without land, and they had to find alternative employment; Norway's eastern rural areas saw the highest emigration rates to the United States. By the 1880s Norway's emigration rate was the second highest in Europe, surpassed only by Ireland; 1.5 per cent of the population had emigrated in 1882; and at the end of the nineteenth century the total was almost half a million people. The United States currently has a larger population with Norwegian origins than Norway itself. Nevertheless, some of these emigrants returned to Norway, bringing valuable knowledge and skills, notably in engineering.

The foundation of social benefits and welfare rights

Even with emigration, remittances sent back to Norway and even newly skilled or moneyed returnees, state support for the poor continued. In the Lutheran tradition, the state had a moral obligation to see to the general wellbeing of their citizens: to care for the poor, protect them, provide education and ensure moral behaviour. States were to discharge this duty by running hospitals and securing the supply of medicines, and later organizing a network of doctors and midwives.

The main difference between the continental, German, Norwegian and Scandinavian welfare states was that, at the end of the nineteenth century, the Scandinavian welfare state had a universalistic dimension. This was due to a close communication between the social democrats, social liberals and reforming conservatives. The Scandinavian countries rapidly followed the changes and proposals made in the 1880s by Bismarck in Germany, the difference being that from the start farmers and all classes were part of the discussion. The Swedish historian Bo Stråth emphasizes that welfare projects stemmed from a 'mixture of self-defined needs among the lower classes and the fear of social and political revolt among the ruling classes. In Scandinavia the gravitation point [...] was closer to the former.'[11]

A close connection between the economy and the state, as well as a long historical Lutheran state tradition, meant that from the very beginning public welfare was perceived as including everyone. This said, a universal welfare system took almost 100 years to complete, resulting in a universal national insurance system in 1967. There were of course conflicts of interest and class struggles following the emergence of a labour class, but the art of compromise is the best description of this development.

In pre-industrial times, there were rules about a minimum level of social and economic welfare, such as looking after elderly or disabled people. Early poverty relief was grounded in a moral view that poverty was something self-inflicted; after 1814 this view was replaced by a belief in 'help to self-reliance', which could of course be difficult for many as industrialization and population increased. The first poverty law came in 1845, and public responsibility for social problems became more common, through laws and financial support, as well as a more pronounced local public responsibility for providing services.

The term 'welfare state' was used for the first time in 1884 during a political debate. The overall picture, however, was that welfare services were undertaken by a large number of 'associations', meaning many initiatives came from political associations and labour unions including the farmer movement, low church movements and so forth. Welfare and poverty relief expanded during the last decades of the nineteenth century. The first labour commission came in 1885, followed by social laws, pensions and safeguarded labour conditions, still in rudimental and non-universal forms. Still, this was the start of a safety net of public welfare.

We cannot leave social policies and welfare without commenting on civil society and what was called *associationerne*. These were all kinds of organizations and initiatives to provide solutions and promote anything from religion to poor relief for sailors. The myriad of associations was a crucial part of modernization and democratization. Due to freedom of speech and freedom of assembly, granted in 1842 by the abolishment of the ban to gather in religious meetings, some claimed that Norway had the best civil society in the world. During the 1840s, participation in local associations exploded. In Oslo, it doubled in ten years. From 1850–1900 the number of national associations went from ten to 145.

These associations could be anything from small clubs to large labour unions, and many of them had welfare as a cause: working for the welfare of prisoners, orphans or other philanthropic aims, often grounded in conservative or religious convictions. Quite a few of them are still significant today, such as The Church City Mission, Blue Cross and the Salvation Army. The main point is that these civil society organizations contributed to welfare in many ways, from founding hospitals to providing educational information about health issues.

It is interesting to relate these associations to the levels of trust in Norway. Contemporary research holds that a foundation for high levels of social trust was built during the second half of the nineteenth century. These associations, apart from their missions, were formidable builders of democracy based on voluntary participation, democratic votes and trust. The relationship between these civil society associations and the state is also important. In Norway, and in the Nordic countries, the states were positively inclined towards these activities. From early on, a valuable coexistence and dispersion of power was established—which later also included large public financing—without the associations losing their independence.

4

THE ROAD TOWARDS DEMOCRACY

In 1884, the civil servants' regime was overthrown by a broad but loose social, political and cultural coalition. The alliance was held together by opposition to civil servants' rule and a desire to democratize Norwegian political affairs. As a common feature, we can speak of a middle-class dominated coalition of counter-cultures which gathered around Venstre, a newly formed political party. Founded in 1884, it was the first modern political party in Norway and came out of the power struggle in the early 1880s. By 1884, political tensions ran high, indeed so high that a Norwegian civil war seemed possible. In the end, however, the overthrow of the old regime turned out to be a constitutional, legal and peaceful affair. This chapter tells how and why pressure for change built throughout the nineteenth century, and the ways in which this crisis was ultimately resolved democratically and without bloodshed.

The (somewhat) loyal opposition

The 1814 Constitution had enfranchised many small farmers. Even so, the first parliamentary elections after 1814 showed that most voters opted for candidates from the social elite. Civil servants were a rather small minority among free Norwegians, but they still managed to secure a strong hold over the Storting for many years after 1814.

However, in the 1833 election farmers dismayed with the bureaucratic elite mobilized and organized voters. The result was a striking number of farmers elected to the parliament. This came as quite a shock, deemed by one contemporary commentator as, 'The triumph of ignorance and the precursor of barbarism.'[1] The 1833 election can also be viewed as a turning point; from this moment on there was a permanent farmer opposition in the Norwegian Storting. All subsequent elections resulted in large numbers of farmers in the parliament, which was quite a challenge for the civil servants' government.

The policy of the farmers was largely based on their own interests. The group was dominated by self-sufficient, independent, property-owning farmers, and not infrequently the farmers' economic interests trumped political principles.

When the civil servant elite started attacking economic privileges in Norwegian society through liberal reform acts, they could largely depend on support from the farmer deputies. One example is artisan privileges, which were abolished from around 1840. Yet this support had its limits, as the farmers' economic interests trumped ideological principles during conflicts. Thus, the Storting farmer politicians prevented all attempts to abolish the odal rights and privileges. There were also characteristic trends when it came to decisions on customs fees, the Norwegian state's largest source of income after 1836. Farmers in the southeastern parts of the country were mainly grain producers, and regularly voted for tariffs on imported grain and against tariffs on imported butter. By contrast, their fellow farmers mainly living in the western parts of Norway, whose livelihood instead came from dairy and livestock, regularly voted against tariffs on grain and for tariffs on butter. The liberalist civil servant politicians in the parliament knew this very well and had to manoeuvre accordingly.

On the other hand, however, farmers' interests had to express themselves in political ideas, and it is possible to see at least some overall principles in the Norwegian farmer opposition.

The farmer politicians in the Storting wanted the level of government fees and taxes to be as low as possible. Moreover, they wanted their communities to be self-governed to the greatest possible extent. Their attitude towards the ruling civil servants was mildly hostile or at least sceptical. In their eyes the regime interfered far too much in the local communities, bothered the farmers with fees and taxes, and represented a culture and a way of life foreign to many farmers.

To summarize, the farmer opposition wanted a small and cheap state in accordance with the views of the *Haugianere*. Yet in quite a few ways this ideal coincided with the economic liberalist ideas of the hegemonic civil servants in mid-nineteenth-century Norway. In the 1830s the regime was able to fulfil some of the opposition's main wishes. Direct state tax was abolished in 1836, and in the following year the Norwegian parliament adopted an important reform: a local self-government act.

This 1837 act (*Formannskapslovene*) was a compromise. On the one hand, there was a traditional bureaucratic wish for central state control, to some extent an administrative legacy from the absolutist regime before 1814. On the other hand, some farmer politicians promoted a proposal that in its consequences would have dissolved the Norwegian state into a multitude of self-governing farmer republics. The final act of 1837 tried to manoeuvre between these extreme positions, resulting in municipalities becoming self-governed in a limited and controlled way.

Even in the relatively egalitarian Norwegian farming communities, the independent, property-owning farmers who dominated the opposition formed an upper layer. Their form of local self-government was democratic within certain parameters but was not a modern form of democracy. For instance, they showed no interest in enfranchising the real underclass in their munici-palities, in other words people without property. Neither did they want to unleash any social unrest. One may say that these farmers as property owners fundamentally identified themselves with the social order of the civil servants' regime. At the very least, we can say that this was a case of strong shared identity, and that this common ground prevented the farmer opposition developing into a real threat to the civil servants' regime. The main though partially political compromise after 1837 was that farmers were largely allowed to govern their local municipalities, while civil servants were largely allowed to govern the state, albeit with some protests and varying degrees of support.

The Thrane movement—an exception to the exception?

In the years 1849–51, Norway experienced its own little taste of the European 1848 revolutions. Ultimately, the revolutionaries were not that revolutionary; they demanded more democracy and more social justice, mainly within the hegemonic liberal ideo-logical frame. The regime's reply was nevertheless largely uncom-promising; one might say uncharacteristically so.

Marcus Thrane (1817–90) was a journalist and intellectual. He was inspired by the 1848 February Revolution in France, with its radical ideas and demands for universal suffrage and social reforms. Thrane started organizing so-called workers associations in early 1849 and met a striking resonance. In a short time, his movement had 30,000 members and 300 associations, producing its own newspaper and holding meetings and rallies in both rural and urban parts of Norway. The Thrane movement was some-what disparate, both socially and ideologically. It was definitely not a workers' movement in a modern sense. The largest social groups were cottagers, small farmers and artisans, demanding universal suffrage, social justice for cottagers and school reforms.

However, in 1849 Europe was in flames and revolution was in the air. The civil servant authorities, as well as many property-owning farmers, were worried. Inside the Thrane movements there were some unruly elements and occasional revolutionary rhetoric. The authorities tried various methods to control the movement, including placing informants inside it. In the summer of 1851, there were rumours of revolutionary action, and the authorities found the time to strike. The leaders of the movement were arrested and later sentenced; Thrane himself received four years in prison. His movement fell apart soon after the arrest, and he later emigrated to the US and stayed there for the rest of his life.

The sentences were deeply political and legally very dubious. Thrane was accused of plotting a revolutionary coup d'état, which was certainly false. Nevertheless, through the arrests and uncompromising attitude towards the Thrane movement, the civil servants' regime had set an example: they would not tolerate any revolutionary threat from below. In the short-term, this was a successful strategy. Many property-owning farmers, frightened of this revolutionary talk, closed ranks with the civil servants and reinforced their support for the regime.

The coming of the left–liberal alliance

Marcus Thrane was no revolutionary, and his movement was not a workers' movement in a more modern sense. Still, the Thrane movement has been considered as a precursor for later socialist movements in Norway, both revolutionary and reformist.

The farmer deputies were not alone in their opposition to the civil servants' government. There were also a few oppositional, left-leaning independent deputies elected from cities and urban areas. During the 1840s–60s some of them tried to build alliances with the Storting farmers, but not much came of it. Between the farmer politicians and the urban, mostly intellectual and academic radical deputies, there was mutual distrust for cultural and ideological reasons. The farmers followed their economic interests and were content with their self-governed municipalities, whereas the radical intellectuals had more sweeping political visions and demanded democratic reforms.

Despite this distrust, a compromise was reached in around 1870. On the one hand, strands of the farmer politicians showed a much more aggressive attitude towards the civil servants' government. On the other hand, some (but not all) in the radical intellectual camp demonstrated a willingness to relax some of their political principles. The result was a big oppositional compromise, albeit an uneasy and fragile one.

Perhaps the most interesting figure in this political landscape is a man called Søren Jaabæk, a farmer from the south-western part of Norway and a member of parliament from 1845. Jaabæk was a self-taught, well-read man; in contrast to most of his fellow farmer deputies, he was also a man of strong ideological principles. In short, his ideological profile was one of political radicalism and extreme liberalism. Where most of his fellow farmer deputies had a rather pragmatic and interest-driven attitude to government spending, Jaabæk took the principle of a small and cheap state seriously. His track record included voting against public spending on railways, artists' grants to authors like Bjørnstjerne Bjørnson, and even agricultural high schools. In this way, he became somewhat notorious and was denounced both as a petty cheapskate and an enemy of progress, culture and civilization. Jaabæk's reasoning, however, was principally liberalist: he regularly voted against everything that, in his opinion, did not belong to a public sphere.

Moreover, in the mid-1860s Jaabæk started to organize societies for disaffected farmers. In a few years, his organization—'Friends of the Farmers'—had recruited 30,000 card-carrying members from nearly all parts of the country. To put this number in perspective, it was almost as many as the total registered voters from rural areas in parliamentary elections during the 1850s and early 1860s. An organized political movement this large was nearly unprecedented in nineteenth-century Norway, bar the Thrane movement twenty years earlier. This exception was of course rather significant, as some observers inside the political elite feared a new revolutionary movement.

Jaabæk's Friends of the Farmers organization was, like Thrane's, not a revolutionary movement. It nevertheless made a big impact at the parliamentary elections of 1868, resulting in heightened political tensions. Jaabæk was the new, undisputed leader of a farmer opposition that was no longer quite so loyal. Some of the radical intellectual politicians, especially the lawyer Johan Sverdrup, tried to use these tensions to their advantage.

As for the radical intellectual deputies, one of their primary demands had been annual parliamentary sessions. In the 1814 Constitution, the Storting was to convene for just a few months every three years and then dissolve. The farmers had consistently voted against this reform and each time managed to stop it, mainly for economic reasons. Their primary fear was that the more frequently the Storting met, the more likely it was that higher taxes would be imposed on farmers. Sverdrup and his oppositional colleagues had regularly voted for modernizing reforms such as public spending on infrastructure. But in 1870, Sverdrup reached out to Jaabæk and made an informal deal: he would vote against public spending on new railway lines if the farmer deputies would vote for annual parliamentary sessions. Presumably this was a recognition on Sverdrup's part of the more consolidated and organized power of the farmer bloc under Jaabæk.

THE NORWEGIAN EXCEPTION?

The deal reached in 1870 was a harbinger of things to come, an oppositional alliance of radical urban intellectuals and farmers. As we shall see, however, this alliance was precarious.

The defeat of the civil servants' regime

Ten years later, the alliance in parliament was tighter, more focused and more aggressive in its opposition to the civil servants' government. The opposition demanded more power to the parliament at the expense of the king and his government. They also demanded a wider franchise, arguing, not unreasonably, that Norwegian society had changed rather substantially since 1814 and voting rights had not.

Traditionally, this transformation from the old, quasi-loyal farmer opposition into part of a new, aggressive political opposition has been partly explained as a result of the nineteenth-century transformation of Norwegian society. The old-style farmer politician was content with governing his local community and wanted little to do with the State and the government's high politics. Yet especially in the second half of the century, rural communities were transformed. The modernization of Norwegian society—through infrastructure like railways, roads and canals, alongside technology, trade and education—meant a more integrated society. Farmers and their rural communities were integrated into wider society, therefore farmer politicians became more aware of and directly interested in national politics.

Previously, the farmer bloc had mainly preserved its own economic interests in the Storting. Then they became more like ideological participants in the national political process. The majority of farmers came down on the side of the political opposition, though a considerable minority supported the government in the 1882 election. It is fair to say that overall the farmers were more politicized, and thus represented more of a threat to the status quo than they had previously.

THE ROAD TOWARDS DEMOCRACY

The oppositional alliance began to call itself the Venstre (left) movement. It was led by Sverdrup, with Jaabæk and other farmer deputies having been side-lined. It won a substantial victory in the hard-fought election of 1882 and started an impeachment process against the civil servants' government. Supporters of the government tried to counter this offensive. One of the results was conservative, pro-government associations across the country. Tensions ran high during the 1882 elections and afterwards, with harsh rhetoric on both sides and spectacular, confrontational public meetings. Norwegian public life became politicized as never before.

During the impeachment process there were even rumours of a coup d'état. Norway's king had played a modest role in Norwegian politics since King Carl Johan's death in the mid-1840s. Yet in the early 1880s a political, divisive king was back. King Oscar II openly sided with his government in the power struggle, and had confidential discussions with Prime Minister Christian August Selmer on how to handle the upcoming impeachment verdict. The king suggested that the government should ignore a removal verdict, and the prime minister agreed. This would have meant a coup d'état and quite possibly an escalation into civil war in Norway; however, the other ministers did not agree and these ideas came to nothing.

Rumours and high tensions persisted. Forces inside the Venstre movement armed themselves by creating gunner associations, openly declaring that these associations had to defend the Storting majority by force if necessary. On the one hand, the impeachment process was about interpreting the Constitution, especially the role of the king and government in the parliamentary legislation. On the other hand, the process was a partisan, political one: the Venstre opposition in the Storting was united against the government and its supporters. The opposition made some unprecedented tactical, but constitutionally legal moves to ensure they held a majority in the Impeachment Court. Loud protests from the government's supporters didn't help, and the expected verdict was reached early in 1884. Ministers in the government were removed from office, sentenced one after another until there was no government left. After some confusion, where efforts to establish a new civil servants' government were met by threats of a new impeachment process, the king capitulated. In the summer of 1884 Johan Sverdrup, the leader of the Venstre alliance, was appointed prime minister.

This is traditionally considered a regime change in Norway. Instead of the civil servants' state, Norway got a parliamentary political system. This was not the case in a strict, constitutional sense, as parliamentarianism was not inscribed into the Constitution, but political realities did indeed change. Since 1884, Norwegian governments have been dependent on support in parliament.

One result of this power struggle was formal political parties in Norway. The oppositional alliance organized themselves into the Venstre party. The supporters of the old government created the Conservative party, Høyre. Before 1884, ministers were appointed individually and often served for decades. They might be considered a peculiar combination of bureaucratic servants and political masters. After 1884, Norwegian governments were based on political parties; they were real cabinets, *kollegier*, rather than boards of individually appointed members.

Perhaps the most important aspect of this power struggle was its peaceful character. As far as we know, not a single shot was fired nor a single person physically harmed. The transition of power was not smooth but it was ultimately peaceful. Lastly, the losers accepted their defeat and did not force the issue. A parallel here might be the Swedish acceptance of the Norwegian 1814 Constitution. Civil servants in post-1814 Norway saw themselves as upholders and enforcers of the rule of law. The law had spoken when the ministers were removed from office, and so they left (albeit some more grudgingly). Later on, the overwhelming majority of the old regime's supporters did accept the new political realities. The Conservatives played the new rules of the parliamentarian game and formed a new government in 1889.

The national democratic coalition

In short, the Venstre alliance of the 1880s may be called a national democratic coalition. It had a common enemy, namely the bureaucratic government. Ideologically, the coalition wanted to develop both chief aspects of the 1814 Constitution: national sovereignty and democratic elements, fused in a joint concept as the sovereignty of the people. In several ways, liberal features were as significant in this coalition as in the civil servant or bureaucratic tradition, but the democratic elements gave the set of liberal ideas in Venstre a different profile.

Rhetorically, the Venstre coalition presented itself as an underclass, challenging the tyranny of the king and the bureaucratic elite. Yet this was not true, at least in a sociological sense. The oppositional coalition consisted of enfranchised members of society, of property owners and learned men. The real underclass did not take part in the power struggle of the 1880s; indeed quite a few of them emigrated to North America. In a sociological sense, we may more accurately call the Venstre movement a coalition of countercultures dominated by the middle class. We could also call it an alternative elite of intellectuals, freeholding farmers and some businessmen. This alternative elite had been a dynamic element after 1814, as new layers of intellectuals had developed, and more and more farmers became active participants in political life.

The alliance was also democratic, in the sense that all its factions wanted to democratize the political system. One form of this was to give the parliament more power at the expense of the king. Another aspect was the matter of expanding voting rights, but there were different opinions inside the coalition on how far to go with this. The most radical elements wanted to immediately give voting rights to all men, and some even to women. Others favoured a more gradual and modest extension. The leader of the coalition, Prime Minister Sverdrup, followed the moderate approach and thereby disappointed quite a few of his followers. Like in 1870, when he had reached out to Jaabæk and the Friends of the Farmers, Sverdrup showed his flexibility. The moderate approach was probably also an effective way to make the new political situation more acceptable for supporters of the old regime.

In other words, the cracks in the coalition quickly became apparent after the victory of 1884.

Venstre was a somewhat disparate movement, with a common enemy but with notable conflict lines. One source of tension was town versus countryside. In a cultural sense, there were urban radical intellectuals on the one hand, and rural Low Church Christians, usually situated in southern and western parts of Norway, on the other. These cultural conflict lines often overlapped with political conflict. The Venstre party split in two soon after its victory, and in the late 1880s and early 1890s there were two Venstre parties, one moderate and one radical. The radical circle became dominant in parliament in most of the 1890s, and secured an important democratic reform, introducing universal male suffrage in 1898. Later the vote was extended to women, with Norway instituting universal suffrage in 1913.

Henrik Ibsen is interesting within this context. Some of his contemporary plays resonated deeply with the radical elements of the Venstre coalition. This was especially the case with *A Doll's House* from 1879, with its insistence on women's liberation and individual choices and responsibilities. Yet *Ghosts* (1881), with its more direct attack on the institution of marriage, was more con-troversial among urban radical intellectuals, and the moderate, Low Church Venstre wing found it abhorrent. Ibsen's reply to this reception, *An Enemy of the People* (1882), attacked majority mob rule both to the left and right. Suffice to say, Ibsen never became a card-carrying party man.

There was also a third distinct current within the coalition: the so-called 'Grundtvigianism', a school of thought inspired by the Danish theologian, poet and philosopher Nicolai Frederik Severin Grundtvig (1783–1872). His influence on Danish culture is massive, especially with regards to education, the role of Christianity and the relation between state, society and the indi-vidual. In the second half of the nineteenth century, his influence on Norwegian political culture was important too, particularly through his pedagogical ideas.

For Grundtvig, popular education should not only be about rationality and science but also poetry and myths. Above all, education should be expressed through the living—that is, the spoken—word: by conversation and discussion, by telling his-torical tales and myths, by poetry and song. There would be no exams in Grundtvig's ideal schools, because the real exam, the real end, was life itself.

Grundtvig's followers established a network of independent schools, so-called Folk High Schools, in Denmark from the 1840s and in Norway from the 1860s. These schools were to provide youth with common values, such as a tolerant, pragmatic Lutheran Christianity, freedom of thought and speech, social emancipation and social justice. These Grundtvigian ideas were in part inspired by Romanticism and Enlightenment, and were decidedly non-revolutionary.

The Folk High School movement played an important part in the Venstre political movement. Thus, this network of indepen-dent High Schools, in practice, became a broad network of

grassroot Venstre institutions. The key word here is independence. These schools were independent of the state; they could
develop their own curricula; and in accordance with Grundtvig's
ideal, teachers and students could freely discuss all sorts of topics. They criticized establishment ideas and institutions including the government, the State Church and the Danish written
language. Many but not all, of these schools openly combined
Grundtvigian ideas with the Sverdrup-led coalition's political
aims. The movement was influenced by both political and cultural radicalism, but was also strongly nationalist in a cultural
sense. Quite a few of its supporters openly favoured the pure
Norwegian *landsmål* language.

On the whole, the Venstre alliance was nationalist and a large
part of its base came from the countercultural *landsmål* movement.
This part of the coalition had aggressive cultural nationalist aims;
they wanted a pure Norwegian written language and, in a more
general sense, to wipe out all Danish cultural traces in Norway.

In addition to this anti-Danish cultural nationalism, the coalition had developed certain political nationalist ideas. The union
with Sweden was not a motivating factor in the formation of the
Venstre opposition, and Swedish politicians and government did
not take part in the power struggle following the election and
impeachment. However, the king did take part, and—as some
Venstre leaders helpfully pointed out—he was a Swede. He was
both King of Norway and Sweden, and it was as the Norwegian
king that he supported his government. Nonetheless, his Venstre
adversaries saw this as misplaced interference from a Swedish king
in internal Norwegian affairs. Thus one important aspect of the
1884 result was that the king's authority, and with it the union
itself, was weakened. Within just twenty years it would collapse.

PART TWO

MODERNITY, 1905–70

THE 1905 MOMENT

HOW TO DISSOLVE A UNION PEACEFULLY

On 7 June 1905 the members of the Norwegian government held an emergency meeting with the members of the Storting to discuss the union between Sweden and Norway. Taking advantage of a constitutional crisis, the Storting unilaterally dissolved the union and handed all the king's constitutional power to the Norwegian government.[1] This was rebellion, pure and simple; the king and the Swedes might have had something to say on the matter.

Arms race

This act of rebellion did not come out of the blue. There had been noticeable tensions between Norway and Sweden since around 1890. On the one hand, a rising political nationalism had manifested itself in and around the Venstre party. In the 1891 Norwegian parliamentary elections, it was split into a moderate and a radical Venstre party. The moderate band soon disappeared, and later in the 1890s the Venstre party became dominated by radicals, who demanded more Norwegian autonomy in the union.

THE NORWEGIAN EXCEPTION?

In their view, the arrangement to have a common foreign ministry and minister meant Swedish hegemony; likewise, after the power struggle of 1884, the Norwegian government was under parliamentarian control. However, in this case the foreign ministry and minister were controlled only by the king.

This Norwegian nationalist offensive triggered a vehement response from Swedish nationalist circles in Norway. They argued that a separate Norwegian foreign minister would mean a break with the union's raison d'être and by necessity lead to the collapse of the union itself. Moreover, the political elite in Sweden was very much dominated by aristocratic, right-wing circles. They rejected the Norwegian political nationalist demands not only because they were Norwegian and nationalistic, but because they were far too democratic.

This contributed to an growing conflict as left-wing, democratic Norwegian nationalism and right-wing, anti-democratic Swedish nationalism made perfect enemies, corroborating and reinforcing each other's visions of the threatening enemy.

In 1895, the tensions between the Venstre-dominated Norwegian Storting and the Swedish Riksdag parliament had escalated to a full-blown crisis. The position of the majority in the Norwegian parliament was that the Storting could appoint separate Norwegian consular representatives in the foreign administration as a unilateral decision. The position of the king and the Swedish parliament was that a unilateral Norwegian decision like this was, in short, illegal. The Swedes made political noise that was interpreted as an open war threat in Norway. The Norwegian parliament made a full and rather embarrassing retreat on 7 June 1895, a date that would become significant.

Afterwards, the Norwegian Storting decided to secure heavy armaments, and the Swedes did likewise. After 1895, the relation between the two union partners' armed forces can be described as an unofficial arms race. Unfortunately, the main grounds for the union in 1814 had been strategic, driven by the idea that the Scandinavian peninsula ought to be united in a military, strategic sense. Such a unit would be easy to defend against military threats from outside, but first and foremost it would put an end to the succession of wars between Norway and Sweden.

On top of this, another strong argument for the union went out of the window. The hegemonic Swedish political elite was not only right-wing, with old-fashioned aristocratic values and a deep distrust of the emerging democracy. In the mid-1890s the parliamentarian majority had also become protectionist in its economic views and policies. In 1895 the Swedish Riksdag decided to repeal the set of laws governing economic relations between the two countries. These laws had essentially created a Norwegian-Swedish common market, and Norwegian adherents of the union argued that they brought economic advantages to Norway.

In these ways, the strategic and economic arguments for the union had become shaky after 1895. In both countries the pro-union position became increasingly difficult to maintain.

The arms race became especially pronounced in 1900, when Norway began updating its old fortresses near the Swedish border and constructed several new defence fortifications along it. With good reason, these fortifications were seen as an affront to the union partner. As a reminder, a shared king was the head of both the Norwegian and Swedish military forces. King Oscar II allegedly exclaimed at an especially critical moment: 'But I cannot go to war against myself!'

Official Norwegian attempts at an explanation were not very credible. Apparently, the fortifications at the Swedish border were a necessary precaution in case a rival, like Russia, invaded Sweden. Then, if this enemy marched westward, they could at least be stopped at the Norwegian border. In reality this scenario was totally implausible, even if Russia was traditionally considered a threat to Sweden.

THE NORWEGIAN EXCEPTION?

During the autumn of 1904 the crisis came to a head. Representatives of the two governments had negotiated long and hard to come up with a definitive solution concerning the issue of foreign policy, particularly Norway's demand for separate consular representation. Under the leadership of Prime Minister Erik Gustaf Boström, the unyielding attitude of the Swedish government provoked even the most faithful Norwegian unionists. Early in 1905, it appeared that the union was finished; in Norway, the union-friendly and compromising Prime Minister Francis Hagerup resigned. Hagerup, a very honourable man, felt that he was no longer the person to lead Norway after the breakdown in negotiations with Sweden, and his colleagues agreed. A new government was formed by Christian Michelsen.

'A tiger will fight'

Michelsen was a shipowner and former Venstre politician. He was afraid of the revolutionary, subversive potential he saw in the emerging socialist movement, and had resigned from the Venstre party mainly because of its leftist policies. In his view, the controversies concerning the union were extremely unfortunate, because they split adherents of established society and took attention away from the real problem, the socialist threat. For Michelsen, it was necessary to get the union question out of the way. There could be only one way forward after the breakdown of the 1904 negotiations with the Swedish government: to get out of the union for good.

Meanwhile, during the spring of 1905, Norwegian public opinion had turned aggressively nationalist and anti-Swedish. The national hero and polar explorer Fridtjof Nansen wrote a series of militant newspaper articles on national honour and the need for immediate action. On National Day, 17 May, he said in a national rally speech:

A tiger will fight for its young as long as it can move a limb; and a people is surely not poorer spirited than a tiger. It will defend its independence and its hearth to the utmost of its abilities. Of this we are sure: come what may, we must and shall defend our independence and right of self-determination in our own affairs. On these rights we must now stand or fall.[2]

In May 1905, a bill establishing a Norwegian consular service was passed by parliament, though everyone knew that it would be vetoed by King Oscar; he did so on 27 May. It was widely recognised that the veto would result in a complete break between king and government and between Sweden and Norway. The Norwegian cabinet refused to countersign the veto and handed in their resignations. Prime Minister Michelsen argued that according to the Constitution, the king could exercise his royal functions only through a cabinet approved by the parliament, which he now lacked. Therefore, he was no longer King of Norway, and without the king the union had ceased to exist. The Storting unanimously confirmed this constitutional interpretation on 7 June and declared the union with Sweden dissolved. Further on, the Storting adopted a declaration that conferred new powers upon the government, giving it the ability 'to exercise, until further notice, the authority and power [that had been] vested in the king in accordance with the Constitution and the Laws of the Realm of Norway'.

The date of 7 June was perhaps not totally coincidental. Indeed, it marked the ten-year anniversary of the Storting's bitter step down from the consular issue.

In Sweden, the declaration was widely viewed as a revolution, and Swedish politicians and press reacted violently. The big question after 7 June was: what will the Swedes do?

In 1905, public opinion abroad was generally ignorant of the relations between Norway and Sweden. A common assumption was that Norway was a sort of Swedish colony, or at least subordinate to Sweden, similar to the relationship between England and Ireland at the time. Prominent Norwegians set out to correct what they viewed as a completely false notion. Fridtjof Nansen published an account of the union conflict in the *London Times* on 25 March, and the paper supported his position with a sympathetic editorial. Nansen's article was also taken up by other European leading newspapers.

On 7 June Nansen published a small book in English, *Norway and the Union with Sweden*. In it he gave an account of the origin and development of the union, to make the causes of the conflict clear and the Norwegian position understandable. The book was also published in German and French. All in all, Nansen's efforts were quite effective Norwegian propaganda, and the Swedes tried to counter with their own well-known explorer, Sven Hedin.

Indeed, both Norway and Sweden sought to gain the support of the Great Powers in Europe through propaganda and diplomatic persuasion. Norway sent Nansen to Great Britain and he helped win the sympathy of both the British public and government for Norway's position. Meanwhile, Sweden had a good relationship with Germany and concentrated its efforts there. If any of the Great Powers had wanted to get involved in a war in Scandinavia, they certainly had the opportunity in the summer of 1905.

The Swedish parliament held an extraordinary session in June and July. Tensions ran high, and a few members wanted to teach the Norwegians a harsh lesson with an immediate and all-out war. Yet a more compromising and thoughtful position prevailed. In short, the majority reaction in the Riksdag can be summarized as follows: (1) The Norwegian Storting's declaration of 7 June is an illegal and revolutionary act, and an insult to the king and Sweden's honour. It is out of the question to accept it. (2) If this means war, we are strong enough to win. (3) However, we will try to avoid a war solely because of Swedish interests. A war will only result in problems for us, in the form of resentful, unruly, rebellious Norwegians.

Instead, the Riksdag declared that Sweden was willing in principle to accept the breakup of the union, but a dissolution had to be based on negotiations rather than the action taken by the Storting on 7 June. It also demanded that Norwegians hold a national plebiscite.

The Swedish reply was quite reasonable but the final demand—the plebiscite—was a big tactical mistake on their part. The Norwegians grabbed the possibility to hold a referendum with both hands. Public opinion in Norway at this time was not definitely pro-Swedish nor pro-union, and the circumstances meant that one had to be extremely strong-willed to vote against the Storting.

The bare facts are these: the plebiscite was held on 13 August. The Norwegians voted 99.95 per cent—368,208 votes to 184—in favour of abolishing the union. Women did not have the right to vote but about 250,000 Norwegian women signed a petition that supported the break-up.[3]

These figures are reminiscent of regimes, like Hitler's Third Reich or Enver Hoxha's Albania, to which Norway wouldn't want to be compared. There was indeed massive propagandistic pressure in connection with the plebiscite, as well as subsequent episodes of public shaming, speculations and accusations about who had been among the 184 unionist diehards. The result was so overwhelming that it was a heavy blow to Swedish unionists. There were of course more than 184 union supporters left in Norway in August 1905, though it is impossible to say how many. It is reasonable to believe, however, that most of them abstained from participating in the plebiscite or perhaps voted with the majority.

Karlstad

Norwegian and Swedish negotiators, led by each country's prime minister, met in the small Swedish town of Karlstad on 31 August.

THE NORWEGIAN EXCEPTION?

The negotiations were tough and had to tackle delicate issues like the status of the Norwegian border fortresses. While the politicians carried on their negotiations in Karlstad, the situation grew very tense. Though they tried to conceal it from one another, both Norway and Sweden began military mobilization. The negotiators were aware that war was indeed a possible outcome, but after some dramatic moments during the negotiations, a compromise solution—the so-called Karlstad Treaty—prevailed.

The agreement stipulated a formally correct dissolution of the union between Sweden and Norway. Both parliaments had to ratify the agreement and declare the union dissolved; in addition, King Oscar II would have to abdicate the Norwegian throne. Further on, the agreement established a demilitarized zone on both sides of the border, as far north as the sixty-first parallel, which meant that the new border defences built by the Norwegians would have to be dismantled. Both parties agreed that future conflicts between them would be settled by an international court. The Swedish Sami reindeer herders were guaranteed the right to let their reindeer graze on the Norwegian side of the border, but the specifics in this matter were not determined until later.

In this way, the Swedish negotiators felt that their honour and the king's honour could be restored. Their interpretation was that the Karlstad agreement had made the Norwegian Storting's 7 June revolutionary act null and void. Most Swedish politicians agreed with this, and the Riksdag ratified the treaty without any dissenting votes.

On the other hand, the agreement was highly controversial in Norway, especially the matter of dismantling the border defences. In the public debate, the opponents (some very loudly) said that this was a sell-out of the nation's honour. Moreover, some of the opponents argued that the whole agreement was a diabolical Swedish trick to disarm Norway, and that the Swedes were most probably planning a military attack when the time was right, Norway's border being defenceless. In what was possibly the most tense and red-hot debate in the history of the Norwegian parliament, the leading MP in the camp against the Karlstad deal declared: 'This agreement is a betrayal! We should have said to the Swedes: You want to dissolve our border fortresses? Well, come and try to take them then'.

Despite opposition like this, the compromise mentality prevailed once more. Both parliaments ratified the agreement, meaning that all obstacles were removed for a legitimate dissolution of the union. On 16 October, the Swedish parliament voted to recognize Norway as an independent nation, and on 27 October, Oscar II abdicated the throne of Norway for himself and all his heirs.

After the dissolution, the Norwegians had to decide what sort of government the newly independent state was to have. Everyone agreed that a swift decision was necessary, and a referendum on this matter was to be held in November. Many nationalists, both supporters and opponents of the Karlstad compromise, had been republicans. Yet in the fierce public debate in the autumn of 1905, several prominent republicans, among them Fridtjof Nansen and Bjørnstjerne Bjørnson, encouraged people to vote for the monarchy. This was for tactical reasons, primarily to gain the support of Great Britain. A new candidate for the Norwegian throne, Prince Carl of Denmark, had been discreetly approached before the Karlstad agreement had been signed. He was married to Princess Maud, third daughter of King Edward VII of Great Britain, and the British king had hinted that he would very much like to see his son-in-law on the Norwegian throne.

And so the second Norwegian referendum in 1905 was held in November. A strong majority voted for a monarchy, which made Norway the only European country with an elected monarchy. The Danish prince and his family arrived in Norway on

25 November. Two days later he swore an oath of allegiance to the Norwegian Constitution, taking for himself the name Haakon VII.

The dynamics of 1905

How could Norway break away from Sweden without an armed conflict? There were several contributing factors. The main one is that the politicians involved in negotiating the separation were willing to compromise. This was the case with the Norwegian Prime Minister Christian Michelsen, whose primary motive was to just get the union question out of the way and concentrate on fighting off socialism; his nationalism was never too emotional or rigid. Possibly more importantly, this was also the case with the Swedish Prime Minister Christian Lundeberg, who can be called a reactionary politician and a right-wing agrarian nationalist. During the crisis of 1895, he had been quite bellicose against Norway. In 1905, however, he and his government chose a peaceful compromise. For Lundeberg and the majority of Sweden's political and military elite, a war in 1905, although possible to win, was simply not in Sweden's interest, certainly less so than a peaceful dissolution of the union. Lundeberg had clearly changed his mind. He may have had second thoughts when the Norwegians showed that they really wanted independence and were willing to fight, as opposed to 1895 when they had backed down fairly quickly.

Of course, many people in Sweden still objected to a war with Norway. This was particularly the case with the labour movement but also with segments of the liberal wing of Swedish politics. The conservative, nationalist elite were aware of these sentiments, which played a part—albeit probably not a decisive one—in their considerations.

The Great Powers showed no interest in an armed conflict in Scandinavia in 1905. The timing was thus excellent for a peaceful solution. Russia, for example, a traditional enemy of Sweden, had more than enough to deal with during the summer and autumn of 1905 thanks to its ongoing war with Japan on the other side of the world.

The attitude of the royal house was also a factor. The elderly King Oscar II was bitter and disappointed, but he was also tired and in poor health in 1905. In short, he didn't have the strength in him to fight for the Norwegian crown. His son Crown Prince Gustav, on the other hand, worked actively toward a peaceful dissolution of the union.

An important and in some ways overriding factor is that the union itself was already loose in 1905. It wasn't worth the hassle for responsible Swedish nationalist politicians to try to hold it together by force. The Swedish protectionist majority in the Riksdag had essentially destroyed the economic arguments for the union in 1895. By 1905 not much remained of the strategic argument either, given the arms race and border fortification race on the Norwegian side. Moreover, it was impossible to ignore the overwhelming anti-union, anti-Swedish public opinion in Norway. There was no conflict concerning territories between the two countries, and there were no problems involving national minorities. In short, Sweden didn't lose much when the union was dissolved.

The dynamics in 1905 are reminiscent of the dynamics in 1814. Early in the year there was resolute, surprising, decisive Norwegian action, establishing a sort of fait accompli. In late summer and autumn, there came tough negotiations with the adversary, trying to defend and preserve the newly established reality. The result: some necessary concessions, and a peaceful compromise overall, resulting in a loose union in 1814 and no union in 1905. In both cases the results were very favourable for Norway, much more so than conceivable alternatives.

6

ENTERING THE TWENTIETH CENTURY

After 1905, Prime Minister Michelsen had got his wish. The union question was out of the way, and Norwegians could concentrate on other things.

The first decade after 1905 was characterized by rapid industrialization in Norway, driven by hydroelectric power. Norway was a country replete with waterfalls, and with the arrival of electricity these could be utilized. Large industries based on cheap electricity were built in remote places around the country, close to waterfalls.

This rapid industrialization was central in modernizing twentieth-century society, building on the first wave of urbanization, infrastructure development and capitalization in the nineteenth century. It created a large working class, a rapidly rising labour movement and resulting social tensions. The countercultures didn't disappear after 1905 either; tensions between towns and rural districts were still palpable, and the cultural conflicts around the written language reached new heights in the 1920s–30s.

For the first time in over 500 years, Norway was completely on its own. At this time the outside world was characterized by unrest and growing tensions between the big European powers.

THE NORWEGIAN EXCEPTION?

The neutral ally

After the dissolution of the union, relations between Norway and Sweden were slightly tense; they had the potential to escalate but did not. A critical period in this regard was of course the First World War.

The newly independent Norway tried to ride two horses concerning foreign policy. On the one hand, the official foreign policy stance was to be strictly neutral. On the other hand, Norway was building a special relationship with Great Britain. The new King Haakon VII was the son-in-law of the British King Edward VII, and his appointment in 1905 secured British goodwill for the newly independent state. Traditionally, both trade and cultural relations between the two states had been good, and after Britain repealed its Navigation Acts in 1849, Norwegian shipping exploited the new free trade conditions.

Sweden, on the other hand, had good relations with Germany. This created a potentially dangerous situation on the Scandinavian peninsula: what would happen in the case of a war between Great Britain and Germany?

When the Great War became a fact in 1914, Norway and her Scandinavian neighbours declared neutrality. Both the Norwegian and the Swedish governments were set on staying neutral. This common attitude, and the common wish to avoid the war spreading to the Scandinavian peninsula, created a friendlier climate between the former union partners. Again, we have to say that compromise and reason prevailed. Again, Norway and Sweden were lucky, as none of the belligerent Great Powers were interested in a war in Scandinavia either.

Yet Norwegian neutrality during the war was, if you had asked the Germans, so-so. Most of the Norwegian elite sympathized with the Allies, especially Great Britain, and this increased when the German unrestricted submarine warfare was put into action.

Quite a few Norwegian trade vessels were sunk by the Germans, and perhaps as many as 1,000 Norwegian sailors perished in these attacks. Further on, several trade deals with the British were interpreted in Berlin as breaches of Norwegian neutrality. A 1960s doctoral dissertation on Norwegian foreign policy during the First World War coined the phrase 'The Neutral Ally'.

The hydropower industrialization

By the time the war ended in 1918, Norway had undergone an enormous transformation, a second wave of industrialization. Being endowed with very high levels of rainfall and many waterfalls, these natural resources were harnessed to the new source of energy—electricity—and industrialization followed. Because of the reliance on waterfalls to power the grid, electricity was brought to remote areas of Norway more quickly than in most countries; and thus so was large industry, based on cheap electricity. This means that, overall, Norwegian living conditions and prosperity improved significantly in the early twentieth century.

There are three important perspectives that explain the second industrialization in Norway at the turn of the century: the role of the state in the economy, the view that industrial companies were not only economic entities but also important socially and politically, and the position and legitimacy of private ownership.

The nineteenth century had established the important role of the state in the economy, and contrary to Sweden and Denmark, Norway did not have a strong, capitalist elite that could privately raise money for large industrial expansions. The state had been used as an important vehicle to establish a modern infrastructure and had facilitated industrial development. It acted as a modernizer, and it was said to be accepted because Norway democratized before she industrialized.

At time of writing, this industrialization could be reproduced large-scale, because of electricity from hydropower. This new transformation, however, was going to require private capital. Between 1900–15, the production of electric power from waterfalls increased eight times. This was of great benefit to industries like smelting plants that needed large quantities of power to melt iron or produce aluminium. Industrial improvement also happened in the important pulp and paper industry.

Those industries were based on the export of raw materials for use in manufacturing elsewhere, but in the twentieth century two new, domestic industries developed. The first was Norsk Hydro, which was founded on Norwegian technology, a change from the nineteenth-century method of adapting systems used in already-industrialized nations like the UK and Germany. The idea was fusing electric power with air to extract nitrogen and produce fertilizers. The first fertilizer plant was constructed in the remote town of Rjukan; it had a waterfall of more than 200 meters that was tamed in the Vemork power plant, later know from the sabotage during the Second World War and the 1965 international film *The Heroes of Telemark*. The second exception was the Søderberg method, which was a self-baking method to form carbon anodes (like aluminium) in the electrochemical industry. It was the basis for Elkem, today one of the world's leading companies in the manufacture of metals and materials. None of these companies were financed by Norwegian capital; the Swedish Wallenberg family, who also owned the mining company Orkla, was a large creditor and owner.

This solution was not debated, but the ownership of natural resources was. Who was to own resources such as hydropower? This industrial adventure was to a large extent financed by foreign investors. Political debates about regulations and concession laws were mostly conducted in the Storting, and the foreign owners had little say. The concession law debates were harsh and gained momentum after 1905. Should foreigners be allowed to buy waterfalls, mines, forests, and land? National interests were important for a new nation that had just got its independence. In the end, these interests turned out to be stronger than a liberal economic exploitation of Norwegian waterfalls, mines and forests.

The debates culminated in a compromise in 1909. Both foreigners and Norwegians had to apply for concessions, on equal terms. There were strict rules if they were granted one, and sub-suppliers, salaries and working conditions were regulated in detail. But the most important condition was the so-called right of reversion—*hjemfallsrett*. After eighty years, the concession ended, and the Norwegian state would take back ownership.

The right of the state to nationalize power plants after eighty years is an example of the importance of keeping the country's natural resources under Norwegian control, and decidedly shows a long-term perspective of national interests. The Norwegian state was liberal and predictable but also pragmatic.

We shall see these themes continued when Norway found oil in 1969. The concession laws marked the continuous public ownership and control over natural resources, and over industrialization more generally.

The discovery and use of hydroelectric power was of immense importance for the creation of the modern Norway; it was a heavy contributor to the rise in living standards; and last but not least, the waterfalls provided the whole country with a cheap and clean energy source. They still do, although some Norwegians will probably protest the 'cheap' part of the description.

An emerging social welfare state

The belief that infrastructure and health care were public responsibilities became stronger after the turn of the century, especially after the First World War. Local governments gradually enlarged their services without political protests, including local telephone services, electricity supply, and fire and police departments. All regarded as natural public services, many became local public responsibilities. There was also a greater acceptance of public health care, most of which had previously been privately managed, often by religious or other non-profit organizations. However, the scope of public services could often lead to economic problems for the local government, which had to be aided by the state especially during the 1920s–30s. The arguments were financial but also political. State interference was used to equalize services between municipalities, gradually pointing to an idea of universality and individual rights. A common system of health care was thought to be more efficient, as well as securing a common level and quality for all citizens, regardless of geography. The road to the welfare state went from a local variety of public and private services to universally standardized, obligatory, tax-financed solutions.

Social welfare was not uniquely Norwegian. During this period welfare and social benefit initiatives were implemented all over Europe, often grounded in a fear of social revolutions. Norway was not an exception but, as we have seen, Norwegians were far from revolutionary uproar. Social liberal thought was quite strong and demands of social insurance and benefits were taken seriously, inspired by many European countries: pension reforms from Denmark, labour insurance schemes from Germany, unemployment benefits from England, and later child benefits from France.

The foundations of what might be called a social fellow citizenship, now the welfare state, was established in the nineteenth century. It was commonly agreed that society should take care of its citizens, provide education and economic support if needed, and thereby also redistribute resources. Social policies during the first decades of the twentieth century primarily concentrated on strengthening and widening existing welfare measures. Welfare insurances continuously came to include new groups.

ENTERING THE TWENTIETH CENTURY

After the first labour commission in the 1880s and 90s, several laws were passed, among them the important accident insurance. Among the main issues discussed were the inspection of factories, regulation of working hours, financial relief under illness, and pensions. The emergence of housing policies, which aimed to give as many as possible the opportunity to own their home, came as early as 1894 with a suggestion of a housing loan fund. We can say that these policies have resulted in a Norwegian exception. More than eighty per cent of Norwegians are today owners of their houses or flats, among the highest ownership rates in the world.

Later, insurance against unemployment became an important debate, and this wasn't so easy to organize. The Labour Party mostly, but not always, argued for universal benefits; though it called only for the inclusion of union members in the case of unemployment benefits. The Conservatives often claimed means testing. Their view was that only people who needed help should get it. The social-liberal Venstre often opted for insurance solutions, and this was the dominating view in the debates. This is also why the first decades of the twentieth century have been called 'the Venstre state', demonstrating the importance of the party even when it was not in government.

In 1909, a general health insurance was finally agreed upon after twenty years, prefiguring the later development of social benefits and other welfare initiatives. Often there was agreement on the main goals, but details stirred conflict. In addition, the costs were a considerable obstacle, because financing was difficult. The main questions dominating the social policy debates were: Who should be insured? Who should pay? And how much?

The first decades of the twentieth century were economically turbulent, and Norwegian unemployment was high in the 1920s–30s. Even if social benefits and welfare were agreed upon, it was difficult to finance them, and they often took a long time to implement.

THE NORWEGIAN EXCEPTION?

In 1912 the social liberal Venstre party was re-elected to government, and the new Prime Minister Gunnar Knudsen announced a plan for radical social reforms. Among his proposals were extensive revisions for health insurance, a new act for insuring single mothers, and free midwife services. Of great importance to this reform agenda was Johan Castberg, his minister of social affairs in the newly established Ministry of Social Policies, who later passed the eponymous Castberg children's laws. These secured the rights of children born out of wedlock, including the ability to inherit from the father and to take his family name. They were the most progressive children's laws in Europe when they were passed in 1915.

The post-First World War economic boom made social policies easier to finance, but this came to an end in 1921. Plans for larger pension schemes were postponed due to public funding problems. Old age pensions had been an important issue for all political parties since the end of the nineteenth century, but faced continuous delays due to financing and debates about insurance- or funds-based programmes, as well as means testing versus universal schemes. However, it was generally accepted that providing pensions was a public responsibility. Finally, an act was passed in 1936.

Overall, the pre-war and interwar period was characterized by the gradual development of a welfare state, subject to much political debate. By contrast, the decades between 1880–1920 were defined by a strong growth in local procurement of common goods, which did not result in political debates. Norwegians had always preferred public procurement over private monopolies, and this was true for local telephone providers, electricity grids, sanitary facilities as well as firefighting and police. It was less true for many welfare services, where liberals wanted private health care to be supplementary to or combined with public services, whereas the Labour Party wanted public solutions. This is true even for contemporary debates in Norway. The second wave of industrialization and the growth of the centralized welfare state were both shaped by the emergence of both the Labour Party and workers as social and political forces in this period.

A new political force

The first attempts at organizing labour in Norway—the Thrane movement for universal suffrage around 1850—were met with repression from the civil servants' state. Later attempts, from the 1870s onward, showed the inherent strength of Norwegian political culture. Both in emerging trade unions and the socialist Labour Party (founded in 1887), Marxist ideas of class struggle and revolution were mostly rejected. The Norwegian Labour Party was inspired by the German Social Democrats (SPD), and its dominant ideas were staunchly reformist. The party argued for political reforms and workers' rights: a fair electoral system, eight-hour workday and so on. The rapid industrialization of Norwegian society between 1905 and the First World War also meant the rapid rise of a working class, and working men mostly voted Labour. The party achieved its first representatives in the Storting in 1903, and by the First World War the labour movement was a major political force in Norway.

Although reformist, the party was a broad socialist tent; there had been left-wing opposition in the party, especially in its youth organization and among some militant trade union members, since before the First World War. This opposition became more vocal during the war and was greatly stimulated by the Russian Bolshevik Revolution in 1917.

The eight-hour day

In 1919, the Storting passed another reform with deep reverberations in the political labour movement. Statutory eight-hour working days had been a central demand of the international labour movement ever since the Socialist Workers' International (the so-called Second International) was formed in 1889. Demonstrations around the world on Labour Day, 1 May, had for several years appealed for the introduction of the eight-hour day. In June 1919 in Norway, the Storting discussed a proposal to make this change.

The tone of this debate was strikingly unanimous on the overall principle, which met the old demands of the labour movement. Labour Party Representative Ole Lian, who was also chairman of the national trade union organization AFL, 'was pleased to note that the demand, which has been raised by workers for many years, will now receive the sanction of society'.

In his opening remarks, Lian pointed out that the eight-hour day was about to be implemented in other countries such as Denmark, Germany, France and the UK. Thus, the reform would not present any problems regarding 'international competition'. The Storting could adopt the eight-hour day without the risk that Norwegian industry 'would fall below the competition'.

This point was also reiterated by the Conservative representative Odd Klingenberg. It can be taken for granted, he said, 'that we soon see 48 hours of weekly working time as normal working hours statutory in all civilized countries'.

It is evident from these arguments that the societal perspective was dominant and accepted in the debate. The eight-hour reform would make workers more motivated at work, and thus more productive. However, competition would not be weakened, because other countries were introducing the same reform as Norway. No other representatives, neither for bourgeois, system-preserving parties nor for the revolutionary class-struggle Labour Party, brought other significant arguments into the debate—at least not regarding the principle of the statutory eight-hour day.

Underlying this reasoning lay the threat of revolution. The working class had to be integrated into the wider community, and then heard when making fair social demands. The unspoken alternative—a warning indicated by the debate—was class struggle and revolution. At last a statutory eight-hour day was passed unanimously, but it wouldn't be enough to stop a crisis around the Labour Party's demands emerging later in the year.

7

THE INTERWAR YEARS

AN EXPANDING POLITICAL SPECTRUM

In the Storting elections of November 1918, right at the end of the First World War, the Labour Party got the largest share of the votes with 31.6 per cent. At the annual party conference a few months earlier, the majority had voted for a revolutionary program, and the party got a new, radical leadership. In November 1918, the largest party in Norway wanted to abolish parliamentary democracy and substitute it with a proletariat dictatorship. Meanwhile, old empires were crumbling and revolutionary fires spread across Europe. No wonder supporters of the established order were sweating.

Open hand and iron fist

From 1906 onwards, the electoral system in Norway was first-past-the-post elections. It was, and remains, an electoral scheme suitable for a two-party system. However, it can also produce many strange results, especially when one or more parties threaten to break the hegemony of the two largest groups.

THE NORWEGIAN EXCEPTION?

The Norwegian Labour Party, which grew very rapidly from a low level, was consistently under-represented in this period. Venstre and the Conservatives kept Labour marginalized in this two-horse-race system. For centre-right supporters of the existing political and social order, all of this combined—the rapid growth of the Labour movement, the strengthening of the left-wing, revolutionary forces inside that movement, and the under-representation of the Labour Party in the parliamentary system—constituted several dilemmas.

The existing society and established political order could, in principle, face what they saw as the revolutionary threat in two ways. One was called 'the iron fist', in other words countering the threat through legal means and, if necessary, military force. The second was what was known at the time as 'the open hand'. This meant offering reforms to the labour movement, and demonstrating that both the working class and the political labour movement should be included in a democratic Norway.

Numerous security measures had been implemented by the government and military leadership in the dramatic year of 1918. The measures were related both to the war and to the perceived socialist threat. In Norway, there were forces that would take a hard and uncompromising stand against what they perceived to be a deadly revolutionary threat, dissatisfied with the authorities' security measures. Nevertheless, the dominant political response in the critical period of 1919–20 was definitely an open hand.

In the 1918 parliamentary elections, Labour took the largest share of the vote with 31.6 per cent, and took eighteen seats out of a total of 126 representatives. Venstre gained the third-biggest share of the vote (28.3 per cent) and became the largest group in the Storting with fifty-one seats. This was a result of the first-past-the-post electoral system, and everyone realized that this outcome was not just unfair representation, but absurd. This came at a time when parliamentary democracy as a political system was under a pressure never felt before in its short-lived history.

For years, the Labour Party had strongly argued for a new, more equitable electoral scheme, more specifically a system of proportional representation. The 1918 election plainly highlighted the failings of the current system, and towards the end of 1919 it seemed that a new electoral system could become reality. On 27 and 28 November, the Storting discussed several received proposals to change the electoral system. This debate is one of the most important in the history of Norwegian democracy.

A necessary sacrifice

The threat of revolution was still a possible reality in November 1919. The Labour Party had consolidated its revolutionary ideological positions, and earlier in the year they joined the newly created Communist International (Comintern). An organized faction of social democrats within the party protested, but to no avail.

Christian Fredrik Michelet from the Conservatives, the chair of the extended Constitutional Committee considering the proposals, made the constitutional stakes clear in his opening remarks. It was about 'nothing less than a partial but profoundly constitutional revision,' he said,[1] a revision 'with the conscious intention of changing the character of this Assembly'. In political terms, a reorganization of the electoral system in a more representative and just direction entailed far more mandates for the declared revolutionary Labour Party, while socially conservative, democratic parties such as Venstre and the Conservatives would lose out. Admittedly, Michelet suggested that it might be more correct to say that a revision of the electoral system would put the Storting 'more in line with the views that are the common rule among the Norwegian people'. Unfortunately for a conservative like Michelet, a substantial proportion of the

Norwegian people in 1919 apparently wanted to abolish the entire Storting. It was perhaps not entirely incidental that he characterized the change of electoral system as a 'radical, I could almost say revolutionary, matter'. Likewise, it was no coincidence that he talked about the existence of a 'state of emergency'.

Anders Buen, one of the Labour Party's most prominent representatives at the Storting in 1919, made the matter clear in a slightly different way. Buen belonged to the non-revolutionary minority at the Labour Party meeting in 1918; but he could warn against, or perhaps more precisely, threaten a revolution. In his opening speech in the debate, Buen pointed out a close connection between the unfair electoral system and the support of revolutionary ideas. He stressed the ways in which the existing electoral system was not fair. While the Labour Party's votes had steadily increased, he said, 'our numbers here in this hall are equally and steadily going down.' This was to give free polemic points to revolutionary forces that wanted to abolish the Storting and all parliamentary democracy. Buen laid the threat of revolution on the table against all attempts to postpone electoral reform:

> If we continue to work on this question in the old way, if there will not be a positive result here, then it is the same as kicking our own legs [...]. I will not dwell on the consequences of that. But that responsibility will then lie with those who have created that situation.

'Electoral reform now, or you get revolution': this was Buen's basic message to representatives who wanted either to keep the existing electoral system or postpone the issue.

One who clearly took these hints was the Conservative Gunder Anton Jahren. Like many other representatives, he noted that there were weaknesses in all the proposals for a new electoral system. It's perfectly possible to vote down every proposal, he said, then we would go to the next elections according to our current electoral system. However, it wouldn't be propitious to do that.

It was not only necessary to give the Labour Party a fair deal in parliamentary democracy, Jahren continued. It was necessary to do so to support the democratic wing in the Labour Party against the revolutionary forces: 'I think one must contribute what one can, to support within reasonable limits the direction that will further the development of society along the parliamentary lines.'

Contributing 'what one can' meant sacrificing an electoral system that favoured the Conservatives and Venstre. Otto Blehr, minister of justice for Venstre as well as former and future prime minister, talked about a 'sacrifice' that was 'necessary for a good and healthy development for our country'.

An interesting take on this matter was provided by the Labour Party representative Magnus Nilssen. The view that can be applied, he noted, is 'that in reality, at its core, the proportional representation system is a fairly strong community preservation system'. Nilssen said that he had increasingly become a supporter of proportional representation, despite the fact that it was an obstacle to the change of society he wanted. The reason was simply that democracy had to be paramount:

> We stand on the basis of the proportional choice system. In other words, we are of the opinion that the will of the people through the right to vote shall be represented in the National Assembly. In other words, the representatives of the National Assembly should be as far as possible an accurate expression of the views held by the people, so that the views expressed there, where applicable, shall be represented in the National Assembly on a proportionate basis. That is the logical consequence, as I mentioned, of common voting rights.

An elaborate interpretation of Magnus Nilssen's reasoning is this: bourgeois democracy is better than undemocratic socialism. The Czech-Austrian Marxist Karl Kautsky had pointed out, in a ruthless criticism of Lenin's Russian Bolsheviks and the entire October Revolution, that the crucial distinction for socialists was between democracy and dictatorship; that socialism could not be conceived without democracy; nor without a widespread 'will to socialism' in the majority of the population.[2] Nilssen's views on the electoral system can be interpreted as a full endorsement of Kautsky's criticism.

Such a principled democratic stance diverged sharply from the revolutionary leadership of the Labour Party in 1919, not to mention the Soviet-Russian Bolsheviks. This reasoning was also a more subtle warning—or, perhaps better, an offer—to the parliamentary majority: if you adopt an electoral reform now, the Labour Party will be built into a representative democracy. If you do not, then you risk a pure Labour Party majority in the parliament in the next elections, meaning anything could happen.

Two votes were crucial. A motion to postpone the case was voted down by eighty-nine against thirty-seven votes. A proposal for a new electoral scheme with proportional elections was adopted by ninety-two against thirty-four votes. Thus, Labour's social democrat MPs got what they wanted. It was no longer quite so easy to argue that the parliamentary system in Norway was undemocratic.

In this way, the democratic, reformist wing of the Labour Party finished the year 1919 with two major victories. Both the central social demand of the eight-hour day and the central political demand were achieved. Parliamentary democracy had shown that it could deliver. The next election, in 1921, would be held under the new proportional system. There was no revolution in Norway, no bloody civil war between the red and the white. The Labour Party had no Lenin and no clear power-grabbing strategy. As far as revolution is concerned, there was only talk. Many European countries experienced armed confrontations between revolutionary and counter-revolutionary forces in the wake of the October Revolution and First World War. Norway was spared confrontations like this, despite a declared revolutionary party receiving support of more than thirty per cent.

In addition, employers in Norway also showed a striking generosity in the wage settlement in 1919. The director of the Employers' Association clearly stated that the costly settlement had to be regarded as an 'insurance premium for work peace and for society's sake'. The Employers' Association magazine wrote that the year 1919 went 'under the sign of the revolution' and that 'marked the policy that our union deliberately laid down'.[3]

The Norwegian labour movement was characterized by a tight relationship between trade unions and the political movement. The relationship was so close that members of the national trade union organization, AFL, automatically became members of the Labour party. Comintern called for an end to this collective membership, a demand which divided the revolutionary forces inside the Labour Party. In 1923, the party withdrew from Comintern, and Moscow loyalists split from the Labour Party and created a new Communist Party. The Communist party soon faded into insignificance, while the Labour Party gradually left its revolutionary positions behind and embraced parliamentary democracy. Many of the social democrats split with the Labour Party in 1921 and for a while formed their own Social Democratic Party.

The revolutionary threat had been substantially weakening since 1921, and by 1923 it had disappeared.

How revolutionary?

How revolutionary was the Labour Party in the most hectic period of 1918–20? Or, more precisely, in what way was the Labour Party revolutionary? Here are some key points. It is striking that the party's general rhetoric, slogans and propaganda were combined with daily work in parliament, municipal councils and trade unions. The connection between general revolutionary rhetoric and daily political activity was not always clear.

Moreover, the party had no coherent strategy to gain power, and was characterized by divisions and various factions. The revolutionary Labour Party was far from Lenin's centralist Russian Bolsheviks. Inside the party there were not only social democrats, but also a pragmatic centrist tendency. The revolutionaries themselves were a heterogeneous bunch, with hard-core Moscow communists, a few left-wing communists and a large syndicalist-inspired wing. In short, the revolutionary forces were divided, and they were continually challenged by non-revolutionary forces within the labour movement.

Furthermore, it is an important point that the Labour Party had developed in a Norwegian political culture, characterized by peaceful solutions and compromises. In a direct confrontation between demands from Moscow/Comintern and the traditional party membership structure, the traditions prevailed.

It may seem paradoxical that the situation in Norway—where the largest socialist party declared itself revolutionary—remained calmer than in countries such as Britain, Germany and France, where the corresponding parties distanced themselves from Comintern and the Bolsheviks. Yet if we perceive that the party members acted within the framework of a common political culture that controlled their actions, even when the rhetoric could occasionally be heated, this becomes much more understandable.

Could the outcome have been different? It is possible that a more confrontational state in 1918–19 could have triggered the use of violence on the left and in turn escalate further. The absence of a political party or movement on the extreme right, able to channel the fear of revolution into political action, is another striking feature. Thus, those who were actual revolutionaries on the left had no extreme, anti-democratic counterpart against whom they could define themselves and from whom they could draw energy. Instead, the main line of conflict was between a large and moderate centre and an extreme left.

Finally, Norway was neutral in the world war. Norwegian society thus avoided the brutalization of social life felt by many warring countries, for example Germany and Italy. As for the economic situation, Norway had no serfdom as in tsarist Russia and no post-war reparations as in Germany.

Looking at these moments in context, it may seem as if the threat of revolution was never imminent. It remained a rather obscure notion with no concrete plans to carry out an insurrection.

However, this is seen retrospectively. People in 1919–20 did not have this perspective. Supporters of the existing social order could not know how this would play out, nor could the declared revolutionaries. They could not tell if they might have to accept the consequences of their revolutionary rhetoric. And one part of this equation was about to change: the rise of a right to counter the socialist left.

Norwegian fascism?

Although the revolutionary threat evaporated in the early 1920s, the idea of it did not. To some extent, such a notion was nourished by the fact that the Labour Party as late as 1932 had not completely abandoned its revolutionary rhetoric. Looking at the overall interwar period, a striking phenomenon is this: there were little or no militant right-wing authoritarian movements in the period 1918–21, when the threat of revolution was acute. The many right-wing authoritarian movements appeared first and foremost after the critical danger had gone.

In the interwar period there existed several groups, parties and movements that can be called right-wing authoritarian. Alternative terms may be nationalist right or right-wing activist groups. Common to them was a strong rejection of the radical labour movement's class struggle and a correspondingly strong fear of the threat of a socialist revolution in Norway. In addition, one can see a scepticism about—for some a blanket rejection of—the existing parliamentary, political democracy. In some, albeit to varying degrees, one can also see a growing rejection of liberalism, individualism and rights. The combination of social liberalism with political authoritarianism was typical of such right-wing movements in the interwar period.

Most right-wing authoritarian movements of the pre-First World War era had been influenced by liberalism. One can see them as further developing the tradition of the Norwegian civil servants' regime between 1814–84, a regime that, in its own way, was both authoritarian and characterized by liberalist ideas. It was in the context of this ideological legacy that right-wing authoritarianism sprang up in the interwar period.

The right-wing authoritarian currents drew on similar leanings from the pre-1914 period. They contained dislike of organized special interests and a marked scepticism of the parliamentary system. In a more positive ideological sense, they were characterized by support for the Norwegian national community and a visible admiration for strong, vigorous governments, not to mention strong, vigorous men. Parts of these currents gathered in the party Frisinnede Venstre (Liberal Left) from 1909.

One part of the political elite in Norway began to fear that the emerging labour movement could threaten the entire established social order; this also applied to some in Venstre. The prominent Venstre politician Christian Michelsen broke with his old party in early 1903, arguing, among other things, that the supporters of the existing order had to stand together against the new threat.

Michelsen became a hero in right-wing authoritarian circles. This was not least due to his powerful leadership in 1905, the year Norway broke from the union with Sweden. In the eyes of his admirers, he had then shown how a nation should be governed and how national interests should be defended. His determination to dissolve the union was not so much Norwegian nationalism for its own sake, but was instead driven by his belief that Norway's political establishment needed to focus not on independence but on stamping out socialism.

The October Revolution and the revolutionary wing victory of the Labour Party, as well as membership in the Communist International, naturally reinforced fear and loathing of revolution and class struggle. The situation was not improved by the parliamentary situation after 1918, where weak minority governments replaced each other. At the same time, working life was characterized by constant, hard conflicts. The 1920s were, more than any other decade, the era of class struggle in Norway. All this allowed for the further development of right-wing ideas in a far more consistent authoritarian direction.

In Europe in 1922, the breakthrough and political triumph of fascism in Italy was a landmark event. Fascism was a powerful response to the threat of a socialist revolution. At an early stage, Mussolini and his movement received support from bourgeois democratic forces. Fascism, however, would not preserve the existing liberal democracy at all. It would create something entirely new—a new type of society with a new type of people, under the auspices of a state that should not only be dictatorial but totalitarian. The fact that Mussolini had to make political compromises in practice did not change these core ideological values.

Mussolini was widely admired. The same was true of a similar movement in Germany that seized power in 1933: Hitler's National Socialism. In a wider sense, one may talk about a generic fascism, an ideological flow that includes the Italian original, German National Socialism, and other more or less similar movements. A common feature in this wider sense is that they were revolutionary in their own way; not looking to preserve existing society, they wanted to create something new.

The admiration for Mussolini and Hitler did not necessarily mean embracing the whole fascist ideology. For right-wing authoritarian circles in Norway during the interwar period, the advent of fascism put forth a crucial, if not always acknowledged, dilemma. Given that one would preserve and strengthen the national community as a superior value, and that Marxism's ideas of class struggle and revolution were a perceived threat to this community, what follows? Should the existing order, with its political institutions, be preserved with slight modifications? Or should one act like Mussolini and declare that the existing liberal-democratic system is unfit to withstand the threat of the revolutionary labour movement and, therefore, it is necessary to reject the whole system and replace it with something new? This was not just about the political system in a narrow sense. Should one maintain at least central parts of the liberalist mindset, including individualistic notions of individuals' rights, of freedom of expression, of organizational freedom, of legal security, of aversion to a comprehensive and intrusive state power? Or should one follow Mussolini's example and reject all of this thought in favour of extreme collectivism?

This was the overall dilemma, expressed here in its pure form. In practice, there were attempts at intermediate positions and sliding transitions. If one wanted to reform the existing political system—for example, by giving the government greater authority—how far could one go before the system was fundamentally changed?

One national hero who, like Michelsen, was an important bearer of right-wing authoritarian ideas, was deeply considering this question in the interwar period: the explorer Fridtjof Nansen. One might think that Nansen would be attracted to fascist ideas. Mussolini not only wanted to replace class struggle, party politics and special interests with national unity. His movement also cultivated values such as courage and manhood, to which Nansen had great affinity. Fascism was distinctly nationalistic, and placed extreme emphasis on action. One might say that if Mussolini had read Nansen's militant writings in February to March 1905, he would have liked what he read.

Nansen, however, did not cave into the solutions of fascism. In his speech at the founding of the nationalist and quite authoritarian movement *Fedrelandslaget* (National League) in 1925, he distanced himself from communism. He also explicitly separated himself from fascist violence and coups: 'But something quite different is when a party wants to impose its teachings on society with brutal force; against them we will stand together. They must, if they try, be beaten, be they fascists or communists.'[4]

There may be many reasons why Nansen rejected fascism's collectivist, violent and revolutionary positions. One important reason seems to be the elitist tradition of ideas that Nansen favoured before and after 1900.

Much of the Norwegian anti-Marxist right-wing in the 1920s was characterized by its combination of liberalist thought and political elitism, endorsed by Fridtjof Nansen. This liberalist, individualistic thought was an ideological buffer against fascism. Nansen, and the majority of his associates and supporters, did not abandon political democracy as a system. They just wanted to reform it and remove what they perceived as weaknesses in the system. Nansen also emphasized the principles of freedom of expression and the rights of individuals.

In many other countries in Europe, for example in Germany and smaller countries like Finland and Hungary, right-wing traditions were more purely authoritarian, and less characterized by liberalist individualism. Fascist and authoritarian, collectivist political solutions gained much greater support in these countries than in Norway, where fascism was only a marginal element in the interwar period. It was no coincidence, therefore, that Fridtjof Nansen never became a fascist.

Nasjonal Samling—the fascist alternative

The most obvious candidate for a powerful Norwegian fascist alternative in the interwar years was Nasjonal Samling (NS), the

National Unity Party. It was founded in 1933 by Vidkun Quisling, a former defence minister in the government led by the Farmer Party, founded in 1920. Quisling had made a name for himself as Fridtjof Nansen's close associate in the humanitarian operations during the famine disaster in Ukraine and Russia around 1920.

From the outset, NS called for close national unity instead of class war and petty party politics, a strong political leadership and measures against the revolutionary forces. The party did not call itself fascist, but its opponents referred to it as fascist and Nazi. Important parts of the party's policies and behaviour also added to such characteristics. The party was ruled by a *fører*—the Norwegian word for führer—a 'leader'. Party members greeted each other with an outstretched right arm. Although the party maintained that this was an old Norwegian greeting, the parallels to Italy and Germany were clear enough. It had as its foremost symbol an Olav cross, usually referred to as the Sun Cross, in red and gold. This was also an old Norwegian symbol, but in the 1930s it definitely had strong associations with foreign models.

The labour movement in Norway regarded NS with fear and disgust. Their reaction varied from warnings and harsh polemics, through mockery, to militant confrontations. In the latter case, there were episodes of physical fights.

For the large bourgeois parties, the matter was somewhat different. They also perceived NS as a highly unwanted competitor and an undemocratic outgrowth. Both in the Conservatives and the Farmer party there were some conciliatory voices towards the NS. During the 1933 parliamentary elections, the Conservatives issued a central ban on organized list collaboration with NS. The local party organization in Bergen defied this ban, but after 1933, the Conservatives' leadership drew clear demarcation lines between their party and NS.

The Farmer party, for its part, entered negotiations on a 'national bloc' with NS and two small right-wing authoritarian organizations in the summer of 1934. However, these negotiations broke down; there were several reasons for this, but the short version is that the political distance between the Farmer party and NS was too great.

Initially, NS hoped to evolve into a large and powerful movement. However, after two electoral defeats in 1933 and 1936—receiving around two per cent of the votes both times—and several internal conflicts and divisions, both ideologically and personally, the party was reduced to a negligible political extremist group from 1937.

A common feature of the many different right-wing authoritarian organizations in the interwar period was their deep concern about the threat of revolution. There was a widespread desire to be tougher in the face of the assumed revolutionary threat, often combined with a desire for a more vigorous government. Yet few developed any ideological alternative to political democracy. Individualist attitudes and liberalist thought constituted an important ideological buffer against the development of fascist ideas. The confidence that the democratic political system, with governments led by Venstre and the Conservatives, was able to defend the existing social order appears to have been great, while the revolutionary threat was real. Nansen was the obvious candidate for a strong national leader; Quisling, to put it mildly, did not have the same appeal.

The 1930s were ideologically more collectivistic than the 1920s. Nevertheless, the main impression is that the liberal tradition on the right in Norway continued to have appeal in this decade. Most right-wing authoritarian movements were influenced by the liberal tradition and did not become fascist or otherwise openly anti-democratic. NS was the obvious exception, but even there the revolutionary fascist thought was not as clearcut as in many similar movements in other countries. NS even tried to adapt external ideological impulses to Norwegian political culture and tradition.

In addition to NS, there were a few fascist and national social-ist groups who had readymade holistic imported ideologies, and no real adaptation to the dominant Norwegian political culture. These, however, remained tiny sects.

At an early stage Quisling made contacts with Mussolini's fascist movement, particularly through organized affiliation to the Rome-controlled organization CAUR, the so-called fascist international. Recent research also indicates that Quisling's movement towards the end of 1935 received money from the Italian embassy in Oslo.[5] However, this was probably a rather modest one-off payment.

Quisling and some of his party members also had some con-tact with Nazi Germany, Mussolini's rival in this ideological ter-rain. From 1937, we can see that NS was more clearly orientated towards Germany. This orientation was organizational, in the form of meetings and contacts, but to some extent also ideologi-cal. For example, anti-Semitism became a more tangible feature of NS from 1935, and it was further intensified from 1937. In the months before the German invasion of Norway on 9 April 1940, NS received substantial financial resources from Germany. Quisling visited Berlin in December 1939, met Hitler and told him that the formally neutral Norwegian government was in cahoots with Great Britain, and that British action in Norway was likely. After this visit, Hitler ordered plans to be drawn up for a German invasion of Norway. As we will see in Chapter 8, Nazi Germany's defeat in 1945 would be the final nail in the coffin for Quisling's NS.

The Crisis Settlement

So, if the far right weren't gaining traction with the electorate in the 1930s, who was? Norway had been struck hard by the eco-nomic crisis after the 1929 crash, and unemployment levels were very high. In addition, a debt crisis ravaged the farming communities. Crisis talk dominated the public debate in the early 1930s. The Labour Party in 1930 presented a radical program to solve the unemployment situation due to the depression, including a socialist economic reform and state-owned enterprises, which caused them to lose many seats. A year later, the largest labour conflict after the First World War included more than 100,000 workers on strike or lockout for five months.

In the 1933 election campaign, the Labour Party had eradicated all revolutionary rhetoric. Instead, the party went to the polls with slogans demanding concrete solutions to the crisis within the current economic framework, as well as full employment and solidarity between town and country. The campaign was a triumph; the Labour Party received forty per cent of the vote and the largest group of delegates in the Storting. The proportional electoral system prevented the party getting an outright majority, however, and Venstre formed a government.

Two years later, after the 1935 election, the Labour Party made a deal with the Farmer Party. In Norway this deal is commonly known as the *Kriseforliket* (Crisis Settlement). The Labour Party formed a government, but guaranteed that many of the Farmer Party's rural crisis demands were met, including more subsidies to the farmers and stronger state interference in agricultural supply. This settlement caused quite a stir. Up until now, the two parties had been fierce enemies in Norway's interwar political landscape. Yet the Labour Party government's policies and style were moderate and conciliatory, and it proved unexpectedly stable.

Just a few days before the Labour Party government took office, with Johan Nygaardsvold as prime minister, a key event took place: the signing of The General Agreement or *Hovedavtalen*. Among the unions on both sides, a common understanding that strikes and lockouts could not continue gradually emerged. This understanding led to negotiations, which lasted over a few years, and finally ended in what is now known as The General Agreement. It included rules of dispute, how negotiations should proceed, and both a right and duty to engage in them. This large compromise settled how labour unions and employer unions should work together, and also how the government should intervene if disagreements could not be solved. In 1915, a labour dispute act had been passed in parliament which implied that the government should endorse the principle of wage negotiations, where the labour unions and employer unions collectively consulted. The act also stated that the government could interfere with compulsory arbitration if the organizations could not agree. This General Agreement formalized and brought into common consensus the principles underpinning the 1915 act.

Thus, the traditional Norwegian political culture, with its emphasis on compromises and peaceful solutions, prevailed even in interwar decades dominated by crisis and political extremism. The Crisis Settlement also implied that more corporative solutions were accepted, especially in farming and fisheries. 1935 was all in all a pivotal year, and many of the economic ideas, corporatism, and workings of the labour market continued to influence politics after the Second World War.

However, disaster then struck in the form of German military forces.

8

THE WAR EXPERIENCE

1940–45

Early in the morning of 9 April 1940, Norway was attacked by Nazi Germany. The first attack wave came from the sea and the air, and it took the Norwegians completely by surprise. The Germans gave the Labour government an ultimatum, which was rejected. The king and cabinet escaped to the inner parts of the country and started organizing an armed resistance.

A new word for traitor

Meanwhile, in the captured capital of Oslo, Vidkun Quisling entered the public scene. On the evening of 9 April, he held a speech on Norwegian radio, declaring himself the new prime minister of Norway and ordering all armed resistance to be cancelled at once. This attempt at a coup d'état hardened the will to fight within the government and presumably among most Norwegians as well. The government hoped for help from the Allies, especially from Great Britain.

The Allied help did arrive, with British forces landing in Norway on 17 April, but it was unfortunately mostly ineffective.

THE NORWEGIAN EXCEPTION?

The main exception was the Northern and strategically important port of Narvik, where Allied and Norwegian forces delivered the first real defeat for German military forces in the Second World War. Alas, when the Germans attacked France in May 1940, the Allies withdrew from Norway. After two months of fighting, the armed forces in Norway capitulated. The king, the crown prince and the government escaped to England, while the crown princess and the children went to the US. The king and the government vowed to continue the fight from exile in London. The date that they left Norway was a fateful one in Norwegian history, 7 June.

Occupied Norway was governed by a German Reichskommissar, a plenipotentiary appointed by, and answering directly to, Hitler himself. However, the occupants needed Norwegian collaborators. Everyone thought that Quisling had acted in accordance with Hitler and the Germans, but a Quisling coup d'état hadn't figured in the German invasion plans. Most probably his attempt had been made without Hitler's knowledge, and certainly without the knowledge of the German generals.

Quisling's coup government in April had never got off the ground. He formally withdrew after only five days, realizing that his coup had no domestic support except from his inner circle, and facing pressure from the German occupants. The Germans seemed eager to find an arrangement with more mainstream political and bureaucratic circles in the occupied parts of the country. The German Reichskommissar, Josef Terboven, disliked Quisling and considered him a fool, detached from the realities of life.

On the other hand, Quisling had admirers in Berlin. After some hefty political intrigues, both in Nazi Germany and in occupied Norway, Hitler decided that Quisling's Nasjonal Samling (NS) was to be the sole legal political party in Norway and the occupants' principal collaborator. On 25 September

1940, Terboven disbanded all other political parties, declared that all political activity from now on had to go through NS and appointed new Norwegian ministers, nearly all of them members of the NS. This was the real start of the national socialist revolution in Norway.

Neutral no more

When Hitler had invaded Poland in 1939 and the new world war had broken out, Norway had declared herself neutral. This time, however, the leanings towards the Allies of Britain and France were even more palpable than in the First World War. The Germans took note this time, too. An episode in February may have been the tipping point for Hitler.

On 16 February 1940, the British destroyer *Cossack* penetrated Norwegian territorial waters on the south-western coast. A German ship, *Altmark*, had been given permission to navigate through Norwegian waters. It had been an auxiliary vessel for the pocket battleship *Graf Spee* and had British prisoners on board, unbeknownst to Norwegian authorities. The Brits forcibly liberated the prisoners, unopposed by the Norwegian navy. When briefed of the incident, Hitler exploded with rage.

Germany had made plans for attacking Norway since December 1939. The navy leadership wanted control of Norway's North Sea ports, and Germany wanted to secure her highly important supply of Swedish iron ore, which in wintertime had to go through the Norwegian port of Narvik. Last, but not least, Vidkun Quisling had warned Hitler of possible British plans for Norway during his clandestine visit to Berlin in December.

After the Altmark incident, Hitler affirmed orders for the invasion of Norway. Meanwhile, the British and the French had also discussed and planned possible military action in Norwegian ports. The Norwegian Storting and Labour government were ignorant of these plans, but aware of rumours concerning the Great Powers and Norway. They still didn't take the rumours seriously enough to order mobilization of the coastal defence, but as the Foreign Minister Halvdan Koht said in a closed meeting just the day before the German invasion: 'If we are going to be dragged into this war, we better make sure we will be on the right side.'[1]

One reason for the leniency of the Norwegian authorities was, of course, that they trusted the British Royal Navy to control the North Sea and prevent a massive German naval attack. Yet this time, the Royal Navy failed. The German invasion in April was as much a shock to the British as to the Norwegians.

The national socialist revolution

Vidkun Quisling's NS party didn't just collaborate with the occupant. It wanted to use the war and the German occupation as an opportunity to create a New Order in Norwegian society, and openly declared that a national socialist revolution was on the table. The main party newspaper, *Fritt Folk* (A Free People), wrote in May 1940:

> We have never recognized Democracy as the true representation of the will of the Norwegian people. [...] How could anyone believe that we, the carriers of national-revolutionary ideas, we who have asked for a cleansing of Norway, could be stopped by such formalities.[2]

The new NS regime immediately started to purge the Norwegian bureaucracy and install a national socialist order everywhere in the local municipalities. The party took, or at least tried to take, control of all important institutions in Norwegian society: courts, trade unions, police, newspapers, publishers, film industry, the Church, schools, and all institutions of research and higher education. The goal was to create a totalitarian, pure national socialist society. Together with the German Reichskommissariat, they made sure that no dissenting voices were allowed.

The NS wanted a clean break with parliamentary democracy. Still, even the revolutionary national socialists did not distance themselves completely from the political culture that had been dominant in Norway since 1814. To the contrary, NS presented itself as the true, sole inheritors of these 1814 beliefs. Their main argument was that these ideas had been distorted and falsified, first by liberals in Venstre and then by socialists in the Labour Party. The party ideologues maintained that there were no provisions for the parliamentary system or political parties in the 1814 Constitution. They also argued that the Führer Principle was deeply rooted in old Norse tradition. Quisling was formally appointed Chief of Government and State early in 1942, and one of his first acts of office was to re-introduce the paragraph in the Constitution that banned Jews from entering the realm. In general, one may say that the NS regime tried to revitalize the authoritarian and elitist strands in the 1814 Constitution and the civil servants' regime. Like Mussolini's original fascists, they saw their revolution as a national rebirth.

Of course, the NS political campaigns took place in a completely new context, and the attempts to position the national socialist revolution within the tradition from 1814 was not particularly convincing. It was plain to see that the national socialist führer state was in principle quite different from the 1814 Constitution's ideas on division of power. The NS openly declared that all liberal elements in the 1814 tradition, with their ideas on individual rights and liberties, were a thing of the past. Still, it is interesting to note that they tried all they could to ground their revolution in old Norwegian traditions.

Moreover, in the cultural sphere, NS had attached itself to nineteenth-century Norwegian cultural nationalism in the 1930s, and this continued during the occupation. Quisling and his party were fairly obsessed with old Norwegian history, especially the Viking age. Very much unlike the nineteenth-century ideologue and nationalist poet Henrik Wergeland, the NS stressed the heroic aspects of Norway's medieval cultural inheritance. They appropriated numerous old symbols and concepts, gave them their own design and placed them into a new, national socialist context. They organized large rallies and meetings in places with high historical, cultural and symbolic significance.

In short, NS redeveloped its close connection with Norwegian medieval traditions in a fierce and rather absurd sense. After 1945, many medieval symbols were in a loose way associated with the NS and therefore brought into disrepute in Norway.

Look to Norway

The NS were completely dependent on the German occupants and often had to grapple with the Reichskommissar. Ideally, Quisling wanted to get rid of Reichkomissar Terboven and rule Norway on his own. To do this, however, he had to convince Hitler that his party was capable of ruling without any German help. Unfortunately for Quisling, Hitler never became fully convinced, and the NS Party and its leader had to accept their German overlords until the end of the war.

The NS party had been a tiny sect before the German invasion. After 9 April, however, and especially after all the other parties were abolished in September 1940, new members flocked to the party. NS had perhaps 1,000 active members before 9 April; at the end of 1940, this had risen to 25,000, and steadily continued to approximately 50,000 in 1943. In a Norwegian context, this was not that bad. The total population in Norway was around three million, and Quisling boasted that the NS was the largest political organization in Norwegian history.

Yet it was not enough. The attempt to transform Norway into a national socialist society was met with little support, to put it mildly, among most of Quisling's compatriots. Although open, active resistance was rather modest and disorganized in the beginning, the openly hostile reactions to the new order were unmistakable.

In 1942, the regime launched an ambitious campaign to control and purify the Church and schools. For the first time in occupied Norway, they were met with widespread and organized civil resistance. The regime tried to use force and at one point deported protesting teachers to the northernmost part of Norway, but to little avail. The resistance was quite successful and boosted anti-Nazi Norwegian morale. As a result, the NS regime, which didn't want to provoke more social unrest, had to delay several of its attempted plans. The peaceful, civil resistance in Norway received attention elsewhere, too. In September 1942, US President Franklin D. Roosevelt held his famous—at least in Norway—'Look to Norway' speech, in which he said:

> If there is anyone who still wonders why this war is being fought, let him look to Norway. If there is anyone who has any delusions that this war could have been averted, let him look to Norway; and if there is anyone who doubts the democratic will to win, again I say, let him look to Norway.[3]

After the German invasion of the Soviet Union in the summer of 1941, Norwegian communists also became an active part of Norwegian resistance. Their main strategy was armed struggle, and they accomplished some spectacular sabotage actions, as well as a protracted guerrilla campaign with base camps in the remote mountains. More democratically-orientated and politically mainstream forces would also organize armed resistance, acting somewhat in accordance with the government-in-exile in London. This primarily took place in late phases of the war, especially the final year. Taken as a whole, however, civil resistance in occupied Norway was much more significant than the armed one.

THE NORWEGIAN EXCEPTION?

Norway's trump card during the war was her shipping fleet. The commercial fleet was one of the largest in the world, and sailed almost everywhere. When the Germans invaded Norway in April 1940, nearly the whole fleet was in foreign ports or at the High Seas. The legal, democratic government demanded loyalty from all captains at sea, and most of them followed suit; nearly every Norwegian ship called at Allied or neutral ports. During the war, the government in-exile controlled the fleet, and Norwegian ships made a heavy contribution to Allied shipping, for instance convoys in the North Atlantic and Soviet ports at the Kola peninsula. Norwegian sailors also paid a heavy price, with merchant sailors comprising about one third of all Norwegians killed during the war.

Most Norwegians rejected the revolution and collaboration proposed by NS. Then again, most Norwegians did not participate in any meaningful form of active resistance either. Many tried to get on with their daily lives as best they could, disliked the Nazis and hoped for better times.

All in all, the German occupation of Norway was relatively mild, compared to most other German-occupied countries. The Nazi race ideology considered Norwegians pure members of the Nordic race. When Terboven was appointed Reichskommissar of Norway in April 1940, Hitler even gave him the task of winning the Norwegians' heart. However, the German occupants used brutal force when it suited them, including torture and terror, usually with their Norwegian collaborators as willing participants.

Norwegian Jews were targeted under the Nazi terror regime more than anyone else. There were around 2,000 Jews living in Norway in 1940. Thankfully, most of them escaped Nazi persecution, but late in 1942 the regime rounded up all the remaining Jews they were able to arrest. Around 775 Norwegian Jews were deported to the death camps in Poland and all of them except twenty-five were killed.

The overall figures are these: around 10,000 Norwegian citizens died as a direct consequence of the war. This figure includes around 2,000 casualties in the Norwegian and Allied armed forces, around 2,000 resistance fighters who were killed or executed, and the Norwegian Jews. It also includes approximately 750 Norwegian civilians killed by allied bomb attacks and at least 500–600 pro-German voluntary fighters in the Waffen-SS on the Eastern Front. Finally, it includes more than 3,500 sailors in the commercial fleet. For tiny, traditionally peaceful Norway, these figures may seem high; for each victim and their families, the violent deaths were a tragedy. Nevertheless, in the broader context of the Second World War, the casualties in Norway were relatively low. Per capita, Norwegian death tolls were around 0.3 per cent, compared to approximately 1.9 per cent in France and 2.4 per cent in the Netherlands. Among German-occupied countries, only Denmark had significantly lower death tolls than Norway.

Post-war purges and a new start

The liberation of Norway was mostly a peaceful and undramatic affair. The main exception is the northernmost part of the country, which was invaded by the Soviet Red Army in October 1944, forcing the Germans to retreat. The Germans used scorched earth tactics and forcibly evacuated the civilian population, but when the war ended, the Red Army exited calmly.

In the rest of the country, the German forces formally and peacefully capitulated on 8 May 1945. Reichskommissar Terboven actually wanted to fight, but Hitler's appointed successor Karl Dönitz ordered him not to do so. The Reichskommissar's response was suicide. Quisling and his government surrendered to free Norwegian police units, which had been organized illegally during the last part of the war. They were reinforced by Norwegians coming back from their exile in Sweden.

THE NORWEGIAN EXCEPTION?

The king returned from his British exile on 7 June: exactly five years after he had left, and exactly forty years after Norway had seceded from the union with Sweden. This date may have been coincidental in 1940, but the triumphant return in 1945 most certainly was not.

The purges after the war had some striking characteristics. Compared to other German-occupied countries, there were few examples of vigilante justice in Norway. On the other hand, many people were prosecuted and sentenced in the legal purge. Membership of the NS party from 9 April 1940 was in itself regarded as a criminal offense, regardless of one's activity as a party member. Nearly 100,000 Norwegians were investigated, and around 50,000 received some form of sentence. Most sentences, however, were not that harsh; there were relatively few death penalties, with twenty-five Norwegians executed in the purge. Most of them were torturers and informers, and only three leading NS politicians were executed, among them Vidkun Quisling.

This was the strictly legal part of the purge. In a more informal sense, former NS members and their families were widely shamed and ostracised in various social settings. They were, or at least most of them felt that they were, left out of the new national community.

Pictures from the liberation in May show cheering crowds with Norwegian flags everywhere. The National Day was celebrated on 17 May 1945 like never before. The political order before 9 April 1940 was quickly restored, reinstating the parties banned by the Reichskommissar. In short, democracy recaptured the most important national symbols and restored its institutions without much ado.

In other words, the main ideas from the Norwegian 1814 tradition were reinforced in 1945, and strongly so. National sovereignty and democracy were seen as two sides of the same coin.

The enemy had not only been an enemy in the traditional sense, but had also tried to replace liberal, parliamentary democracy with a national socialist führer state. The NS had presented their anti-democratic, authoritarian ideas as the alternative in the 1930s, they had collaborated with the enemy during the occupation, and they had lost. As a result of this, all sorts of Nazi and fascist ideas in post-war Norway have been associated with the stigma of treason and have been widely discredited.

One important lesson from the Norwegian war experience was that compromises don't always work. On 10 April 1940, a peaceful solution to the German invasion was still on the table; it would be something similar to Denmark, where the king and the government accepted the German ultimatum of 9 April. Informal deliberations between the fleeing Labour government and the Germans had stalled, largely because of the king. He said no when the Germans had demanded a prominent place for Quisling in a new Norwegian government. In the summer of 1940, another royal 'no' was extremely important both for public morale in Norway and for the outcome of the occupation itself. After the king and government escaped to England, remaining members of the Storting negotiated with representatives of the German Reichskommissariat. The Germans put pressure on the Norwegians and demanded the king's abdication. A small majority of the remaining MPs showed a willingness to accept the German demands, even for abdication; they saw this as the only way to avoid a pure German regime or a Quisling government in occupied Norway. However, the king once again refused in a forceful radio speech from London. In the end, negotiations broke down, and Reichskommissar Terboven declared that NS was to be the sole legal Norwegian political force. The king was also cheered as a unifying national symbol—something he had not been before 1940—when he triumphantly returned from his exile in England.

THE NORWEGIAN EXCEPTION?

The Norwegian negotiators in the summer of 1940 were clearly led by Terboven; a puppet regime and military occupation were on the cards for Germany the whole time. The somewhat naïve democratic Norwegian politicians, used to peaceful negotiations and compromise solutions, didn't see through this. Apparently, the traditional Norwegian compromising attitude didn't work with an adversary as brutal and cunning as the German Nazis in 1940.

9

THE POST-WAR DECADES

HEYDAY OF SOCIAL DEMOCRACY

In many countries, the post-war decades were a prosperous period. In France they are referred to as *Les Trente Glorieuses*—the thirty glorious years. Countries were rebuilding after the war, and the period was characterized by a strong belief in what politics could and should do. In Norway too, the period between 1945–70 was characterized by equality, economic growth and larger welfare reforms.

Fellesprogrammet—officially called the 'Cooperation program for the reconstruction from 1945'—was a democratic development and reformulation of the original ideas from 1814. The emphasis on state control and governance remained strong, and is still the political norm when it comes to larger social reforms. The main ideological expression in the program was agreed upon by all political parties, even including the Communists. The program stated that, as a result of war and occupation, Norwegians were 'one people despite differences in outlook on life and conditions and despite old struggles'. This experience of community was something to preserve for the future. It further linked

Norwegian community to 'the democratic principles that have been expressed in the Eidsvoll Constitution and the further development of democracy until 1940'.

When the Labour Party was in government from 1935–40, its rhetoric had been more radical than its policy. As the historian Einar Lie writes:

> The Labour Party reformism in office [before the war] confirms that the threat of fundamental changes in the political and economic system was to a large extent unrealistic. The rhetoric was still radical but the political practices in economic policies were not radically different from what the right-wing parties had stood for. The substantial changes came after the war, brought about by the specific economic and political situation that had been created.[1]

As we shall see, within this post-war context, the Labour Party's self-image became the self-image of the nation, resulting in the political and civil collectivism that marked the 1950s and 60s. These decades can be characterized as the cooperative and collectivistic period of Norwegian history. The belief that social development could be governed and adjusted in detail was strong. The general economic growth, high employment rate, and growth in living standards during this period contributed to making the rhetoric even more powerful. The argument was that active policies made positive development possible. The slogan belonging to the Labour Party, 'building the country', had a strong appeal.

A shared political project

The Second World War changed Norwegian society. Liberals had argued for a national identity opposing the Labour Party's international class solidarity. They had also argued for local initiatives, civil society and traditional values such as family and church.

The war changed these positions. The social democrats' ambitions prevailed in the large nation-building project of the post-war decade. Many initiatives had been interrupted during the war and were taken up again in the program.

As for national consciousness, the Second World War and the German occupation left Norwegians with a shared experience that for five years had bound the nation together, except for those few who had decided to cooperate with the Germans. Most people felt that this sense of Norwegian identity should be maintained, smoothing the political differences that had been present before the war.

The political program was prepared by a committee, representing the four political parties that had agreed upon a political truce in 1940: the Labour Party, the Conservatives, Venstre and the Farmer Party. Their proposal was ready in the autumn of 1944, but we must note that many elements were gathered from the work of leading Labour Party members in exile in London from 1942–43. They were partly inspired by the British liberal politician William Beveridge who, in 1942, published 'Social Insurance and Allied Services', better known as the Beveridge Report. This report became the basis for the post-war British welfare state, built by the Labour government elected in a landslide in July 1945. In Norway, too, it was the Labour Party that benefited electorally from reconstruction policy—not surprisingly, because *Fellesprogrammet* had a clear social democratic leaning, building on the Labour Union war blue book which stated economic guidelines and principles for rebuilding the country. Together with the Labour Party, the Labour Union had during 1944 prepared a 'blue book', with the aim of suggesting economic policies that interfered extensively in the market economy to ensure a rational, efficient rebuilding of industries and infrastructure. Economic plans were to be followed, production to be controlled, and important economic decisions to be political rather than commercial.

The spirit of the program was that Norwegians were a *folk*, in the typical Norwegian sense of the word, despite differences in economic conditions or old political conflicts: 'In the Norwegian mind a sense of community is created that no violent power could dismantle.' The language was symbolic and emotional, and continued with the following call: 'In the light of future challenges, we will call upon the same readiness to make sacrifice, the same companionship and the same will to endure hardship and to stay together.' This may seem conformist, and it was added that debate was natural in a liberal society and that no one wanted political uniformity. Political parties should have the right to defend views unrestrictedly in line with the principles of liberal democracy.

In hindsight, this political manifesto does not highlight plurality and debate. The war had united Norwegians and given them a strong sense of unity, probably the strongest in Norwegian history. The idea was that all Norwegians shared a collective identity despite earlier class struggles and backgrounds; the Quislings, however, were not included.

After the war, it was difficult for political opponents to argue against these policies due to their own lack of success in economic policy during the 1930s. The acceptance of stronger political interference had grown during the pre-war decade, which benefited the social democrats.

Fellesprogrammet described how the country should be rebuilt economically. All resources were to be employed, both public and private, which of course meant rigid control and structured, detailed plans. Two ideas are worth mentioning: employment for all and a fair distribution of wealth and resources. The second idea is political because it questions what is fair. Which resources should be redistributed, and when does redistribution conflict with the principle of private property rights? Employment for all also took a strong political view on the kind of employment that was needed: employing people in work that benefited the goal of rebuilding the country. Both ideas were supposed to work together to create a viable and prosperous future for Norway.

It was the Labour Party—a political party that only a few decades earlier had accepted the international communist decree Comintern—which used the principles of market capitalism to reunite the nation after the Second World War. The framework of the Labour Party program, such as the demolition of the capitalistic economy, were gone. Intentions to regulate and control the economy were still prevalent, but private property rights and the principles of a market economy were accepted. The conservative defence of liberal principles, property rights, and opposition to the strong corporate elements of economic policy, ensured that the Labour Party quite quickly abandoned the idea that 'capitalism was unfit to secure peace and prosperity'.

Since *Fellesprogrammet* was agreed upon by all the political parties, disagreements between them became less pronounced. In the new climate of national togetherness, it was not *comme il faut* to disagree or raise political debates, leaving the political sphere of the first post-war years almost non-political. The Labour Party held the dominant position with an absolute majority in the parliament from 1945–61. The social democrats also dominated in neighbouring Denmark, but not to the same extent. Danish governments were shifting, and the political landscape was more diverse. The hegemonic social democrat position was stronger in Norway.

Norway had a long history of accepting state interference in difficult times, even when public finances were weak. The state was never seen as 'malevolent', and even liberals could accept the need to intervene. This contributed to the extraordinary role of the state in the late 1940s and beginning of the 1950s.

First and foremost, key aspects of the Norwegian rebuilding processes were efficiency, planning, technology and structure.

Public welfare was to supply security for everyone. The political slogan of the time was 'join forces and pull together'. The feeling of a new start was far-reaching, and the Labour Party had the power to decide how this should happen. The Labour Party politician Ronald Bye pronounced that, 'my father did not believe in God but he believed in Gerhardsen [the Labour Party prime minister after the war, in power for a total of 17 years], and it was sort of the way it was in the family'.[2]

The overall direction of economic policy actually had a strong continuity from the 1930s, with planning, tight governance and control. At the same time, however, the Labour Party became less socialistic, accepting the need for an open, liberal economy with private ownership. The liberal defence for a capitalistic economy might appear to have vanished in the post-war planning regime, but this was not the case. The Conservatives played an important role in moderating the Labour Party, which eventually left eager planning policies. The Norwegian historian Even Lange has called the Labour Party 'the least dogmatic social democrats in Europe'.[3] The party nearly always cooperated better with the Conservatives and the centre-right than with the far-left socialists. Their willingness to compromise and moderate themselves led to strong development and growth.

A generation of technocrats

The generation that lived through the Second World War had a common and special experience that would strongly influence Norwegian politics in the post-war decades. The war also created a generational change; younger people who had only experienced periods of unrest and war came into office, taking central political positions and assignments elsewhere in public life and society. Prominent figures like Erik Brofoss (Central Bank Governor and Minister of Finance), Trygve Bratteli (Prime

Minister from the Labour Party), Haakon Lie (Labour Party General Secretary) and Jens Christian Hauge (Head of Resistance during the war, Minister of Defence and Minister of Justice) were all in their thirties in 1945. Prime Minister Einar Gerhardsen was forty-five. The crisis of war had not only influenced politicians, but also academics in many social and economic disciplines. They joined forces with politicians and supported their chosen policies through analysis and independent proposals. The economic protagonist was professor of economics and Nobel laureate, Ragnar Frisch, who had a long-term influence on Labour Party politics from the 1930s onwards. Frisch was known for his work in econometrics and macroeconomic planning, and the ideals of planning the economy also nourished this belief in other social sciences.

Science and technology were applied to serve politics. Neutral, professional advice and arguments were to be used not only in economics but in a wide range of social and labour market policies. To a certain extent, one might say that the first post-war years were pragmatic and technocratic, especially if compared to the harsher ideological debates that characterized the 1930s. Politics was based on rational, industrial thinking, on expert advice and analysis. Bureaucrats and administrative bodies were tailored to different administrative tasks that expanded through the 1950s–60s, following increasing living standards and economic growth.

An example of this optimistic technocratic control was Karl Evang, the public director of Norwegian health care from 1938–72. He was a bureaucrat who marked Norwegian health care and social policies for more than thirty years. His mantra was that health care services and policies should be governed by medical expertise, and thereby depoliticized. Evang had wide authorizations as the most senior civil servant in the Ministry of Social Affairs and could personally propose legislation and financial budgets to the Minister, for initiatives concerning health care, vaccination programs, medical education, and health information campaigns. Institutionalized, regulated social policies were seen in the education system: dental care, breakfast in primary schools, education of health personnel, and the creation of a system for young doctors to practise all over Norway after finishing their education. It also influenced housing policies, with the aim of telling people what was in their best interest and thereby ameliorating the public health (*folkehelsen*). Norwegian health care under Evang was unified and centralized—not just the curative care but also preventive measures. This naturally fitted into the vision of a welfare state that seamlessly offered high-quality health care to all citizens, regardless of income, status or geographic residence. The directory of health care was the organizational peak of the pyramid, covering the whole country and implicitly making it paternalistic: health became a public responsibility, and how you chose to live was thus a public concern.

The bureaucracy was strong, competent and highly qualified, but during the post-war decades the willingness of the Labour Party to let the bureaucrats administer political planning and control could easily become problematic. The bureaucracy grew in scope and size as the willingness to build a strong system was great. To a large extent, this happened without losing the generally high trust among Norwegians and the democratic political power to set goals. Nevertheless, a well-functioning bureaucracy has a responsibility to use its discretionary powers wisely, and keeps and gains trust while doing so.

The use of bureaucratic power in a democracy is usually not problematic. All decisions cannot be made through democratic processes, as this may well lead to chaos. On the other hand, a bureaucracy that is left on its own and gets its powers from general political instructions is authoritarian, like the communist system in the Soviet Union. Bureaucracies are nonetheless indispensable in modern complex societies. The law cannot account for all eventualities, and all modern societies largely delegate the power of decision to experts and bureaucrats. The bureaucracy therefore always operates between the goals of efficient decision making and democracy, which often contradict when it comes to administrative power.

The pressure on civil society to be a sphere of morality and identity was the result of the entry of experts. The instrumental society created in the welfare state was connected to the rational and the professional. The consequence was that the balance between the state and civil society became more distorted than before. Science and technology were used in the service of politics, favouring neutral, professional advice and arguments. As the sociologist Rune Slagstad pointed out: 'The formation and the moral education of the population—*folkedannelsen*—became an integrated part of the social democratic project but it gradually lost its power to shape society. A technocratic elite became hegemonic'.[4] This sums up the post-war development.

Economic regulation and control

The culture of collaboration in Norwegian politics grew substantially in the post-war period, because there was great acceptance of using bureaucratic means to govern society. A competent, educated bureaucracy was seen as capable of implementing politics with a relatively high level of autonomy. Political signals were given through so-called enabling acts, imposed despite ardent protests from the political opposition. The most famous of them was the price law. In the 1940s shortage economy, it was all about covering basic needs, solved by rationalization and tight governance of supply. The price regulations were seen as a means to regulate demand not covered by the supply. The idea of the law was based on the wish to distribute the few available goods fairly, not according to the ability to pay. The price law gave the bureaucrats the power to decide the general level of prices; they could also withdraw profits from businesses if they saw fit, even if the activity was legal. The bureaucracy had the means to conduct distribution policies and regulate the profits of private businesses. What constituted too high a profit was never revealed. A professor of economics, Wilhelm Keilhau, gave the following comment to the proposal of a new price act in 1953:

> The proposal will in reality rely on the academics without an independent experience from business life, [without knowledge of working conditions, without knowledge of specific industries, and without economic responsibility] to wheel and deal with the Norwegian economic life—based on 'discretion'. A more perverse social system has never been suggested.[5]

Initially, the act gave an extensive framework for detailed intervention, which created debate. There was great willingness to regulate, but it quickly became clear in practice that implementation would be complicated, and the proposals faced opposition. It was impossible for the politicians and the bureaucrats to get an overview of the economy. Any attempt at correct planning of prices would be doomed to err.

Even though Labour had left behind its revolutionary ideology, the Conservatives still explicitly denounced what they saw as a 'socialist planned economy'. Their program emphasized a free market, stating that 'no one is more suitable to create the necessary efficiency in production and supply than private businesses.' There were great objections to the extensive economic governance of business. In addition, the laws gave authority to the administration, which could act with wide powers. According to the Conservatives, the principles of rule of law were eliminated. Public governance and intervention outmanoeuvred democracy and justice.

An important question raised was the evaluation of the economic condition after the war: was it as weak as it seemed?

Goods viewed as luxury goods, such as cars, were regulated until 1960, and during the next decade the number of cars almost tripled. If you were to buy a car before this point, you had to go through a thorough application process to verify that you needed it. However, it became clear quite quickly that the desire to plan or stimulate production did not work in practice. Norway was not the only country that wanted to regulate the economy immediately after the war—as a natural continuity of the war economy—but the chief objection in this context was that the regulation regime continued long after it was strictly necessary. Pre-war levels of production and consumption were reached in 1946, and in hindsight one might ask if the regulations lasted too long, and if a less tight market control would have generated higher economic growth. European countries in general regained the pre-war level in 1947. Norwegian industrial production sites were not as damaged as the Central-European ones and, in addition, transport and infrastructure had also been improved throughout the war. Following an in-depth and harsh debate in the wake of the proposal for permanent price and regulation legislation in 1953, this legislation was effectively abandoned. The established governance system continued, but without the same radical intervention. Regulation of goods became less common, but at the same time an extensive system of credit regulations was developed.

The regulation was not merely part of economic life. Committees were formed to organize many social areas and these initiatives experienced explosive growth. In 1936 before the war, 250 such government bodies existed, whereas in 1951 the number had doubled. It continued in this way: by the beginning of the 1980s, more than 1,000 different committees and organizations had influence on politics, whether directly or indirectly. This influence cannot be overstated; it could be said that in certain cases it was an even more important source of political power than that elected in parliament, one example being Evang and health care.

In the post-war period between 1950–70, Norwegians witnessed a high growth in living standards compared to earlier periods in history, just like most Western-European countries. It must be added, however, that the growth in Norway was lower than in most other comparable countries. While Japan and West Germany had their specific challenges after the war, their economies grew by nine and six per cent between 1950–73 respectively. Overall the world had an average annual growth rate of 4.9 per cent. Norway had an annual average growth rate of only 4.12 per cent, lower than the European average, and probably caused by a tighter state control of the economy that perhaps hindered a better growth rate.

A collective compassion and duty to care

The dominance of the Labour Party after the war had the consequence that society, nation and state became synonyms. National values and national identity were partly replaced by a social democratic understanding of the state as the bearer of Norwegian identity. It was easier to accept public interference and responsibilities when the public sector was seen as something shared and beneficial. At the same time, the balance of power in society shifted. NGOs and voluntary initiatives and organizations were increasingly drawn into the social democracy as a means of achieving goals in welfare policies. Consequently, they lost their independent position. Public services and responsibilities grew in correlation with the expansion of the welfare state. Accordingly, solidarity was connected to the welfare state and no longer exclusively to labour unions: social democracy and the welfare state became twins. This 'union' had far-reaching significance for the liberal understanding of community and society with distinctive spheres of the public, the civil, and the private. Solidarity was fulfilled through public policies, rather than something that manifested itself in social relations.

The main principles of the welfare state, the goal of full employment and the fight against poverty were all common political ground. Venstre had for instance argued all along for universal principles in welfare policies. By the end of the 1960s, when a conservative government introduced what was referred to as National Insurance or *Folketrygden* (note again the use of *folk*), a system that organized all benefits from unemployment pay to pensions and sick leave compensation, Venstre emphasized the need for non-exclusion over means testing measures.

The idea of a unified system for social security had been part of the political programs for both the Conservatives and the Labour party since the late 1940s, but it had taken time to agree upon all the details, especially the financing.

The national insurance system included all-important and wide-ranging rights that had earlier been passed into a coherent system of benefits, many of which originated from local rights agreed upon before the Second World War. In many ways, the guarantee of rights was a counterpart of bureaucratic autonomy and power. The politicians were able to ensure these through political decisions and detailed regulations, which meant that there was limited scope for legal or administrative decisions based on judgement.

The welfare state expansion can be seen as a large, collective project with the aim of supplying security and equal treatment for all social classes. It also had an individual aspect. Everyone was to be liberated from earlier dependencies, whether that was their family or employer. The paradox that gradually appeared was that the more equality that was offered, the more independent everyone became. The welfare state development was a 'peculiar combination of liberalism and socialism': the socialist, collective idea of equality and the liberal idea of rights and individualism, 'a kind of universalism—equal rights for all citizens within the nation—obtained by a collective arrangement that should advocate individual freedom.'[6] Universalism is built on the rule of law, liberal civil rights and the protection of the individual against the power of the state. It is a mixture of individual independence and a collective framework. Norwegians and Nordic historians alike point to this as an important reflection of Norwegian society, which has strong historical traditions both of liberal governance and collectivism.

The development of welfare services made voluntary suppliers of health care and similar services become more instrumental. This implied that the suppliers gradually lost their independent status, either disappearing or becoming incorporated into the new large welfare system. The political aim was to make sure that everyone received the services and benefits to which they were entitled, and the responsibility for that was public. In reality, many services were still provided by private companies and charitable institutions. These gradually received public financing and started operating on behalf of the welfare state.

The welfare state was perceived as the great national community; the governments of the post-war decades, dominated by Labour, made it seem a beyond political choice and a pillar of national cohesion.

From the 1950s, leisure became an important domain, even in politics. Norwegians wanted to spend their time off work outside—literally speaking. Small, primitive houses (*hytte*) were constructed near the coast and in the mountains. Mountain resorts, not luxurious hotels, unified Norwegians. How leisure time was spent was not entirely free from ideology. Prime Minister Einar Gerhardsen had written a book in the 1930s called *The Representative*, where leisure and hobbies such as music, sports and outdoor life were seen as activities that would develop the individual into a valuable member of society. It became a public responsibility to make sure that everyone had an opportunity to participate. In the political program of *Fellesprogrammet*, leisure was described as follows:

> Libraries, academies, sports organizations and other youth organizations should join together and discuss leisure and how they can contribute to give young people a meaningful education and a healthy recreation. Sports federations should be rebuilt and developed in order to become strong institutions for physical education as well as for the education of comradeship and competition.[7]

In addition, arts institutions were strengthened to make culture available to all. Previously, culture had been connected to enlightenment institutions, to popular movements and to labour movements, and was now being promoted by public measures. Leisure was first connected to physical health but was rapidly also connected to spiritual and cultural activities. Culture soon became a description of both arts and sports, and cultural policies worked towards distribution and democratization. Nevertheless, it was initially difficult to see the difference between bourgeois culture and culture for everyone to enjoy. Ironically, *A Doll's House* by Henrik Ibsen (1879), which was a bourgeois revolt against social conventions, became the first project to be promoted all over the country by the newly established Riksteater (1948)—a theatre that moved around the country with performances in order to 'promote the idea of theatre to every town and village'.

Norway has hosted the Olympic Winter Games twice with great success, in 1952 and 1994. Local arenas for sports were built all over the country, and the winners became national heroes. This could have collided with the basic logic of social control and fear of diversity, which is encompassed in the *Jantelov*—the law of Jante—expressed in the writings of the Norwegian-Danish author Axel Sandemose in the 1930s. Its first law states that you should not think highly of yourself or believe that you are better than others. The still prevalent myth is that everyone in Norway is 'born with skis', despite many Norwegians having never tried it. Skiing and outdoor life is accessible to everyone, and snow covers the country through the winter. Norwegian skiers and ice skaters are still seen as hardworking and worthy winners, and even if they earn a lot of money, few complain about inequality and undeserved payment.

Civil communities had strong links to earlier groups including the temperance movement, language movements, and a myriad of humanitarian and religious organizations. These gradually lost their status during the first half of the twentieth century, and the three decades between 1950–80 removed them even further from local societies and their historic 'habitations'. The labour movement as a voluntary community was also weakened, but many of their central issues had been directed to the welfare state, with their solidarity channelled into this system. An important mental shift occurred in the same period. Because of the dominant instrumental view of the welfare state, different civil communities were viewed as 'supporters of claims on benefits or welfare services from special interest groups that were to be fulfilled by the welfare state'. These organizations and their growing dependence on public goodwill, both in terms of economic support and recognition, strengthened the role of the welfare state as the coordinator of different collective interests. These two developments mutually enhanced each other at the expense of an independent civil sphere. Generally speaking, many civil organizations 'compete' to obtain grants from the state budget, which ensures their financing but also makes them more dependent.

This expansion of the state's tasks and areas of activity is one trend of the post-war period. A more specific trend is the arrangement between the state and special interest groups, not least the strict regulation of the relationship between the state, the labour unions and the employers' unions. We seem to have a form of corporatism here, albeit a democratic corporatism, with strong roots in traditional Norwegian culture and society.

Post-war Norwegian identity

The feeling of a national 'we', a common identity, had never been as strong as in the first decade after the war. Labour, in government throughout the post-war 1940s and 50s, merged their idea of the nation with the solidarity of labourers, becoming a *folk*-party. Since most of the population were workers, this appeal was strong. The overwhelming experience of a common fate during the war became a shared notion of performance and solutions, so strong that it may be understood as a new ideology or a new collectivism.

Dugnad (voluntary community work) is a Norwegian civil tradition as old as Christianity. The concept of voluntary work is not unique and similar ideas can be found in many countries. Yet the idea itself and how Norwegians perceive it are unique in some ways, because people were historically isolated, dispersed and had to cope without external help. For centuries, the king was in Denmark and central authorities were few and far away. One had to find the means to carry out larger tasks. *Dugnad* is closely linked to a shared common project where all could participate with whatever means they had. It was reciprocal in some ways: one year you help, the next year you get help, and all was voluntary. The word *dugnad* comes from virtue, implying a moral duty to contribute to your community. It is still prominent in Norwegian society, but wealth also threatens the will to participate, as it might be tempting to pay one's way out instead of participating in manual labour. This trait of Norwegian identity is important in order to illustrate a strong, often moral, sense of equality.

A state secretary from the Conservatives has said the 'social democratic idea of equality was like an image of everyone standing on the same line'.[8] Such a comment contains an underlying acceptance of equality and homogeneity and a strong unification: everyone does equally well or badly, no one is ahead of anyone else, and the offer one receives is the same. Standardized universal solutions were meant to guarantee safety, but they also erased differences in quality. The basic social democratic assumption was that universal solutions would provide the best services and ensure quality for all, because given a choice, the well-off might choose differently and thereby undermine the universal services.

Both collectivism and corporatism are concepts associated with authoritarian, fascist political systems and lines of thought. We thus have to repeat that anti-democratic ideas were widely discredited in Norway after the Second World War. Norwegian mainstream collectivist and corporatist currents after 1945 were distinctly democratic. Classic liberal ideas, on the other hand, did not exactly have their heyday in post-war Norway.

Per Kleppe, former Minister of Finance from the 1970s Labour Party, claimed the following:

> When the historian Francis Sejersted talks about the happiest moment of the social democracy in the 1950s, it is a misunderstanding. It was not the happiest moment, it came later. Happy moments must be connected to the fact that the people you fight for and that you represent, the working class in a wide sense, get better education, better housing and better income. This moment came later.[9]

In a certain sense, this is also the paradox of social democracy. When the social democratic struggles had successfully increased wealth and education for all, the voters no longer wanted social democratic policies. The mental revolution of the 1970s was a transition from equality and unity to freedom and diversity. The freedom revolution implied a fundamental revolt against the ideals of equality and unity, with many arguing that they had led to an unpleasant conformity. 'Freedom of choice' became the new buzzword. People were supposed to take greater control of their lives.

PART THREE

STILL AN EXCEPTION?
THE 1970s TO THE PRESENT

10

THE NEW CONSENSUS OF THE 70s AND 80s

From 1945–63, Norway had different social democratic govern-ments. The Labour Party led with a parliamentary majority, but in the late summer of 1963, a small but important change took place. A government formed by the Conservatives, Venstre, the Christian Democrats, and the Centre Party (formerly the Farmer Party) marked the end of the Labour Party dominance. They came to power because of the King's Bay case at Svalbard. King's Bay was a coal mine owned by the state, and on 5 November 1962, an explosion killed twenty-one miners. It soon became a ques-tion about responsibility and lack of security measures, and a vote of no confidence was passed concerning the handling of the accident. After eighteen years with a social democrat majority in parliament, it suddenly became clear that other governments were possible. Voters increasingly perceived an arrogance in the Labour Party, being so used to winning that they had taken power for granted. Even though the Labour Party regained gov-ernment very quickly, after just twenty-eight days, its position and status were weakened.

The twenty years following the short-lived 1963 coalition pro-duced mostly minority Labour governments, interrupted by two further centre-right coalitions: first from 1965–71, and again briefly in 1972–73. The prime minister in 1965–71, Per Borten, came from the Centre Party. In 1972, the 'no' vote in the Europe referendum (discussed below) forced the Labour government to resign, replaced with a transitional government led by a Christian Democrat prime minister. Elections the following year returned Labour to power, but by the end of the 1970s, it was clear how far Norway had shifted from the social-democrat consensus of the post-war period.

1970s discontent and the end of consensus

1970 can be seen as a pivotal year, not because something extraordinary happened, but because it came between two identity-forming events: the 1968 protests and the Norwegian EEC vote in 1972. The 1970s also marked the transition to a society where liberal values, like freedom and diversity, were much more prevalent than in the post-war decades. Labour's economic policies did not work the way they had after the war. With the 1973 oil crisis, Norwegian shipping saw their ships in the docks waiting for employment, and heavily subsidized industries got into trouble.

The 'Labour Party State' had been founded on a compromise between socialist and liberal-conservative ideas, tied to a socialist industrialism. The condition was industrial growth, the right to welfare benefits and a growing private purchasing power. All three were strained in the beginning of the 1970s, and solutions did not come from the social democrats. 'The fulfilment of melancholy' is the name of a chapter in *Norwegian History of Ideas* by the sociologist Andreas Hompland. He describes the sadness many social democrats felt at the beginning of the 1970s.

A caricature of Norwegians in the 1970s was the image of a homogenous population, a stable and transparent community, and a welfare state that was believed to promote 'the good life'. 1970 is in many ways a symbol of the triumph of social democracy, as described in this quote:

> Towering over the national community was one TV-channel with a handful of program hosts—Erik Bye, Rolf Kirkevaag and a few others. They were symbols that united the nation and they formed a common identity both for politics and culture. Above them stood Prime Minister Einar Gerhardsen and the King, both of them eating bread with the traditional brown cheese like everyone else for lunch.[1]

However, this covered an underlying discontent, a revolt against authorities and against extensive political governance. The backlash first came in the form of the Norwegian variant of the 1968 student revolt, which originally started that spring in Paris university campuses when students protested against the education system. In the aftermath of 1968 in Norway, different youth protests manifested themselves from 1970–73 as a radical left-wing populist protest, and a left-leaning nationalist resistance against the social democratic post-war state. The 1968 revolt in this context was, according to Norwegian sociology, more identity-based and cultural than explicitly political:

> Maybe the most prominent heritage of '1968' is the cultural heritage—a value—and attitude change manifesting itself in increased tolerance and acceptance of diversity and differentness when it came to clothes, hairstyles, sexuality and living arrangements.[2]

Green protests started in the 1970s at the same time that Norway discovered oil and gas. Climate issues collided with industrial modernization and energy demands. The summer of 1970 witnessed the first spectacular protest against a power plant being built for hydroelectric power, which would result in constructing a dam and destroying nature in the area. The protesters tied themselves to construction machinery at the Mardøla river and refused to leave. Industrialization and economic growth battled against the protection of nature. Later in the decade, problems of acid rain made Norwegians aware of the fact that climate and environmental issues were international, not only local. Initiatives like 'Limits to Growth' and 'Future in Our Hands' found resonance because, as we have seen, Norwegians have an almost religious approach to nature and outdoor life: they are part of what it means to be Norwegian. Norway was therefore one of the first countries in the world to get its own Ministry of Environment in 1972. Labour's Gro Harlem Brundtland, who would later become the country's first female prime minister, became Minister for the Environment in 1974 and would later be Chairman of the 1978 UN Commission for Environment and Development, the Brundtland Commission.

The rebirth of all prior Norwegian political debates

The rise of these progressive movements coincided with the 1972 debate and referendum on membership of the European Economic Community (EEC). The plebiscite raised political debate in Norway to a new level, not only about the pros and cons for entering the EEC, but about the core of Norwegian political values. The 1972 debate can be called the rebirth of all prior Norwegian political debates.

In 1970, the Norwegian parliament had voted 132 against seventeen to renew the application to join the EEC (blocked by France's Charles de Gaulle in 1967). Negotiations went on until January 1972, and the process brought down two Norwegian governments. The Prime Minister Per Borten, from the Centre Party, was responsible for the negotiations. His party was among the key protesters of EEC membership. In January 1971, he showed classified information from the Norwegian ambassador to Brussels about the negotiations to the leader of the People's Movement for No to EEC on a flight to Copenhagen.

This led to his resignation, and the Labour Party took over with the pro-EEC Prime Minister Trygve Bratteli, who finished the negotiations but later resigned when Norway did not vote to join the EEC.

The campaign to join the EEC failed for the same reasons that the 2016 Brexit campaign in the UK succeeded: Europe was perceived as protecting and furthering an urban, cosmopolitan elite and corporate interests. The Norwegians who advocated for the country's membership wanted to avoid tariffs, to secure admittance to the market, and to have a vote and be part of the decision-making processes.

Thus, as with Brexit, the pro-Europe camp was dominated by big business and the establishment parties, trade-friendly industrialists and employers unions, as well as bureaucrats and the major national newspapers. However, they were poorly organized. Genuine ideological pro-Europeans—who argued for the idea of Europe and saw the union as a peace initiative—were harder to find, even though the pro-Europeans also argued that the EEC was a project for peace in Europe.

Those against joining the EEC rallied around such slogans as 'against the power of money' or the 'rich man's club'. The 'no' side quickly connected to their favourite idea, *grasrota*—the grass root or the people's voice—in opposition to the elites, who were accused of wanting to centralize, to give power to EEC to decide Norwegian politics, and to give up Norwegian sovereignty. District politics, agriculture and fisheries sectors were all natural allies in the fight against membership (the old Farmer Party and the Centre Party were of course united in the protest). Also affiliated with this side were national special interest drives such as the language movement, which was stronger in the rural areas; the lay Lutheran movement, fighting liberal theology from Oslo; and the temperance movement, working against the prevalent view on alcohol in the cities.

The protesters argued for import protection, for sovereignty and for local control. One could also find issues that had no direct connection to the membership question, but which nevertheless were merged into something to oppose. Environment protectionists (like feminists and the women's movement) also connected their views with the 'no' campaign, even though it was not clear at this time whether protections would be stronger within the national state or in the European community. Saying no to the EEC, to nuclear weapons, and to NATO often coincided. All in all, the focus on sovereignty meant that 'no' became synonymous with saying 'yes' to being Norwegian. Hence the 1972 debate was very much controlled by the 'no' camp. While Denmark and the UK voted to join, the Norwegian result was 53.5 per cent to stay out and 46.5 per cent to join. As a result, EEC membership was removed from political debate and became taboo for almost two decades. The debate had been hard, and feelings were strong.

As well as splitting Norwegian society in two, political parties found themselves fragmented by the debate. The Christian People's Party, a Lutheran party with some fundamentalist followers who saw the EEC as the Antichrist, mainly voted 'no' but had a few 'yes' voters. The official party lines for both the Labour Party and the Conservatives were pro-Europe, but the Labour Party was divided, and quite a few members were 'no' voters. Venstre was deeply divided on the EEC question, splitting into two parties in 1972; it would struggle for decades to unite. As a consequence of these disagreements within the existing parties, new ones were founded after the agonizing debates.

A weaker Labour Party and the birth of new political parties

Though government kept changing hands in the 1970s between Labour and the centre-right establishment, new parties and new ideas rose up in the post-referendum years. There was an expansion of the party-political left, parallel with the growth of progressive movements within civil society. In 1975, what is today known as the Socialist Left Party was formed by a left-wing coalition of 'no' voters, uniting Norway's two socialist parties. The Communist Party had existed since 1923 and had a representative in the parliament until 1961, but chose to remain independent of the Socialist Left Party. However, the line between the socialists and the communists became clearer when a new party, the Socialist People's Party, was founded in 1961.

Then, in 1973, another left-wing party emerged in the wake of the referendum. A strong revival in some youth milieus of communism and far-left socialism was common to many Western countries in the 1970s. Yet Norway had its own characteristics, and the dominant ideology on the far left was Maoism. The Norwegian Maoist party AKP(ml)—Workers Communist Party Marxist-Leninist—was founded in 1973, but Maoist organizations had been active since the late 1960s. Throughout the 1970s, this party was arguably the strongest of its kind in Western Europe. Norwegian Maoists adored Mao's China, Pol Pot's regime in Cambodia and, until the split with China in 1977, Enver Hoxha's Stalinist regime in Albania. The party was an almost religious sect which never had parliamentary representation in the 1970s, but had far-reaching influence for decades in culture, literature and academic circles, as well as in journalism and media.

On the other hand, the most significant development to come out of the 1972 referendum was the foundation of another new party, one that was not on the left but which shared with the new socialist parties a rejection of the status quo. The party was named after its protagonist Anders Lange and was first and foremost a populist protest party. Later renamed the Progress Party, their key issues were easily found in the continuation of the party's original name: '[a party] for substantial reductions of taxes, tariffs, and public interference'. They were 'libertarian' in the sense of wanting to reduce state and all public interference in private life, and in their opposition to paternalism. Anders Lange was a controversial figure who had been active in the National League in the 1930s. When first formed in 1973, the Progress Party was more focused on opposing taxes in general, as well as tariffs on cars, petrol, alcohol and tobacco. It tended to gain about four per cent of the vote until immigration became an issue in the late 1980s. At this point the party received twelve per cent of the vote because they opposed immigration and became the primary proponents of a strict Norwegian immigration policy, a position they have held since the 1990s.

Overall, the trend in the 1970s was a movement away from the social-democrat consensus, toward greater openness and freedom (whether in a market liberal sense, or a protection-of-the-marginalized sense). This gradual liberalization over the decade prepared the ground for more long-term liberal politics, and what has been referred to as the 'right wave'. In the 1977 election, the centre-right would win the most votes, but not enough to displace Labour from government; in 1981, the Progress Party would see its popularity grow, and the Conservatives would take power.

The Labour Party became more radical in its economic policies after the oil crisis in 1973, radical here meaning more socialist and leaning towards economic planning. The Labour Party advanced proposals of nationalized banks and insurance companies, large-scale public acquisitions of industries, and obligatory appointment of public representatives and employee-representatives to boards in private companies. It was an ideological minefield of reforms that touched upon property rights and nationalization. Radical suggestions were also put forward in security policies, criminal justice, concession regulations and in the governance of housing cooperatives. This made it easier for centre-right parties to put forward ideological arguments, creating a clearer distance and making room for political alternatives.

When recovering from occupation and war, improvement is not hard to achieve. In hindsight, however, the social democrats held on to the idea of planning beyond the necessary need for recovery, and coupled with the idea of a continuous progress that was also shared by liberals, positive results were not so evident. Extensive public interference was also riskier because it could fail. The invested prestige and forces created high expectations that were hard to meet. The increasing complexity and scope of the welfare state demanded more bureaucratic administration and control. The centre-right and the populist Progress Party both campaigned against this trend throughout the decade. They argued that policies adapted to increase efficiency were ineffective because the bureaucracy was not able to cope. It was not only state bureaucracy that received criticism; indeed (over)regulated capitalism had proven inefficient. The identity crisis of social democracy came about because full employment was not reached, nor a crisis-free economy, and regulated capitalism was failing to address the crises of the 1970s.

This criticism from the right, and the partial reversal in the ideological sphere, was of course a common phenomenon in Western countries. Statist solutions and arrangements didn't work anymore, classic liberal ideas had their revival, Hayek and Friedman became ideological gurus, while Reagan and Thatcher won convincing political victories. In the case of Norway, these ideological trends had deep historical roots in the ideas of 1814, especially in the pragmatic liberalist and modernizing ideas of the civil servants' regime later in the nineteenth century.

Modern society and individual freedom

A different Norway was formed in the 1980s–90s, based on ideas diverging from those that characterized the post-war decades.

THE NORWEGIAN EXCEPTION?

When the Conservatives won the election in 1981, the post-1972–73 radicalization came to an end. A former member of the youth organization Red Pioneers says that it was a strange situation for him to go from planning a communist revolution to celebrating his graduation from upper-secondary school with a huge, commercial, party (a Norwegian tradition known as the *russ*). He describes his personal transition from the 1970s to the 1980s in the following way:

> I was enlisted as a member of Red Pioneers from the age of seven or eight, a kind of guerrilla group that should prepare itself for revolution. We saw war-movies, visited the Chinese Embassy, and participated in protest marches against the super-power politics in the third world, and against porn. The grown-ups discussed politics, read Marx, and distributed clandestine newspapers at night. Then came the 1980s. No one talked about revolution anymore. It was like a strange and slightly embarrassing dream that had lasted some years, and that was gone. And that was well.[3]

The next decades were the years of market economy principles in politics, modernizing the economy in many ways; the process continued even when the Labour Party regained power in 1986. To simplify, society became more individualistic and pluralistic, with a greater emphasis on freedom of choice. This didn't mean that the 1970s currents of protest and culture of dissent disappeared—quite the opposite. The 1968 generation made their mark on cultural and literary life for decades after that protest year. Radical, often socialist ideas were prominent in poetry, novels and children's literature.

1968 had its legacy in several critical movements, most visibly the women's liberation movement and the green movement. These generally opposed, among other things, authorities, tight administration and homogeneity; revolutionary ideas were also clearly manifested in literature. A reduced belief in the authorities became key. Religious and political ideals, as well as ideas about health, leisure and family life, changed. It was a liberal reaction to social democratic authority but also to conservative traditions. Freedom of choice, tolerance and pluralism were especially visible in lifestyle choices and acceptance of different forms of family life.

Liberalising but no neo-liberalism

Alongside this cultural and social liberalization, the government focused on market liberalization. Broadly speaking, politicians' focus went from production and supplier interests to a greater awareness of consumer policies during the 1970s and onwards. Norwegians became more interested in securing consumer rights in many new fields of social life. At the same time, they became more demanding when it came to the scope and quality of public services. The liberal shift was clear: more rights were ensured by law when the economic responsibility of fulfilling them was possible. The ideological divide was still between those who wanted 'one size for all' and those who wanted 'pluralism and choice'.

Norwegians were pragmatic, and Norway never got the neo-liberal turn of Thatcher and Reagan. It is simplistic to assume that the right-turn in Norwegian politics was all about neo-liberalism, such as the idea that everyone should become market consumers. Those who see the 1980s liberalization as a problematic replacement of the state by the market also see the demand for choice as something negative. Those who were against the 1980s Norwegian market liberalism claimed that the proponents of freedom of choice argued for a perverted form of freedom, delineating everyone as customers in a market.

The belief in every citizen's possibilities was hegemonic throughout the 1980s. The most important argument from the Conservatives before the 1981 elections was that the pronounced scepticism towards public administration in many domains had its roots in the limitations of personal choice. The political toolbox of the Labour Party had become obsolete, only able to offer more of the same. The Conservatives and their political allies grew in confidence and offered new ideas, solutions and policies. Metaphorically speaking, the new political solutions were in accordance with the needs of society and the mentality of the people. Collective identities from the post-war social democracy were losing ground. This was the beginning of a development that has lasted until the time of writing, where many of the former markers of identity have lost power, and where it has become the responsibility of every individual to create their own identity.

Norwegian governments have up to the 2020s shifted between a socialist bloc and a liberal-conservative bloc. Each government has had to rely on smaller parties. The political discussions might seem harsh and divisive, but in hindsight it is fair to say that the 1980s were also characterized by compromise. At the core of debates was a fundamental question about balance between the state, the market and the civil spheres of power and responsibility. Generally, centre-right parties and moderate social democrats will argue for liberalization in some cases, yet at other times be willing to follow social democrats in increasing public responsibilities and budgets.

Once in government, the Conservatives continued their and the Progress Party's critique of Norwegian bureaucracy. Astrid Gjertsen, the efficient and outspoken Minister of Consumer Rights and Government Administration (a title that no longer exists), duly pointed to the fact that government officials had been operating in much the same way since the war. In an interview she gave an example to illustrate her point, a social security office that closed once or twice a week in order to catch up with a growing backlog. Other public offices had opening hours that made it increasingly difficult for the public

to access their services. Gjertsen pointed out an apparent dis-
cord between available public services and the need for the
public to be served satisfactorily.

The Conservatives wanted decentralization to reduce the
power of central bureaucracy and the civil service, and simplify
regulations both for the sake of the rule of law and to avoid
excessive state intervention. The Progress Party gave the harshest
criticism and made a smaller state explicit in the party program
from its foundation until 1997. During the 1970s–90s they promoted efficiency to reach this goal, while the 1980s promoted
privatization.

*Conservative modernization followed by social democratic
renewal and reform*

In 1984, the Conservative-led Willoch-government presented
their program to modernize the public sector. The goal was to
reform public administration and to scale down the public sector
through privatization. In addition, many visible initiatives were
taken to deregulate and liberalize more generally, including policies deregulating credit and currency, and housing policies which
completely changed that market. The liberalization of television
and radio brought the state monopoly to an end, utterly changing Norwegian media, although the state-financed broadcaster
NRK still holds a dominant position forty years later. A practical
deregulation came with the liberalization of opening hours. The
abolition of the 'closing hours act' had symbolic significance and
profoundly changed everyday life for Norwegians.

Many deregulations could be carried out because of developments in technology (breaking up the NRK-monopoly), international competition (interest rate policies, the abolition of maximum price regulations), and changes in the housing market,
which had gone from a grey market where cash circulated to a

well-functioning housing market. These deregulations were overdue and became easy political successes. They also contained an underlying ideological wish to liberalize.

In 1989, an Official Norwegian Report named *Better government in the public sector* was published. The author was Tormod Hermansen, one of the leading market-technocratic reformists. Hermansen can be connected to the state-owned oil company Statoil, to the Norwegian Banks' Guarantee Fund and to the Post Bank. The background for this green paper was an increasing criticism of the governing of public institutions, government agencies and enterprises. It proposed several measures to improve administration, systems, and to more efficiently use public resources. About twenty-five years later, Hermansen would comment that it was natural to ask questions and propose new solutions in 1989, and he concluded that the proposed guidelines were followed for many processes in the subsequent decades. Some examples include several bank mergers in 1998, the new Energy Act from 1991, and the transformation of the public telecom service to Telenor in 1995.

Ultimately it was the Labour Party that led the deregulation processes beginning in the 1980s. After losing power in 1981, they needed to renew their political program. The consensus had definitively shifted in Norwegian society and policy, and it was clear to the social democrats that they would have to respond. The Conservatives may have started the reforms, but Labour returned to power in the late 1980s, and the figure who oversaw much of the deregulation process was the party's leader Gro Harlem Brundtland, prime minister in 1981, 1986–89 and 1990–96. From 1985, she promoted a campaign called 'Action Freedom' and revitalized the social democratic ideology. A more centre-oriented Labour Party emerged, one that had taken into account the general wishes for individualism, freedom of choice and plurality. Nevertheless, the policies of this time were revitalized Labour, with a clear ongoing role for the state.

The former willingness to govern through a large public sector was transformed into a readiness to introduce market logic in many areas within it. Efficiency, clearer roles and responsibilities, competition and adaptation to consumer needs were keys to a greater market orientation. The authors of a book called *Neoliberalism: Ideas and Political Reality* conclude that, even though New Public Management was a trend in Western democracies from the 1980s onwards, Norway did not see extensive privatization of public enterprises, nor a larger private sector at the expense of a public sector.[4]

This should not imply that there have been no changes in public responsibilities in principles of government. The user-friendly turn in public services has become much greater, as has an orientation towards the citizens' demands, their choices and their individual needs. The alternative has never been a return to the models of public government that existed before the 1980s. Rather, it has been to ameliorate and develop public services in health care, childcare and education, and to institute new areas of state oversight related to individual rights. One of the most obvious of these has been gender equality.

Norwegian gender equality

Feminism is not a recent phenomenon. Norway enfranchised women in 1913, and throughout the 1960s and 70s, women entered higher education in large numbers. There was a shift in ideas about the role of women alongside the publication of Simone de Beauvoir's *Le Deuxième Sexe* and Betty Friedan's *The Feminine Mystique*, as well as the 1968 movement and a demand for gender equality. Of course, this demand is not exclusively Norwegian, but it can be said that the foundation for gender equality and for women's participation was particularly strong in Norway. In the 1950s and 60s, few women were employed and the divorce rate was low. The role of the housewife had become professionalized; she was analyzed and studied like an industrial worker, driving a healthy society and contributing to the GDP. A mother in difficult situations had rights such as housewife payment, housewife vacation and home help, all connected to her status as mother; she was entitled to a small payment and vacation, during which she got a replacement at home, and this replacement would also occur if she got ill. On the one hand, women before 1970 were mostly housewives; on the other hand, even the housewives enjoyed better rights than in most countries, and an increasing number of young women chose a different path.

The housewife was a historical exception: women entered universities, demanding employment and equality. The economic growth in the 1970s was followed by full employment and a steep rise in education levels, in what can be called an education boom. The possibility of free higher education spurred people, especially women, to undertake higher education. Supplying the means and opportunity to study meant that education was open to all. This greatly influenced women's participation in the workforce as well as the high level of gender equality and the broad social consensus valuing it from this period onwards. The first women's march to mark International Women's Day on 8 March took place in 1971.

These demands quickly found their way into politics. Equality was to be obtained through politics and by law; it was called state feminism, and the Labour Party were strong proponents of actively using politics to achieve gender equality. This was quite a shift for the party, who proclaimed before the war that married women could not work, and who during the 1950s strongly recommended the ideal of the '1-2-3-4-family': one breadwinning man, two children, a three-room flat, and a four-wheel car. The Conservatives mainly adhered to the housewife ideal after the war, but progressive women in all parties gradually came forth with more liberal views of gender equality.

In 1972, Norway established the Gender Equality Council, among the first of its kind globally. In 1978, Norway passed the Gender Equality Act. The Equal Opportunities Commissioner was appointed in 1979 to check that no gender discrimination occurred. Paramount was the fight for free abortion, resulting in the law of elective abortion in 1978. In Norway, when people oppose this law for whatever religious or ethical reason, they immediately meet strong protests. Only in 2018 did the question of selective twin abortion result in a huge and uncompromising debate.

In 1986, Gro Harlem Brundtland became the first female prime minister in Norway, and she presented a government where eight out of eighteen ministers were women. When it comes to gender equality in Norway, there are women leading politics, and the top positions on both sides in several of the largest labour and employer unions were occupied by women until recently. However, although Norwegians passed a quota law of forty per cent women on company boards, the private sector is still lagging when it comes to women in chief positions.

At the time of writing, women participate in the workforce. They do more part-time work and have a higher sick leave frequency, but their participation is paramount to the labour force. The statistics of women's wages indicate that pay is lower in the public than in the private sector. On the other hand, the public sector—with its shorter working hours, and possibilities for part-time work—makes it easier to combine family and working life for many women.

Parental leave was not introduced until the end of the 1970s. Mothers' leave was changed to a parental leave of eighteen weeks, shorter than in Sweden which at the time allowed seven months' parental leave. Norway gradually increased the duration and in

1992 it was thirty-five weeks. The implication is that family politics came in response to women entering the workforce. In 1993, a critical reform was implemented when a special quota was introduced for fathers; this has since been increased, and today the total leave with full payment is forty-nine weeks. Each parent has an equal quota of weeks, and one third of the weeks can be allocated freely. Mostly the mothers add these free weeks to their quota, indicating that fathers use their designated time and the mothers use the rest.

A generous parental leave makes it possible for a mother to stay at home for almost a year, sharing some weeks with the father, then a full-coverage kindergarten takes over until the child starts school at the age of 6 years old. The parental leave pay is generous and, in addition, a non-taxable monthly payment is given to all parents regardless of income or economic position until the child is 18 years old. Moreover, parents that don't use the kindergarten when the child is 12 months old may choose to receive a cash payment until the child is 2 years old while staying at home. This is not in line with the principle of *arbeidslinjen*—that it should always be more beneficial economically to work than not.

The gender equality policies have strongly influenced how family life should be lived, and choices that do not conform—like receiving cash payment until the child is 2 years old instead of sending them to kindergarten, starting work before the end of parental leave, or buying help for housework and childcare—are 'socially sanctioned'. The economic side of the picture is that women earn less than men and taxes are high, which makes the trade-off between work and taking care of children smaller. Instead of buying expensive childcare help, it is better to work part time, which again influences careers. There are also some unintended consequences of the gender equality policies. There are few female entrepreneurs and relatively few female managers in the private sector; women dominate public sector services like childcare, health care, elderly care and primary education. In some sectors, women make up almost ninety per cent of the workforce.

For some time the Norwegian fertility rate has been among the highest in Europe, although behind France, but has recently decreased and as of 2019 is 1.56. This shows that generous family policies do not necessarily lead to larger families. Norwegians behave almost exactly as the system intends: they don't have children before they are employed, because the payment for parental leave is much larger than the upfront payment you receive if you are unemployed. They let their children start in kindergarten at the age of 12 months; mothers and fathers share the prescribed quotas for parental leave with few exceptions; and almost everyone in work chooses to send their child to kindergarten rather than accept the cash payment for staying at home with them.

In many ways, the policies concerning women introduced in the 1980s and early 1990s exemplified the compromise that Labour, and Norwegian government in general, came to make, with the state as a firmly supportive steering hand that neither withdrew from the market nor gripped it with an iron fist. The large reform and modernization processes would continue into the new millennium, independently of different governments. Both the Labour Party and the Conservatives were to a certain extent inspired by international trends and New Public Management, and it is beyond doubt that these changes would not have happened if the two parties did not essentially agree on how changes should be implemented. The Norwegian political pragmatism would work well throughout the 1990s. Gro Harlem Brundtland argued for a pragmatic administration of affairs, not an ideological one.

The right-left axis in economic policies has been relatively stable throughout the twentieth century. According to the political scientists that analyzed Norwegian 'neo-liberalism' and market capitalism, however, it is the left-wing parties in particular that 'seem to have changed their political profile towards a greater acceptance of parts of the neo-liberal program'.[5] They add that the Norwegian political centre over time has been more pronounced compared to other Western-European countries. This includes the Norwegian manifestation of what can be said to be a light version of New Public Management. In many ways, therefore, the 1980s marked a time of change and progression. However, while this trend continued through the next decade and beyond, the 1990s would also see Norway's attention return to an old question: its relationship with Europe.

11

NORWAY AND THE WORLD

EUROPE AND OIL AT THE TURN OF THE MILLENNIUM

The 1990s marked a great paradox in Norway: Norwegians managed to reject European membership for a second time in a 1994 referendum; but also signed a single market agreement with the EU, making Norway the most adaptive European country of all, but without any say. As we shall see, one of the main arguments for not joining has been sovereignty, particularly in relation to the oil wealth that fully started coming in from the mid-1990s. One may ask if this is exactly what we have been ceding. Overall, the picture we will see emerging in this chapter is of Norway ending the twentieth century and entering the twenty-first with some definitive decisions about its place in the world, concerning both the country's relationship with Europe and how to handle its new-found prosperity.

Both in 1972 and 1994, political and economic elites were defeated by a populist coalition centred around long folk-movement traditions from the nineteenth century. In both cases the left, especially the far left, voted against Norwegian membership of the EEC/EU. This phenomenon had deep roots in Norwegian history and political culture. Norwegian nationalism was leftist in the years up to and including 1905. Friends and supporters of the union with Sweden could be found on the right side of the political spectrum. After independence, nationalism and democracy were seen as two sides of the same coin, both by Norwegian nationalists themselves and by their fiercest opponents in Sweden. In the interwar years Norwegian nationalism was more diversified in a political sense, containing right-wing, authoritarian and pro-fascist voices and movements. After the Second World War, however, the idea that Norwegian independence and democracy were inseparable was strongly reinforced. In the 1972 and 1994 debates, these important currents in Norwegian political culture reappeared. Norwegian nationalism has largely been more democratic and leftist than in other countries, while the Norwegian left has mainly been more nationalist than other countries' political left.

To reiterate: from the late Middle Ages to 1905, Norway was under foreign control and did not have to be the leader in any international relationship. After 1905, when Norway gained independence from the union with Sweden, Norwegian foreign policy was grounded in a desire to stay neutral. At the same time, this neutrality was not that strict, especially during the First World War. Norway further developed a special relationship with Great Britain, and may well be called a neutral ally. During the Second World War, Nazi Germany ended all pretensions of Norwegian neutrality.

When the Cold War emerged after 1945, there was fierce political debate about Norwegian foreign policy. The debate was especially fierce and especially decisive within the Labour Party, in connection with the establishment of the NATO defence alliance in 1949. The left wing of the party wanted to stay neutral, like our neighbour Sweden. Some of the leading Labour Party politicians had developed good relations with the US during the war and argued that a Western defence alliance was essential for

Norwegian security. One deciding factor, perhaps, was the Communist coup d'état in Czechoslovakia in early 1948. A majority inside the Labour Party voted to abandon traditional neutrality and embrace NATO membership. Thus, Norwegian foreign policy became less ambivalent, at least in this particular area. Norway was no longer a neutral ally but an ally of the West.

The European debates

Norway has been a loyal NATO member since 1949. The former Labour Party Prime Minister, Jens Stoltenberg, has been the head of the organization since 2014. At the same time, various governments have tried to maintain a cordial relationship with our north-eastern neighbour the Soviet Union, later Russia. This was the case during the Cold War and is still the case at the time of writing. There have been and still are some tensions. In the twenty-first century, these mainly exist in connection with the Spitsbergen/Svalbard islands, presently concerning fishing rights and oil in the Barents Sea.

Overall, though, Norway is clearly firmly committed to the trans-Atlantic alliance. But why do many Norwegians still believe that the country is better off outside the EU? A Norwegian social scientist remarked that, 'Norwegian self-understanding is best pronounced in "permanent special treatments"' and added, 'Enthusiasm for Europe is as faded as the memory of 1914 or 1905, whereas 1940–45 is still strong.'[1] The answer is that Norwegians oppose the EU, but they like Europe. There are deep trends in Norwegian history that can be connected to the European debates, first and foremost to the democratic, left-leaning nationalism and to the circumstances in 1814, 1905 and 1945.

This is the story of the most divisive political debates during the last fifty years and how Norway ended up with an extensive Europeanization.

THE NORWEGIAN EXCEPTION?

Norway's relation to the EU—the new name for the EEC after 1993—describes in many ways Norwegians' modern relation to nation, folk, sovereignty and state. *Annerledeslandet* has been the nickname for Norway, literally meaning 'the different country'. It is not as if Norway is not a European country with long historical and cultural connections with Europe. Many parts of Norway, especially along the long coastline, have historically been very international and outward facing. Trade and international contact by sea have traditionally built Norwegian identity; Norway became an important seafaring nation and, later, an oil and gas nation. Fisheries have always been important. Norway is dependent on the sea, and on extensive international contact, trade and communication. Yet Norwegian international relationships, particularly with Europe, have not been easy. Norway has never been proactive in her relationship with Europe. One important reason may be that Norwegians have been the underdog in two unions, first with Denmark and then with Sweden. Supranational organization is often met with scepticism. Denmark and Sweden both chose to join the European Union, while Norwegians have voted 'no' in two referenda.

The strong resistance to joining, both in 1972 and in 1994 with the newly rebranded EU, is due to fear of unions or loss of what Norwegians call *sjølvråderetten* (self-rule/self-government)—a term that indicates the Norwegian independent will. In 1994, the debate over EU membership was framed much as it had been in 1972. The slogan went as follows: 'Yes to *folkestyre*—the people's government—no to union'. The opponents were afraid of giving up sovereignty and to lose what they called the possibility for democracy. They mobilized across the country, particularly in all affairs seen as typically Norwegian, like geographic distances and district politics, conveyed through the farmer and all that he symbolized, the long coastline, the sea and the fisheries. European integration was perceived to ruin all this, in its essence ruining Norway. The EEC became the proxy for dimensions like local-national, national-global and independence-cooperation. The question was what constituted the Norwegian identity.

Norway had built Western alliances since the early twentieth century, with the UK and later also the US. After the war Norway received help from the Marshall Plan, like many Western European countries, but in many ways Norwegians were not so occupied with European affairs, except for the UK. It must also be remembered that Queen Maud of Norway was a British princess and that the relationship between Norway and UK was close during the war.

In 1957, the Treaty of Rome that founded the EEC was signed by six countries. A few years later the UK wanted to join, and so did the Norwegian government. In the 1960s, Norwegian protesters claimed that the Treaty of Rome would create space for international capitalists and make it difficult for Norway to follow her line of politics. Arguments about freedom, self-sufficiency and of guarding the Norwegian Constitution were also frequent. Even though the EEC of the 1960s did not resemble the twenty-first century's integrated EU, the feeling of the protesters was that a membership would open Norway to foreign capitalists and remove the possibility of an independent economic and social policy. The first application was sent in 1962, but de Gaulle refused to accept the UK in 1963; hence also the Norwegian application, because in the 1960s Norway had a policy of following the UK and the other Scandinavian countries when it came to questions of economic integration, tariffs and trade.

Norway became a member of EFTA—the European Free Trade Association—in 1960, neither fully inside or outside the EEC. The EFTA membership initially paused protesters and bred hope of joining the EEC in those who wanted membership, but the pause did not last long. Norway applied for membership again in 1967, but once again de Gaulle interrupted the application process. The negotiations over Norway's new application in 1971–72 brought down two Norwegian governments in quick succession, the second when the pro-EEC Labour prime minister failed to convince the country in the 1972 referendum.

The people's movement 'No to EEC' gathered 130,000 members, which is a lot in a population of around four million at the time. The 'no' camp was well organized and had deep-rooted potential for mobilization. They were a motley crew; the divide was not along usual political lines. Among the protesters, one could find left-wing radical academics, leftist civil servants and many, but not all, of the labour unions, as well as local farmers, fishermen, and those in the low-church movements—all of them afraid of losing sovereignty, and the power and capitalism for which the EEC stood. The emerging grassroots/elites divide was in some ways along the traditional right-left-axis, but more along lines recognizable from the nineteenth century. Opposition in south-western parts of Norway was expected because the nationalist and religious countercultures of the nineteenth century still enjoyed support in these areas. One might ask how it was possible to unite an internationally oriented socialism and a 'no' project that had a closed, local perspective building on romantic, national ideas. Suddenly, the intellectual socialists and the Centre Party farmers were bedfellows. Women tended to vote 'no', and the same was true for people working in the public sector.

Geographically, the 'no' side was found in the northern and south-western parts of Norway, whereas the 'yes' side was concentrated in urban areas, especially around the capital Oslo. In 1972, the votes for 'no' were sixty-seven per cent in the northernmost region and twenty-nine per cent in Oslo; in 1994, it was sixty-seven per cent and twenty-five per cent respectively. To sum up, the opponents of EU membership were concerned about the partition of the country into well-developed centres and less well-

endowed peripheries with their fishing interests and more traditional cultural attitudes. Thanks to these peripheral interests,
voters were not found across the political spectrum but were
mainly on the left and centre-left. The people voting 'yes' were
business-friendly, mostly conservative or social democratic. This
picture was more or less the same in 1972 and 1994.

One thing that did change between the two referenda was the
perception of Europe among environmentalists. As we've seen, in
1972 the nascent green movement sided with the 'no' campaign,
but in 1994, the divide over questions about climate and environment were deeper, naturally because these issues had been less
pronounced in 1972. The environmental movements had voted
'no' in 1972, but in 1994 several ardent opposers had changed to
'yes', arguing that the environment was better off with Norway
remaining within the European Union. Nevertheless, this was
not enough to turn the polls in favour of 'yes'.

Conservatives overwhelmingly voted 'yes' both in 1972 and
1994. Norwegian conservatives have mainly been less nationalist
and more influenced by liberal, cosmopolitan ideas than many
conservatives in other countries. This is an important political-
cultural current going back to the late eighteenth century, most
clearly expressed in the nineteenth-century civil servants' regime.
The liberal strands in Norwegian conservatism were surely under
pressure in the inter-war years. But since 1945 these currents,
like other aspects of the 1814 ideas, have also been reinforced.

Both 'yes' voters and 'no' voters had concerns about agriculture, because of climatic and geographical circumstances that
make it difficult to compete internationally. Fisheries were also a
concern; this later changed because of fish farming, which is
industrial and able to compete. Finally, Norwegians have always
been concerned about how drawing closer to Europe might affect
Norway's control of its energy sources, hydroelectric power, and
more recently also oil and gas. As we will see, this latest windfall

for Norway would be an important factor in Norway's second 'no' vote in 1994.

The North Sea treasure

The debate about the European Union (EEC) in 1972 was probably the single year after the Second World War when debates were harshest, and the fronts were the most uncompromising. It had been a question of life and death for Norway as a nation. When the Europe question arose again twenty-two years later, all the same sentiments, arguments and divisions came back to the forefront of politics. Yet this time they seemed to be even more pressing because, by the EU referendum of 1994, Norway had become rich.

Norway found oil in the North Sea on 23 December 1969. Quite quickly, it became clear that the country's petroleum and gas reserves were huge. The US company Phillips Petroleum was engaged, and drilled the well that started it all. It was later said that the Ekofisk oil field changed Phillips and Norway. The sectors in the Ekofisk and later Frigg, a bit further north in the North Sea, were mainly given to foreign companies, since Norway did not have the expertise in geology nor in oil services more generally. This was to change substantially in the decade after the first discovery.

Soon, a political goal of national control was established and accepted by all political parties. It took the form of protectionism and privileges for Norwegian companies. It was important to gain national control by building up a competent and capable oil and gas sector. Back to our title, the North Sea oil represents a Norwegian exception: immense luck this time combined with successful politics and an understanding of what was needed.

Statoil was founded as a state-owned company and covered all oil- and gas-related activities. The main goal was to ensure national control of the production of oil, and when it came to disagreements about Statoil, these were more about how to create it than the fact that it should be done. The same was true when it came to control of the revenue from oil: it soon became clear that a sovereign wealth fund should be established, to decouple production and its revenues from spending, thus preserving the wealth that would be generated by the industry for Norway's future generations. This was politically agreed in 1990, when the Government Petroleum Fund, or 'the oil fund' for short, was created with Norway's central Norges Bank. In other words, there was a strong sense from the start of the oil period that the Norwegian nation-state needed to look after its windfall carefully, preserving Norway's interests.

All over again

According to many, oil and gas were not to be shared with Europe. In 1993, when the European Union was founded, Norway prepared for another membership referendum. This time around, both proponents and opponents of Norwegian EU membership used nationalist arguments to a greater extent than in 1972. They agreed that Norway was the best country in the world and had to continue to be so. The disagreement between them was how this could be maintained, being the 'outside country' or the 'different country' within the union.

After the Berlin Wall fell in 1989 the former Eastern European countries wanted to join, and EEC had become larger, counting twelve countries as members. Once again, Norway entered the European debate, but this time the EEA (European Economic Area) agreement was prepared and signed in May 1992 between the EEC—about to become the EU—and the EFTA countries. The EEA was the solution established to bring EFTA signatories into the new EU single market. It came into force from January

1994, but soon the only remaining EFTA countries were Norway, Iceland and Liechtenstein.

Nevertheless, a majority vote in the Storting consisting of the Conservatives, the Progress Party and the Labour Party decided to apply for Norwegian membership in 1992. Two years later, the Labour Party government decided to hold a referendum on 28 November 1994. In that year, surveys showed that if Finland and Sweden became EU members, Norway would probably do so as well. Again, the debate followed the same lines as in 1972, albeit not so harshly. Television had taken over, and the two protagonists became the Prime Minister, Gro Harlem Brundtland, and the Centre Party leader, Anne Enger Lahnstein. Those in favour of joining the EU argued that, now that Norway was a member of the European single market, it was more important to be part of the decision-making processes within the EU. The 'no' side argument was broadened by the protection of the oil and gas industry and its revenues. The Labour Party was divided once again. Brundtland said 'yes' in April 1994 and, at the same time, 2,500 protesters showed up at the Labour Party meeting.

The most important reason why the 'no' side ultimately won was their ability to appeal to the sense of being Norwegian. One may argue that the 'yes' campaign never really understood this: their arguments were too rational and intellectual. 'Union' was a term that had strong connotations for Norwegians, signifying the end of the union with Denmark in 1814 and with Sweden in 1905. In the aftermath of yet another 'no' result in the referendum, it was said that the Norwegians were a lost cause the moment the EEC became the European Union. The argument went that joining something with the tainted phrase 'union' was impossible for many Norwegians. However, this argument did not explain why most voters in countries like Ireland, Estonia, Latvia and Lithuania, which had similarly been part of the United Kingdom and the Soviet Union respectively, were apparently not affected by the word 'union'.

The result this time was 52.2 per cent 'no' and 47.8 'yes', even closer than in 1972. The voter turnout in 1994 was eighty-nine per cent, which is extremely high. After this second referendum, once again the EU question became political taboo.

The great Norwegian self-delusion—being both inside and outside

Two things happened in the wake of 1994. Norway entered into the EEA agreement and the free-travel Schengen zone, and EU debates disappeared almost completely, only emerging around the Brexit vote in 2016.

How has Norway chosen to relate to what might jokingly be named 'abroad'? The former leader of the European Movement, Paal J. Frisvold, explains how Norway time and time again has chosen to evade, to reluctantly follow, and not really 'belong to Europe'. Frisvold explains that the term 'association' has a positive connotation for Norwegians: Norway is then only partly committing herself rather than going all in. It gives Norwegians the opportunity to be in-between, neither outside nor inside.

When the idea of the EEA was launched in January 1989 by Jacques Delors, the president in the EU commission, and the Norwegian Prime Minister Gro Harlem Brundtland, who at the time was president of the EFTA Council, people expected that it would be possible to find a common mechanism for decisions in matters concerning both EFTA and the EU. These expectations had been based on a speech that Jacques Delors had held in the European Parliament on 17 January 1989 in which he said, '... we can look for a new, more structured partnership [with the EFTA countries] with common decision-making and administrative institutions to make our activities more effective and to highlight the political dimension of our cooperation in the economic, social, financial and cultural spheres.'[2]

The irony, depending on what you voted for in 1994, is that Norway in many aspects did become part of the European

Union, under the EEA that brought it into the single market. It is a very strange agreement, making the EU issue apolitical and pragmatic. At the beginning of the process to set up the single market, EFTA had been a seven-country bloc, but as other members like Sweden and Finland joined the EU itself in 1995, Norway was left as one of a couple of countries remaining under the EEA. It became a special deal.

The most extensive description and analysis of the Norwegian relationship with the EU was carried out in 2012, when a publicly appointed committee produced an Official Norwegian Report of more than 1,000 pages, fittingly named *Outside and Inside*. As anticipated, no one batted an eyelid. After more than twenty years with the EEA agreement, the green paper described the relationship as follows:

> Norway is both outside and inside the EU—at the same time. On the one hand, Norway is not a member of the EU. Norway does not participate in the decision-making processes within the EU and does not take part in the important parts of the cooperation, such as the Euro and the European foreign policies. Norway has formally a more independent position than the EU-countries and has to some extent had the possibility to choose what to join and what to reject. On the other hand, Norway is tightly connected to the EU. Norway has agreed to approximately 75 per cent of the EU-acts compared to the member states that have 100 per cent but they have been implemented more efficiently than many member states have done. From an EU-perspective, Norway is the closest connected country to the union without being a member. As the European foreign service states on their homepage: 'Norway is as integrated in European policy and economy as any non-member State can be.'[3]

Norway is more than ever a part of the global development. The 'yes' voters may applaud the fact that even though Norway is outside, there are large differences between theory and reality. The idea of self-governance and the national community is challenged by the fact that Norway is more closely connected to Europe than she has ever been in history.

Liberals generally find themselves favouring the 'yes' position, because they tend to be internationally oriented. The interesting question regarding Norway will be if the socialist left will still say 'no' and, on the other hand, if some conservatives might end up as 'no' voters. A fear of losing a sovereign national state and power is a common conservative view. Even on the traditionally union-friendly Norwegian right, there have been some dissenting voices, especially among self-declared national conservatives inside the Progress Party.

The democratic paradox of our relation to the EU stems from the fact that agreements that should secure Norwegian interests and values are, in their structure and consequences, deeply problematic for Norwegian democracy, since we have no vote. On the other hand, these agreements have parliamentary foundations and public support. The democratic deficit in the EU has decreased, but at the same time the democratic deficit in Norway's agreements with the EU has increased.

Since the EEA began in 1994, Norway has imported more than three quarters of the EU laws, making it the most adaptive country by far. In addition to incorporating more than 10,000 decrees, the most visible side of the single market is the free movement of labour. More than six per cent of the population in Norway are EU/EEA citizens, and Norway has been one of the most popular destinations within the single market, especially from the countries that joined the EU in 2004, like Poland and Lithuania. Ever since 2004, right up to the outbreak of the COVID-19 pandemic in 2020, Norway has been the country with the most migrants from Eastern-Europe compared to inhabitants.

In addition, almost eighty per cent of Norwegian exports go to the EU. Two thirds of Norwegian investments abroad go to the EU, with more than seventy-five per cent of this related to oil and gas.

THE NORWEGIAN EXCEPTION?

The paradox is that Norway until recently has had almost no discussion about the most important international relations, and no political debate after 1994. Almost no European perspectives are discussed in textbooks at school, which may prove problematic if the debate re-emerges. Another paradox is that the support for the single market has never been stronger, with sixty per cent wanting to stay with the single market versus 21.5 per cent for 'no'. The support for the EU turns these numbers upside down, with sixty-five per cent saying no to EU membership and twenty-five per cent wanting to join.[4] After the Brexit chaos in the UK, however, there are voices opting to revalue the EEA agreement, and some are even arguing that Norway might obtain a better trade agreement.

Norway has adapted, and the consequence is that Norway is not a high priority in Brussels. As they say, the only problem with Norway is that there is no problem with Norway.

Norway is a small country in the world

In 1972, the Christian People's Party Prime Minister Lars Korvald concluded in a speech that Norway was a small country in the world. That is still true. Norway is completely dependent on the rest of the world, but she is geopolitically important because of her long coastline and access to the Arctic. Moreover, as a producer of oil and gas, Norway is both an important energy exporter and a large financial investor through her sovereign wealth fund.

Yet Norway is also vulnerable, because most of the export consists of raw materials in various forms, hence subject to often volatile international pricing. It is paradoxical that a small country like Norway, which depends on trade and international relations, sees itself as a leading country internationally, especially when it comes to peace negotiations and foreign aid, both with a deep moral undertone.

Norway had the first Secretary General in the UN, Trygve Lie, and has had a seat at the Security Council four times, which is in the upper half of European countries. In June 2020, Norway was elected for a Security Council seat for the fifth time. A small country in Northern Europe, never the dominant power in any constellation, was chosen by the Swede Alfred Nobel as the country to host the Nobel Peace Prize committee. Although it is not clear why Nobel did this, it has given Norway an image as a peaceful nation and one that seeks compromises. Norwegians have internalized a sense of moral superiority in international affairs, especially after the Oslo Accord, the peace process between Israel and Palestine, was signed in 1992.

As we mentioned in the Introduction, Norway is symbolized by nature rather than culture and has historically had an inferiority complex. However, over the last fifty years Norway has gradually become very rich; this may improve its self-image as it is no longer the Scandinavian little brother. On the other hand, this has introduced a new sentiment into national culture about Norway's place in the world: guilt. Norway has been a colony but has never had colonies, at least not since the Middle Ages. Thus it has not had to face up to the same problematic history and legacies as most wealthy Western European nations. Yet today the new-found oil wealth, and its contribution to the climate crisis, gives Norwegians a bad conscience. As we will see in the concluding chapter, Norway's continued export of oil to other countries is now colliding with its global green image, as international momentum builds in the fight against climate change. This is not a simple matter for Norway: as we are about to see, the country's oil industry and subsequent wealth are deeply intertwined with its economy as a whole.

The North Sea oil and the art of sharing and securing wealth

How has a small country like Norway handled the exploration of its vast reserves of oil and gas? It was of course lucky to discover these resources, but can Norwegians' successful management of their wealth be attributed to luck? We will argue that the strong institutions and the strong foundations of liberal democracy that were in place before the discovery in 1969 are of crucial importance to understand how Norwegians have been able to extract and employ riches from the oil.

When a country discovers an important natural resource, it may be a curse and a catalyst for corruption and exploitation, not beneficial to society. However, Norway has ensured that its oil story has been a success story thanks to two things: the state's role from the start in controlling the exploitation and sale of oil and gas; and two key decisions in 2001, limiting the state's involvement and use of the sovereign wealth fund in the twenty-first century.

The large Norwegian state has deep historical origins, which are still prevalent. To understand why Norway has a large, state-owned oil sector and owns almost half of the Norwegian Stock Exchange, it is necessary to consider how Norwegians think about the role of the state and its legitimacy.

The public debate about oil has, ever since its discovery, been focused on how to use the revenue, closely connected to the question of how to organize the oil sector. In 2001, two landmark decisions were made about these very issues, implementing a vision of a stable future for the industry and for the wealth derived from it. Yet even before that, going back to the first decades after Norway won the big lottery of natural resources, there were important questions concerning international presence, private ownership, and how to build local competence and knowhow. These needed to be addressed right from the start of the 'age of oil', and the path chosen after 1969 for both the oil industry and wealth was deeply informed by Norwegian political and economic tradition.

Historically strong belief in the state and its bureaucracy

The Norwegian Constitution is 200 years old. Early on Norwegians coupled economic independence and political rights, which accounted for a considerable part of the male population when it came to suffrage. We did not have a nobility of importance, nor an economic elite. The bureaucracy was considered trustworthy from early on, and corruption was largely abolished only a few decades after the Constitution of 1814.

The Norwegian bureaucratic elites were liberal, but not in the British classical liberal sense. The state was actively used as a vehicle to build infrastructure and finance large projects—such as roads, ports and railways—in order to democratically facilitate economic growth. The 'Bergensbanen' railway from Oslo to Bergen took half of the 1909 state budget, or around 2.5 per cent of GDP, to construct.

From the nineteenth century, the picture of a strong but benevolent and useful state appeared. Norway was democratic before she became industrialized, and Norwegians trusted the state and its bureaucrats to protect them. State loans and guarantees were made, and this continued through the early twentieth century and after the Second World War, with high levels of public investments often combined with favourable financial terms.

A long historical perspective shows a clear continuity from the renewable power plants producing electricity from waterfalls, to the non-renewable oil and gas. Norwegians have persistently wanted national control, especially when it comes to natural resources. This inclination has been stronger in Norway than in most other countries. As has been noted in the EU debates, control over both extraction and vital decision-making is paramount, resulting in a large public oil sector. Large, private or foreign companies have always been met with a certain amount of scepticism. In comparison, large, publicly owned companies have been regarded more positively. Public control, either through ownership or through parliamentary rules and laws, has been important ever since the nineteenth century.

Due to Norway's 400 years in union with Denmark, and then ninety years with Sweden, Norwegians generally oppose being ruled by others, which was apparent in the EU debates. As we have seen, the national orientation can be traced in several restrictive concession laws from the early 1900s which regulated waterfalls and ownership.

After the discovery of oil in 1969, the state stepped in, as it had during the period of industrialization, to take care of national interests. A system of tax incentives and favourable test drilling rules were established, and soon made the whole fast-growing chain of oil-related activities profitable for the new sector, from the drilling to the sale. Within the first decades a large sector of Norwegian oil service companies was formed, helped by protectionist policies, with the state-owned company Statoil as the largest player. Norway became a professional oil- and gas-producing country, with Statoil acting as a hub for the quick building of expertise, ensuring that suppliers would be Norwegian. For the first decade after oil was discovered, a traditional protectionist policy was followed, in line with the general consensus of the 1970s in favour of state intervention. Norwegian businesses were subsidized with beneficial credit rates, tax incentives and other concessions. But as we saw in Chapter 10, from the 1980s onwards the Norwegian state loosened its control over the market. International legislation and EEC/EU principles of a level playing field influenced policy, but also a domestic recognition of the difficulties of protectionism.

The normalization of oil and gas production during the 1980s as well as the collapse of global oil prices in 1986—following the economic crises and industrial slowdown of the 1970s—diminished the need to further control extraction of oil by Norwegians, and the presence of international companies was seen as important. An argument for the privatization of the oil sector was the various role of the state as owner, lawgiver, controller and tax collector when it came to the oil industry. There were calls for a partial privatization of Statoil. Professor of Economic History Einar Lie, writes that, in the 1990s, it was estimated that the revenues from Statoil would represent as much as seventy per cent of the total revenues from the oil production and equal all revenues from land-based activities regardless of sector.[5]

By 2001, Statoil was deemed to be too powerful and was broken up. One part of Statoil became directly owned by the state, whereas it later became partly privatized and changed its name to Equinor in 2018. Ultimately, this arrangement did not solve the basic disputes regarding the Norwegian state's different roles in the oil industry; as long as the state is a huge owner of commercial companies, such conflicts will exist. However, it marked a new status quo for the twenty-first century in Norway's handling of its oil production, and the same year would see a new principle established for the handling of the oil wealth, too.

The management of wealth and the restrictions on using it

The first decades after the discovery of the oil reserves had made deficits rather than profits for the state. Investments were enormous and had to occur before revenue could be generated. Nevertheless, it was clear even then that oil would substantially alter the Norwegian economy. As early as in 1974, a white paper had argued that future surpluses would need to be invested in assets abroad, in the interests of both the economy and coming generations, and it launched the political slogan of the decade: 'building a better Norway'. As we know, in 1990 the Government Pension Fund Global, commonly known as the oil fund, had been established (with no deposits) to hold the nation's long-term savings; it soon became clear that it would increase rapidly.

In 1995, the government had announced the prospect of transfers to the fund for the very first time, which happened in 1996. This raised the question of how the fund should be managed in the new millennium.

Professor Einar Lie, in his book about Norges Bank, argues that there were fears that such a large investor as the fund would acquire too much influence and undermine democratic control and credibility.[6] Lie adds that historians often remark that business interests have low legitimacy in Norway compared to other countries. Ideas from the nineteenth century and the civil servants' state maintained that power and influence of great importance to society must be under direct democratic control to have legitimacy. Business interests must therefore be controlled as democratically as possible and not be allowed to be too powerful. The Ministry of Finance is both a policymaker and a regulator of the financial sector, and has always been concerned about potential concentration of financial power. An example mentioned by Lie was that in the 1990s, there had been active initiatives to limit the growth of the three biggest Norwegian banks in order to make smaller and regional banks thrive.

A committee was formed to investigate how the fund should be managed. It concluded in 1997 that a separate organization from the central bank had to be set up and become as international and professional as possible. The Norges Bank Investment Management (NBIM) was created as a separate part of the central bank, charged with managing the oil fund and the state's foreign exchange reserves. Lie further remarks that: 'neither the civil servants at the Ministry of Finance nor the Bank's own management seem to have been in any doubt that the fund should be managed by the Bank.'[7] As remarked above, the legitimacy of power is linked to democratic institutions, and the civil servants, including NBIM, are supposed to work for the common good. A saying about former NBIM CEO Yngve Slyngstad

(2008–20) is that he never talked about politics, whereas the CEO who followed him, the former international investment fund manager Nicolai Tangen, raised a huge debate when he proclaimed that he wanted a 100 per cent inheritance tax. He soon discovered that the CEO of NBIM, like other civil servants, are not supposed to talk about politics in the public debate or generally interfere in politics.

In addition, a set of rules were decided upon to govern how NBIM should go about its business. There were two particularly important conditions. Firstly, all investments should be in international markets; this was to avoid an overheating of the Norwegian economy through excessive domestic investment. Secondly, sixty per cent of this should be invested in equities. These conditions were designed to guarantee stability and avoid putting all of Norway's eggs in one basket, but they have been controversial because stock markets are seen as high-risk for a sovereign fund that was set up for generations. In addition, ethical debates about the kind of investments that could be made resulted in the foundation of The Council of Ethics in 2003. In 2014 it was decided that The Council of Ethics would come to advise Norges Bank (The Central Bank), which would make the final decision. Today NBIM operates as a highly competent international fund manager.

More importantly, it was decided that returns from the fund were to be transparent if they were to be used in the state budget. In 2001, this principle was established as the *handlingsregel*, which is essentially a fiscal rule of conduct saying that a maximum of four per cent of the annual net returns from the oil fund could be used in the annual state budget. Four per cent was chosen because at the time it seemed a fair estimate on what the net revenue would be over time. It was also specifically mentioned that the extra oil revenues should be applied not only as a patch to cover up state budget deficits, but to enhance growth.

Highlighted measures were tax reductions and investment in infrastructure, research and general education. The idea was to encourage governments to take a long-term view of Norway's development, rather than taking advantage of the oil wealth to splurge all at once.

Both decisions—to put the revenue in a sovereign fund invested internationally, and to limit the rate at which the oil fund could be spent—were designed to head off one problem: the Dutch disease. This is the nickname for a situation where greatly stepped-up development and rapid growth of one sector (in this case oil and gas) adversely affects the rest of the economy, creating a problem for the other export industries exposed to competition. Because of the great value of oil or any other natural resource, it becomes hard for ordinary export industries as the prices they offer in the international market are too high because of the currency. If this goes unchecked it can lead to unemployment, because the struggling sectors can only cover their reduced income by moving manufacturing jobs abroad where labour is cheaper.

A second risk with the sudden arrival of a highly valuable new resource is that the state responds with extremely high spending elsewhere in the budget. This is what the Dutch government did after the discovery of a giant natural gas field in 1959, but it causes a problem: it floods the rest of the economy with more money than it can absorb, overheating it, and such a policy is then very hard to reverse without harm. A return to normal activity is difficult to achieve without cutting costs, reducing benefits and increasing unemployment. Norway had several means of preventing the other sectors of the economy from collapsing due to the loss of price competition in the export market. One of these was the Norwegian system for wage coordination, based on the idea that increases in wages must be adjusted to what the export industries can support over time. Together with the sovereign oil fund and fiscal rule, this has prevented the Dutch disease.

By controlling the rate at which money passes from the oil sector into state revenue, the internationally invested oil fund and the fiscal rule limiting its expenditure both ensure that the 'boom' is not brought into the economy all at once, keeping some kind of balance and ensuring long-term security. The fiscal rule allowed for flexibility of business cycles, seen as an average over time. It has been reduced from four per cent to three per cent, both because the yield is low and because the fund itself has grown enormously, which means that the Norwegian economy cannot absorb even three per cent of the returns. It is possibly not even conservative enough.

The fiscal rule is currently uncontroversial. Various governments, comprising parties of the centre-right and centre-left, have embraced the rule and prepared their national budgets according to it. Nevertheless, after almost twenty years with the fiscal rule, we can see a pattern. Most of the extra money has been used directly on spending in the state budget, regardless of which party is in government. There are differences, however, in how tax cuts are prioritized. There were almost none in the eight years of social democrats from 2005–13, but the conservatives actively made cuts before and after this period.

The fiscal rule is a source of pride to Norwegians. They talk about it as being responsible and tie it to a generational perspective. The natural resources should generally be managed with a long-term view in mind. The farmer (*bonde*), whom we have discussed in earlier chapters, is someone who leaves the farm, by odal rights, to the next generation in the same or even in a better state. This is an old and prominent virtue for Norwegians, which can probably be explained by the fact that Norway has been endowed with natural resources and that the Norwegian economy has always been tied to production and trade of natural resources, from timber, fish and hydropower to oil and gas.

THE NORWEGIAN EXCEPTION?

Norwegian ethics

Finally, there is the question of ethics. As mentioned, concentration of capital is perceived with scepticism. Norway has established an international reputation for non-corruption and as an upholder of principles. The Nobel Peace Prize committee is Norwegian, and the country has hosted and led international peace negotiations. Thus, in the view of Norwegians, ethical standards need to be high. Yet being able to invest internationally without meeting ethical dilemmas is difficult. The oil fund is buying shares, properties and doing investments all over the world. How shall Norway invest? Which ethical considerations shall be made? Norway is a high-cost country whose income levels are more than fifty per cent higher than the countries with which she is trading. Norway, which did not have colonies and even lacked sovereignty itself, now holds a modern colonial position, living by the work of others through the returns from the oil fund. The only thing that can soften the picture is that Norwegians see themselves as professional investors, complying with high ethical standards and promoting fair and transparent business for long-term relations.

There is also a kind of ethical dilemma in how Norway's oil is handled domestically. The 'black gold' may have postponed or delayed necessary readjustments of industries. The public sector and the immensely productive oil industry are huge, while the private mainland-based sector is struggling with productivity. This is problematic with regard to the egalitarian perception that Norwegians have of themselves. Nevertheless, the blessings of oil are many: the level of social conflict is low because it has been possible to accommodate many demands, in everything from generous social benefits—the sick leave benefit is for instance 100 per cent paid for—to free or heavily subsidized health care, parental leave and kindergartens, to mention just a few. Norway ranks highest among the OECD countries both on public employment and on the size of public expenses in relation to GDP.

This is how Norwegians like to be seen: a small, rich country promoting high trading standards abroad and equality of living standards at home. As we will see in Chapter 13, however, the oil is posing a new ethical question for Norway as the world confronts the climate crisis.

12

PEACEFUL COEXISTENCE OR POLARIZATION?

IMMIGRATION AND IDENTITY

On 22 July 2011, the thirty-two-year-old Anders Behring Breivik killed seventy-seven people in an act of terrorism in Norway. Eight people were killed by a car bomb placed at the main government building in downtown Oslo, before sixty-nine more were gunned down in a shooting rampage at a summer political youth camp at the island Utøya, outside Oslo. In addition, about 100 people were wounded. After the court found him to be legally sane, the terrorist received the maximum allowed sentence of twenty-one years in prison; this will probably be followed by preventive detention, in effect possibly amounting to life imprisonment.

Without getting into legal definitions and professional psychiatric diagnoses, it seems reasonable to suggest that Breivik's act of terrorism, especially the massacre at Utøya, bears witness to a very warped mind. He was a lone wolf, planning and carrying out his act of terrorism on his own. His attack was directed at the centre of political power in Norway, the main government building in Oslo, and at those he saw as the future governmental leaders of Norway: the members of the Labour Party's youth organization AUF, who had gathered at the summer camp at Utøya.

Shortly before carrying out his acts of terror, Breivik posted a 1,500-page ideological manifesto online with the title *2083, A European Declaration of Independence*. This was a statement marked by cutting and pasting, with references to multiple authors and exhibiting varying levels of intellectual calibre. Large portions of the text had been written by others, presumably without the knowledge and permission of the author. The statement nonetheless added up to a kind of coherent whole.

The most obvious aspect of the manifesto is the attack on Breivik's enemies, that is, on Islam and what he sees as the politically correct elite of Western Europe—in his language, 'cultural Marxists' and/or 'multiculturalists'. Also obvious is the extreme conspiracy theory on which this image of the enemy is built. According to Breivik and his sources, a cultural-Marxist, multicultural elite in Europe, as well as political leaders in the Muslim world, have conspired to break down and destroy dominant Western and European values through mass immigration of Muslims to Europe. According to this conspiracy, the purpose is to build up a new society where Europe becomes part of the Arabic world: 'Eurabia'.

In his manifesto, Breivik draws up apocalyptic visions. Europe, Western Europe in particular, is in a free fall toward its destruction. At one point he uses particularly telling language: 'Keep in mind that these regimes we are fighting have and are still committing genocide against the indigenous peoples of Europe by exposing them to 25 million Muslims'.

This apocalyptic vision of existing Western European regimes committing genocide against their own native population was to give Breivik, along with his ideological comrades in arms, the right and duty to use all necessary means. They belong to a select, self-appointed elite who have grasped 'How the World Works', including its problems and their solution:

> As a Justiciar Knight you are operating as a jury, judge and executioner on behalf of all free Europeans. Never forget that it is not only your right to act against the tyranny of the cultural Marxist/multiculturalist elites of Europe, it is your duty to do so.

In light of the mass murder of 22 July 2011, his formulations like the following are especially grotesque: 'There are situations in which cruelty is necessary and refusing to apply necessary cruelty is a betrayal of the people whom you wish to protect.'

Summing up a consideration of his moral right to carry out acts of cruelty, Breivik concludes with these words:

> In many ways, morality has lost its meaning in our struggle. The question of good and evil is reduced to one simple choice. For every free patriotic European, only one choice remains: Survive or perish.[1]

So how could peaceful, prosperous, harmonious Norway produce a human monster like this? His is a psychological case, but it is of note that his ideas—extreme and grotesque as they are—have a certain logic and meaning. He was not acting completely randomly, but responding to what he saw as an existential crisis for Norway and for white Christian Europe.

A very, very dark underbelly?

Breivik was not the first in Norway's recent history to engage in a violent act of intolerance and right-wing extremism. Norway has experienced neo-Nazi violence since the 1970s. In the early 1990s, several old churches in Norway were set on fire. It appeared that these church burnings were closely connected to a small milieu of young musical artists, who played a form of heavy metal music commonly referred to as black metal. Their lyrics, their appearances, their rites and practices and their overriding ideology were a rather unhealthy mix of Satanism, old Norse religion and mythology, neo-Nazism and a few elements of their own making. The idea of burning churches was meant as an anti-Christian statement and a call for action. At least some of them really meant what their blood-dripping lyrics said; they had a deep-felt hatred of Christianity. The arsonists' favourite targets were the so-called *stavkirker*—medieval churches built of wood with very characteristic structures, some of the oldest wood buildings still in existence—and symbols of Christianity's triumph over the Norse religion.

Largely, the reactions to this Norwegian black metal scene and its actions were shock and horror. For some youths around the world, however, it also generated fascination and inspiration.

The core milieu was dissolved after one of the leaders, Varg Vikernes, killed another central figure, Øystein Aarseth, in 1993. Vikernes was and is commonly known as 'The Count'. For a while, his artistic alias was 'Count Grishnackh', named after the prominent (and of course evil) Orc captain in Tolkien's *Lord of the Rings*. Ironically, his given first name was Kristian, which in Norwegian literally means 'Christian', a less than fitting name for an anti-Christian ideologue and activist. Vikernes thus changed his name into Varg, an old Norse word for wolf.

Vikernes was sentenced to sixteen years in prison for murder and church burnings. After his release, he moved to France. He still lives there, now under a new name, making music and writing ideological manifestos. Black metal has continued to thrive as a niche heavy metal genre, with Norway still being seen as an inspirational centre, and with Norwegian bands like Emperor, Dimmu Borgir and Aarseth's and Vikernes' old band Mayhem at the forefront. However, the movement is now considered a more ordinary, commercial enterprise, stripped of most of its early 1990s ideological baggage and especially its criminal, church-burning aspects.

PEACEFUL COEXISTENCE OR POLARIZATION?

A massacre of left-wing teenagers at a summer camp and the burning of medieval churches. Of course there are significant differences between Breivik and Vikernes, but the acts committed by both were shocking and, at least in Norway, demonstrated unprecedented forms of extremism, with one of them including the horrors of mass killing.

In 2014, a Norwegian called Anders Cameroon Dale was listed on the US State Department's Specially Designated Global Terrorist list as well as a similar UN terrorist list. Not only a namesake of Breivik, Dale is also just a few months older. This other Anders grew up near Oslo. Like Breivik, he dabbled in party politics in his youth; Breivik was briefly member of the Progress Party, Dale was member of the Green Party in Norway and stood as a low-level candidate for the municipal elections in Oslo in 2007. In 2008, the older left-winger converted to Islam—a politicized, radicalized, eventually terrorist form of Islam.

Dale joined Al-Qaeda in the Arab Peninsula in 2008, left Norway for Yemen, became a bomb-making expert, was allegedly associated with several terrorist activities—among them plans for the London Olympics in 2012—and made it to that very exclusive Global Terrorist list in 2014. His present whereabouts, if he is still alive, are unknown to us. There have been other native Norwegian converts with violent Islamist leanings. Most, but not all, of these terrorists or terrorist supporters have been affiliated with the so-called Islamic State.

One recent manifestation worth mentioning in this context is the terrorist action committed by twenty-two-year-old Philip Manshaus. On 10 August 2019 he killed his seventeen-year-old stepsister Johanne and then attacked a nearby mosque, armed with a shotgun and a rifle. He was overpowered by people in the mosque before he could seriously harm anyone there, so the only person he managed to kill was Johanne. She was adopted, with a Chinese background, and the killer's expressed motivation was purely racist. Like Breivik, Manshaus was alone and seemed to come from nowhere. He had also been radicalized on the internet. His foremost role model was Brenton Tarrant, the anti-Muslim terrorist from New Zealand. Like Tarrant, Manshaus subscribed to the 'great replacement' conspiracy theory (a white nationalist narrative of white Europeans being wiped out by high Muslim immigration and birth rates), but as the killing of his stepsister indicates, he had a broader ideological motivation than just hatred of Muslims. Unlike Breivik in 2011, his brand of right-wing extremism was neo-Nazism, and he had unsuccessfully applied for membership in the neo-Nazi organization *Den nordiske motstandsbevegelsen* (The Nordic Resistance Movement).

Are all these just coincidences? After all, there are extremists, outsiders and terrorists everywhere in modern Western countries. Political extremism, too, has not been unknown in Norwegian history—after all, we Norwegians gave the world the word 'quisling'.

Still, the shocking violence and unprecedented terrorist thinking doesn't fit in with traditional Norwegian extremism, like the communist revolutionaries in the 1920s or later. In its own way, Islamist terrorism is, of course, also a new kind of innovative extremist ideology in Norway, something quite different from the traditional left-wing and right-wing extremism. So what is it with Norway? How can an affluent, successful, peaceful, harmonious society like this produce terrorists like Anders Breivik, Anders Dale, and Vikernes? Are there any specific patterns here?

A closer examination will leave little doubt that Breivik shares essential mental and ideological tendencies with other terrorists, irrespective of whether they can claim an ideological justification. Viewed in these terms, he fits nicely in a category that might be called 'the mentality of the terrorist'. If we want to pursue this line of thought further, it might be fruitful to see Breivik as a terroristic variant of a modern human type called 'the outsider' in Colin Wilson's terminology: a person who feels himself outside and unable to find himself at home anywhere in the modern world. The others more or less fit in this model too.

For the last couple of years before his terrorist act, Breivik had isolated himself. He had moved home to his mother and spent most of his time surfing the internet. Apparently, he had radicalized, and planned his terrorist activity without engaging with any bits of what we may call the Norwegian public debate, not even the dark, marginalized and extreme corners of it. In this sense he was an outsider, and perhaps, between his social situation and his psychological condition, he would have developed a violent, radical outlook in whatever society he lived.

On the other hand, he is also one of us Norwegians. Perhaps there is something about the hegemonic culture, the safe, peaceful, consensual, welfare-societal, compromise culture of present-day Norway that drives troubled individuals to radicalization. The right-wing black metal extremists who burned churches in the 1990s did not just say they hated Christianity itself, but also the hegemonic Christian-based culture in modern Norway. Maybe it takes extraordinary efforts to make a real break with such an unusually strong national consensus, to send a 'Fuck you' message to Norwegian society.

The last decades' demographic changes

Norwegian society has always been one of the most ethnically homogeneous in Europe. Immigrants did come to Norway in the past, not least Swedes but in earlier times also the Danes, Germans and Dutch. By the modern era, however, they were no longer considered immigrant populations, having assimilated and intermarried to the point where they were indistinguishable from other Norwegians; their own nationalities were of the same majority race and religion as Norway. What remained of the

221

Jewish minority after the war had also very much integrated into Norwegian society. In 1970, the Sami population was the only ethnic minority of any size, making up around 10,000–15,000 of at that time around 3.8 million Norwegians. Another minority group in the north, the ethnic Finns, was even smaller. At the time of writing, just fifty years later, there are roughly one million immigrants and children of immigrants living in Norway. This is a large number in what has always been a very small population: one million represents almost a fifth of all Norwegian residents, compared to the UK with around fourteen per cent and France with only twelve percent.

Many are Europeans, like Poles and Lithuanians, but also our neighbours from Sweden, working here as a result of the EEA/EU agreement. Since 2004, Europeans have been able to work and live in Norway, and Poles soon became the largest immigrant population. Around 100,000 Poles are living in Norway, followed by Lithuanians and Swedes. Others are immigrants from all over the world, many of them refugees, asylum seekers and their families. The first substantial group of non-European migrants to Norway were Pakistanis, who first came as immigrants seeking work in around 1970. In 2016, according to official statistics, there were approximately 266,000 persons with Asian backgrounds and 115,000 persons with African backgrounds living in Norway. Many of them have been granted Norwegian citizenship. From 1990–2019, roughly 130,000 persons from Asian and African countries were granted asylum in Norway. In the same period, roughly 160,000 relatives were allowed to settle in Norway on family reunion grounds. In other words, just in the last thirty years, Norway's ethnic-minority population has increased tenfold from 1970. Norway was not unaffected by the aftermaths of the Arab Spring and the subsequent migration crisis in the mid- to late-2010s in Europe. In only 2015, 30,000 asylum seekers came to

Norway, mostly from Syria. According to the Pew Research Center, Norway had the fourth highest per capita rate of asylum seekers in Europe in 2015.[2]

Solely due to this great intensification of immigration, Norway has experienced a rapid population increase. It has gone from having roughly 4.35 million inhabitants in 1995 to around 5.37 million in 2020. The speed and scale of the transformation has led some to question whether the immigration and integration policies of bygone eras can still apply in the twenty-first century.

Since the late 1970s, integration, and not assimilation, has been official Norwegian policy towards immigrants and refugees. Assimilation has been considered abuse against people from non-Norwegian cultures, and immigrants have been encouraged to hold on to essential parts of their own culture. There are still political debates about how successful or unsuccessful this integration policy has been, and the rapid increase in immigration in the twenty-first century has only reignited these arguments.

Does this large-scale migration constitute a problem, or is immigration overall beneficial or necessary to Norwegian society and culture? Questions are raised about how much money immigration is costing the Norwegian state, and if the government should try to produce some sort of official immigration account. Further, if there are problems concerning integration of immigrants and ethnic minorities, what sort of problems are they, and in what way are they related to cultural traits among the minorities versus social and economic conditions of the Norwegian system? Norway is in a single market with the EU, thus EU citizens can work in Norway and come and go as they please. When it comes to non-European immigration, the question is whether immigration should be somewhat reduced, or if Norwegian borders should be opened further for refugees and asylum seekers.

THE NORWEGIAN EXCEPTION?

Assimilation, integration or falling out?

Some Norwegians may argue that the acceptance of immigration is dependent on a certain assimilation, not only economically but culturally. The latter has not been *comme il faut* to say, but looking at the long-term consequences of immigration, a gradual assimilation, in a loose and wide sense, may be happening for those who succeed in Norwegian society. One factor that can be said to contribute is that most Norwegians own their housing, which is also eventually the case for quite a few immigrants. Owning a house or a flat makes settlement patterns varied, and 'ghettos' or parallel communities are to a large extent avoided. However, it is no secret that work is the best way to integrate or, in the long run, assimilate. This is where Norway's recent decades of immigration explosion meet a particularly Norwegian problem.

There are several factors making it difficult for immigrants to obtain employment in Norway; these are inherent to Norwegian society as a whole, but exacerbated in the case of immigrants by the particular barriers they often face: lower education or qualification levels, and lower language skills. These confine many immigrants to low-skilled or unskilled labour, but Norwegian social security schemes, housing benefits and so on are so favourable that many without special qualifications in the Norwegian labour market—whether Norwegian-born or immigrants—will lack motivation to find work when all that is available are the lowest-paid, unskilled jobs.

Also, the wage structure is compressed. The difference in pay between low-skilled and high-skilled labour is much smaller than in many other countries. This is a good thing in general, leading to higher levels of equality, but it also means that high-skilled workers are not all segregated into specific small and extremely well-paid sectors. They also work in lower-skilled jobs that still pay well, and in which they are considered highly competent. This may hinder low-skilled labourers from entering or remaining in the labour market, because they compete with more productive workers. The model is designed in such a way that the labour force excludes rather than includes unproductive workers; because again, those finding it hard to keep a job can rely on the generosity of the state.

Employment figures for some ethnic groups—people from countries like Somalia, Iraq and Syria—are low or very low. Immigrants from outside Europe have never become net economic contributors as a group, which means that they are a strain on the Norwegian welfare state. Of course, one could say this is also true for Norwegians born in Norway, as long as the budgets are supplied with oil revenues. However, the many native Norwegians living on unemployment benefit and gaining from the welfare state do not rely on having a job and a workplace to help them be part of Norwegian society. They speak the language, they have been raised in the Norwegian education system, and they have family ties. Extensive programs and economic benefits are put in place to ease and enhance immigrant working participation. Compared to the input, however, the results are so far not very good.

Quite a few immigrants have been living in Norway long enough to have children that are coming of age. If we look at how these Norwegians with immigrant parents are doing, a mixed picture emerges. On the one hand, some are truly successful. They have high social mobility, work hard and are well represented in higher education. Education is clearly the key to success, and many have ambitious parents that encourage them to do well. Other key elements are interactions with Norwegians through school, organized sports or other activities, as well as neighbourhoods—taking part in *dugnad*, for example—and work. These developments are encouraging, but they do not form the whole picture. Second-generation immigrants are also over-represented in statistics of dropouts from secondary education, those convicted of crime, and the unemployed.

Of course, Norway has oil money to soften at least some of these problems. Anti-immigration voices may point to this very fact being part of the overall problem; Norway gives asylum seekers and other migrants very generous economic and social benefits, perhaps the most generous in Europe. The welfare state is highly benevolent to all residents and citizens of Norway, but as we have seen in the previous chapter, only a small percentage of the state budget comes from the oil fund. Those who are in work pay high taxes in return for the benefits of the welfare state. One of the big questions concerning immigration is if the Norwegian oil revenue will be sufficient in the long run, if these trends of high immigration and low immigrant employment continue; or if the Norwegian welfare state system will have to be amended. This question may of course be even more pertinent to ask if, as expected, oil production and revenue are reduced or even phased out in the near future.

Identity politics and polarization

Another big question is how cultural relations between some of these new ethnic minorities and the relatively homogeneous Norwegian society will develop in the future. There are cultural factors concerning immigrants that reinforce differences and problems. As we saw in extreme form with the manifesto of Breivik, the core question is often how to deal with and integrate 'Islamic' values in a modern, secular Norwegian society. It is important to point out that Muslims in modern Norway are not a homogeneous group; numbers from Statistics Norway indicate that around 200,000 are members of Muslim congregations, which implies around four per cent of the Norwegian population. Islam is interpreted and practised in various ways. Not all Norwegian Muslims feel that sentiments expressed by Muslim organizations and leaders of mosques represent their own views—even if these spokesmen claim to represent all Norwegian Muslims, and even if Norwegian authorities accept that they do so.

Nevertheless, certain practices and attitudes that are associated with traditional societies and Islam have been held up as barriers to the integration of Muslim immigrants into Norwegian society. For example, some Pakistani families continue the tradition of arranged marriages, quite often with relatives from Pakistan. There are around 40,000 Pakistanis in Norway, and almost half of them are born in Norway. Seven out of ten choose their partner among other Pakistanis living in Norway, and one out of five girls marries a man from Pakistan. This statistic in itself is no proof of arranged marriages, though many were in fact arranged. What this definitely does tell us, though, is that while waves of migrants from past centuries, like Swedes, have assimilated by intermarrying, newer ethnic minorities in Norway like Pakistanis often prefer to marry within their own ethnic communities.

One problem raised in connection with this, fairly or unfairly, is gender equality. Another is the possibility of varying degrees of social coercion against young people, who grow up in Norway and want to express their freedom to choose partners and lifestyles in a modern secular society.

The idea of liberal, democratic and secular values clashing with Islam is often at the heart of moments of tension, for instance over free speech. In 1989, around 3,000 Muslims in Oslo demonstrated to stop the Norwegian edition of Salman Rushdie's novel *The Satanic Verses* being published. The demonstrations were largely peaceful, but feelings ran high, and this was clearly something new in modern, liberal, secularized Norway. Four years later the Norwegian publisher of *The Satanic*

Verses, William Nygaard, was shot and nearly killed. The culprit got away and is presumably still at large.

In early 2006, there were significant tensions when several Norwegian newspapers re-published the Danish Muhammad cartoons. In the Middle East, there were violent demonstrations against Norway, and the Norwegian Embassy in Damascus was attacked and burned down. The Foreign Minister, Jonas Gahr Støre, tried to explain the Norwegian position on the Arabic news stations Al-Arabiya and Al-Jazeera in an interview some, but not all, Norwegians deemed as much too apologetic to intolerant, anti-liberal forces. Representatives of Islamic mosques, on the other hand, demanded stronger protection and greater respect for the Islamic faith.

On the other hand, in 2015, after the killing of Jews in Paris and the attack on *Charlie Hebdo*, Muslims initiated a human ring around the Synagogue in Oslo in solidarity with the victims and to show their contempt for the Islamic terrorist actions in Paris.

It is still disagreements about this development that have influenced public debate about Islam in Norway. What may be a bit less controversial, however, is that all these issues have had strong polarizing effects. This polarization doesn't seem to diminish, even if one of the most prominent governmental buzzwords in these matters is dialogue. Some of the public opinions in these matters are less than civil, and the rapid emergence of social media in the 2010s has hardly helped matters. It is worth pointing out that such polarization is not a matter of a monolithic ethnic Norwegian majority versus minority groups. There is a wide spectrum of positions among ethnic Norwegians, and there are also various points of view among minorities. Nevertheless, two increasingly remote and mutually hostile camps have been developing.

There are two increasingly different views of the crisis in Norwegian, Western and global society. In one corner there is deep dissatisfaction with perceived political correctness and broad societal currents like immigration and globalization. In another there are demands for stronger measures against perceived racism and hate speech.

Racism does, of course, exist in Norway. The question open to debate is the kinds of racism that are prevalent and to what extent they are expressed. Racism manifests itself in various ways: prejudice and discrimination against individuals with minority backgrounds; inflammatory and hateful language, especially in social media and online but also in society at large; and organized anti-immigrant, especially anti-Muslim, groups. The tiny group '*Stopp islamiseringen av Norge*' (Stop Islamization of Norway) has held several provocative stunts with inflammatory speeches and burning of Qurans. As we have seen, there are also manifestations of right-wing extremist violence. So far, however, it seems that most of these groups are a marginal phenomenon, outside mainstream political discourse. Then again, like all other modern Western societies, what we can call systemic racial inequality may be part of Norwegian society, though in the public debate there are controversies regarding this. The question is how far it exists, in what ways it manifests itself, and what measures the government can take to combat it.

One may argue that phenomena like the polarization of politics and identity politics, so prevalent in the US and the UK, have not been that noticeable in Norwegian society. Many, perhaps most Norwegians still find their information through traditional media rather than social media. Debates about immigration have been held in the open, as well as on social media and in darker corners of the internet. So far disputes have been mainly verbal and non-violent. Breivik's 2011 attack was a catastrophic exception, though as we have seen with Philip Manshaus, not the only one. Unlike the American and British situation, where extreme populist forces have quickly absorbed the disenchanted working class, in Norway a much-strengthened Centre Party has been there to receive some traditional Labour voters.

Even the populist Progress Party has been something of an exception in the flora of right-wing populist European parties, like The Sweden Democrats, Sannfinnene, Rassemblement National or Alternative für Deutschland. Among Norway's mainstream democratic political parties, it has profiled itself as the anti-immigration party, or at least the party most sceptical of non-Western immigration. This has especially been the case since the late 1980s. The party had its best election result in 2009 with twenty-three per cent of the vote. From 2013–20, the party was part of a centre-right coalition government, but non-Western immigration to Norway did not go down in this period. Nevertheless, the party has still been less radical, less nationalist and more influenced by liberalist strands of thought than the other parties, as has Norwegian nationalism.

There are, at the time of writing, different ideological tendencies inside the Progress Party. It is possible to identify a national conservative wing, more in line with parties like the Sweden Democrats and the Danish People's Party. At times there have been tensions within the party, and even defections, due to disagreements on politics and strategy, but none large enough to create either a more prominent liberalist party or a more extreme right-wing party. Outside of this there are also several miniscule parties with a clearer nationalist leaning, as well as websites and social media communities one may characterize as nationalist, right-wing populist or, in some cases, deeply xenophobic and right-wing radical. Inside these milieus there are especially strong concerns about globalization, Norwegian membership in the European Economic Area (of which the Progress Party is in favour) and last, but not least, the presence of Islam and Muslims in Norway.

So far, people with these leanings both inside and outside of the Progress Party have not been able or willing to create a coherent political force. However, there may indeed be an opening for a right-wing populist party to the right of the Progress Party, some existing groups may develop into one or it may be a new party altogether, which in a relatively short time could find its way to parliamentary representation (the threshold is four per cent). If so, in this regard Norway would be less of an exception compared, for instance, to her Scandinavian neighbours.

We may also find strands of thought grounded in identity politics in some leftist and left-liberal milieus. Some people argue that the traditional left-right axis of politics existing since at least the 1880s could crumble and give way to identity politics, and that political polarization would rapidly increase. In 2015, The Labour Party was one of the largest social democratic parties in Europe and by far the largest party in Norway, an exception compared to most other European countries. This is no longer the case; at the time of writing the Labour Party has lost its pole position. While some of the party's voters did find their way to the Centre Party, others seem to have defected to parties further to the left. This may signal that the political landscape in Norway is changing, becoming more polarized and more focused on identity politics, aligning with most other Western countries. What is certain is that Norwegians will have to decide how they want to respond to the unprecedented and sudden shifts brought about by fifty years of immigration.

Agreement in realpolitik—disagreement in rhetoric

What the future will bring is hard to predict. Currently, one might say that traditional Progress Party rhetoric has become more mainstream, suggesting a strict regime for immigration from outside the EU and limiting refugee quotas to international agreements. Moreover, stronger demands in the integration process have become better accepted. In political debates, these topics are highly controversial. Two parties in the centre-right government, Venstre since 2018 and the Christian Democrats since 2019, argue for doing considerably more to help refugees and asylum seekers from Africa and the Middle East in Norway. The left wing of the Labour Party and the other left-wing parties tend to have similar rhetoric and immigration politics. The Conservatives are generally more restrictive and have proposed limits to immigration, referring to the economic, social and cultural capacity of society to integrate immigrants. The Centre Party's rhetoric is also largely on the restrictive side. The centre-right of the Labour Party, at least in practical politics, resembles the Conservatives.

In short, immigration and integration questions have come to divide Norwegian politics; yet the rhetoric may be slightly more divisive than the practical politics. Also, in these sensitive and highly controversial areas, mainstream Norwegian political forces have been able to find compromises. Since 2006, Norway has had a centre-left government with the left-wing Socialist Left Party, and a centre-right government including the right-wing Progress Party. Despite this, there has been no big shift regarding immigration and integration politics. Not even the refugee crisis in 2015 was able to bring on full-scale polarization in the Norwegian political landscape.

13

THE NORWEGIAN EXCEPTION?

The lucky but clever follower

Has Norway been simply lucky, or have Norwegians been clever and seized opportunities when they came around? The probable answer is that the country has had a large amount of luck, but that Norwegians have been able to make circumstances valuable. The Navigation Act in 1849 was a golden opportunity for shipping and trade at a time when postcolonial Norway was looking to modernize rapidly. Norwegian waterfalls became silver when they could be used to produce electricity after 1905, just in time for the newly independent Norway to go through a process of large-scale industrialization. In 1969 we found yet another treasure in the North Sea, just as the post-war social democratic economics no longer seemed to be working. Lastly, since 1814, Norwegians have been blessed with peaceful neighbours: Sweden, especially in 1905, and Denmark and Russia more generally.

At the same time, people have seen these opportunities and acted. As we have shown, a political culture that promoted compromise, and politicians that were mostly pragmatic and loyal in their decision-making, contributed to political and economic development. Their values were embedded in the shared 1814 experience, with its important ideas of freedom and equality. From the union with Sweden, the language question and the ousting of the civil servants in the nineteenth century, to the international rise of fascism, the turn to market liberalism and the relationship with Europe in the twentieth century, the losing side in national divisions accepts defeat and a stable consensus always seems to emerge. So far this has even held true for the deep polarizations of identity politics in the twenty-first century.

Even if Norway has been peaceful for more than two centuries, with the exception of the Second World War, the same cannot be said for politics. Uncompromising forces have fought for their views many times, and the paths that were followed could have been dramatically different if these views had become predominant. Around 1850, the civil servants' state uncompromisingly put down the Thrane movement, and in 1884 we could have faced a civil war. It did not happen. Strong cultural nationalism had a harmonizing effect on most Norwegians, but it is also important to remember that it had a darker side too, most obviously in the treatment of Jews. The interwar period was tainted by rather pronounced anti-Semitism, and Norwegians cannot be proud of the paragraph in the 1814 Constitution that prohibited Jews from coming to Norway. One could argue that the identity politics and hate crimes of recent years are also connected to this strong national culture, both in terms of extremists' pride in 'pure Norwegianness' and in terms of a reaction against what they see as censorship from the moralizing, conforming majority.

What lies ahead? Will Norway still be lucky or are new circumstances emerging that will be less favourable than in the past 200 years? Maybe it will turn out that Norway is not as exceptional as one might think. We will explore some issues that might change Norway in the future. First there is the substantial and rapid loss of homogeneity in society, both through the growth of cultural and ethnic minorities and through the polarization of politics around questions of identity; can social trust and the tradition of compromise and consensus survive these transitions? Norway has had a political system that has served her well for two centuries, and transitions have been made without severe conflicts. Will Norway be able to keep a political system that can handle conflicts and find viable solutions? Will Norway still be among the world's most stable democracies?

Then there is climate change: has it made Norway's most profitable industry a liability? How can Norwegians transform to other industries something that has been immensely valuable economically, and how fast will it have to be done? The Norwegian Sovereign Wealth Fund has made it possible to finance Norwegian welfare in an unprecedented way. Will Norway be able to make necessary adjustments to the budgets when public finances will have to adapt to a slowdown of oil revenues?

Finally, this slowdown will be particularly challenging alongside an ageing population and a growing unemployed immigrant population; it would lead to a reduction in the workforce and tax base and put increased pressure on the extremely generous welfare state. Can Norway keep its high level of equality?

The withering of the Norwegian gold—trust?

The high level of trust in society is said to be the Norwegian gold. Trust is difficult to measure, but it is a key word in Norway. According to surveys of trust, it has for decades consistently had much higher levels of trust than the US, for instance. Recent similar European surveys show that Norway comes third after Denmark and Finland with values over 6.5 on a scale from one to ten.[1] It is possible to say that this represents a Nordic exception, since the top four countries in European surveys belong to this region.

THE NORWEGIAN EXCEPTION?

Social scientists and historians constantly discuss why this is, posing questions like, 'Have politics created trust, or is it the other way around?' Scholars in Denmark and Sweden who looked into trust among Scandinavian Americans found that Norwegians who emigrated to the US still have a higher level of trust than their fellow Americans, many generations after they left Norway, implying that they brought it with them from Scandinavia.[2] The answer, then, can be that initial high levels of trust have historically made it easier to implement policies including universal health care, pensions and so forth. This creates a circle of trust, because governments deliver and improve or support people's lives. Once you are in this positive spiral, trust makes politics work, feeding back to trust in the state or what we might label institutions, and in bureaucracy and judiciary in general. Trust is connected to history, to well-functioning institutions, to a strong civil society and to a shared feeling of identity.

Norwegians trust each other and they trust the state. The social contract is based on this and is the reason the large welfare state is accepted. Norway has a lot to lose if levels of social trust diminish, because Norwegian society is modelled around it and depends on it.

The trust in the state is resilient; it has continued most likely due to high education levels, low unemployment and economic equality. Even during the COVID-19 pandemic, trust levels have remained high despite Norwegians going through several lockdowns. The next level is interpersonal trust, which is believed to be very important for society, and which facilitates everyday and professional life. For Norwegians, both the general trust we have in institutions and the particular trust we show each other are high.

In 2012, three Norwegian social scientists introduced a third level: community trust. This is the trust towards our neighbours outside the interpersonal level, to those who live in our neighbourhood and whom we might meet on the street. It has decreased slightly, especially in neighbourhoods with high levels of cultural heterogeneity, often connected to immigration. This community level is also connected to the *dugnad*, a shared common project where all could participate with whatever means they had: if people don't trust their community, why should they make an effort to help out? If we lose our feeling of a shared identity, of being Norwegian and included in society, the overall levels of trust may very well decrease. The polarization of politics and the growth of identity politics explored in Chapter 12 both pose this threat.

Another possible disruption of Norwegian national cohesion and social trust is the axis of the centre and the periphery, which as we saw in Chapter 11 is pivotal for Norwegian identity and understanding of politics. The opposition from the farmers, both as part of the nineteenth-century left-liberal alliance and in the Farmers party (later the Centre Party), has always advocated for the districts and the periphery. They have seen themselves as independent and opposed to free trade, and have been preoccupied with Norwegian independence. With a few permutations on the way, their aim since the early nineteenth century has been self-governing local communities and the ability to live where they have been living for generations. Surnames from all over Norway, even the smallest places, are still in use. Upholding settlement patterns as opposed to urbanization is the credo.

The tension between the urban and the rural has been intense for centuries. A common joke is that whenever a small place gets a tunnel or a bridge, people immediately move away, contrary to the intention of connecting people in remote places to the mainland or the closest town. A popular TV series has the illustrative name *Where no one could believe it is possible to live*—and believe us, there are many of them. Statistics show that Norwegians are moving to urban areas, but in politics the districts still have strong voices.

THE NORWEGIAN EXCEPTION?

A new protest, following old political lines and fuelled by the Centre Party, is the opposition to change and to centralization, which in a Norwegian context often means that public services are reorganized into larger units and localized in fewer places. Norwegian district policies have been strong, in sharp contrast to Swedish policies which have centralized and not subsidized districts. The protest is first and foremost expressed by the Centre Party, and can be seen as a protest against globalization, against immigration and against change. This is why the Norwegian periphery was against joining the EEC in 1972 and the EU in 1994.

Another type of protest that emerged in rural areas at the time of the EEC referendum, and which is still part of Norwegian public debate today, concerns climate and environment. Such protests have only grown louder as international momentum builds in the fight against climate change, and this brings us to the second great challenge facing Norway in the twenty-first century: what to do about the oil.

From black gold to dirty polluter?

Many Norwegians grew up with the idea that Norway was the 'cleanest' country in the world. Nature was all around, waterfalls secured clean and renewable energy, and only a few (and unseen) larger industrial sites were polluters. Even the oil industry has been out of sight for most Norwegians. The production itself takes place at sea, far from our daily lives, and Norwegians are not consuming the 'dirty' oil.

Therefore, both production and consumption are decoupled from Norwegians, but the revenues they generate are not. Until recently this was uncontroversial, but the oil and gas industry increasingly faces criticism. This debate surfaced after the Paris Climate Agreement in 2016 and it has become acute since. Are

THE NORWEGIAN EXCEPTION?

Norwegians hypocrites, preoccupied with emission neutrality at home while exporting carbon abroad to other countries that are not so lucky?

Even without the need to address the climate crisis, the oil will not last forever. Yet given the size and importance of oil to the Norwegian economy, it is clear that a phasing-out must be discussed. Green political parties argue for the shutdown of an industry that provides an enormous proportion of the country's wealth. It guarantees around 160,000 people employment out of a workforce of 2.7 million, and has a productivity far higher than the now slowing overall rate of 0.7 per cent, because the high value of oil means that alternative employment will not be in such a profitable sector.[3] Auxiliary industries connected to oil services also employ many people. On 25 October 2019, the fiftieth anniversary of Phillips Petroleum's discovery of the Ekofisk oilfield, the Norwegian Oil Fund passed ten trillion kroner, around one trillion pounds sterling. This is more than seven times the size of the state budget, and almost three times the size of mainland GDP.

Hence it is no easy thing for Norway to give up its oil, but the problem is not going away. Late in 2020, the UN published the annual Human Development Index (HDI), which created a stir. Norway was still number one—a position we had held since 2001—but on a new planetary pressures-adjusted index (PHDI), we had fallen to number sixteen. The reason was that the UN PHDI also measures sustainability, carbon emissions and use of resources. Even if such indexes are just a ranking, it may send signals about a tougher future for oil and gas extraction and the use of non-renewable resources more generally.

When the COVID-19 pandemic hit and Norway simultaneously experienced a steep fall in oil prices, the dilemmas of oil production and climate change came to the fore. Some thought that the pandemic represented an opportunity to reduce oil and gas production and speed up the green change in the energy sector, whilst others argued for the importance of facilitating new investments in oil and gas to ensure economic growth and employment. So far, the oil industry has won this debate, in part by arguing that continued oil production is necessary to enhance investments in new green energy to replace coal as an energy source on the continent.

Investments in oil and gas are long term, and decisions taken now will have to calculate a long-term horizon. This is also true for windmills, which are increasingly part of the Norwegian energy debate. Since Norway has connected the electricity grid to the continent in order to export energy via cables, it must produce more energy than is consumed domestically. There are several possibilities: expanding or ameliorating the hydropower production and/or constructing windmills. The conflict lies in protection of the environment and irreplaceable interventions in nature, which is also why Norwegian politicians have so far decided not to search for oil and gas near the famous Lofoten, Senja and Vesterålen archipelagos.

The tensions between those who want to terminate oil production and those who say that it is necessary to help other countries move away from coal can split political parties and, to a certain extent, generations. Climate change concerns younger people to a greater extent, but so do the long-term consequences for the welfare state. Between the need to phase out oil and the parallel pressure of demographic changes, what will become of Norwegian prosperity?

Sound finances or brutal downscaling of welfare?

Norway is an outlier when it comes to how its inhabitants perceive society. When answering surveys, the majority of the population says that Norwegian society is egalitarian. In a survey referred to in a book by Norwegian sociologists, French and British respondents claim that their societies are like pyramids with a small elite on the top, and a large share at the bottom.[4] Only one in ten Norwegians claims the same; close to ninety per cent believe that there are few at the bottom and most people are in the middle. In comparison, only twenty per cent of British and twelve per cent of French respondents believe the same. Norwegians' answer that ambitions and hard work are the key to social and economic mobility also distinguishes us from other countries.

As we saw in the Introduction, global rankings suggest that Norwegians are not wrong to characterize their society in this way. Levels of inequality are low. Norway also has a high score on social mobility. For instance, Norwegians value education lower than most other countries, yet the education level has risen. The share of people with higher education increased from thirteen per cent in 1985 to thirty per cent in 2014. Over the last sixty years, it has doubled itself forty times. With low inequality and high education levels, we probably won't see increased social mobility in the future; but this is not necessarily a bad thing as long as the levels of equality remain high. It is the combination of low social mobility and high levels of inequality that creates social and economic problems. So the question is, will Norway be able to keep up the equality ensured by the current welfare state?

The Norwegian state budget in 2021 is more than 1,500 billion Norwegian kroner (118 billion pounds sterling). Public budgets have increased from fifty-one per cent of mainland GDP in 1978 to fifty-eight per cent in 2020. This is the largest share of all OECD countries. A large public sector indicates that many tasks and responsibilities have been assigned to it. If we measure public sector employment as a share of total employment, only Denmark is ahead of Norway. Almost thirty-five per cent of the total workforce are in the public sector, the largest percentage of all OECD countries. The expenditure on public services as a percentage of mainland GDP is thirty-two per cent, whereas the average in the OECD is twenty-three per cent.

Norway's tax level is lower than the size of the public sector should suggest, because there is always money thanks to the oil fund, and the state budget increases. Norwegians don't seem to have the normal prioritizing debates about public spending because, until now, there has been so much public money that most demands have been satisfied. The budget deficit between public income from mainland GDP and public expenses is continually growing. From around 2005–20 the gap has widened from roughly four per cent to roughly ten per cent (not including the COVID-19 economic measures). So far, however, the deficit has been covered by using revenue from the oil fund.

As long as Norwegians use the politically-decided revenue— the fiscal rule—of three per cent, the budget deficit will increase because the oil fund is still increasing. When the COVID-19 pandemic hit in March 2020, Norwegian politicians opened the oil fund tap, and used over forty per cent more of the oil fund's annual transfers; this is still allowed according to the fiscal rule, because one can use more in time of crisis. The question is when the transfers should stop or be reduced, and if any of them will become permanent. Even if the 'input' side of the equation (oil revenue) remains steady, the 'output' (demand for state funds) looks set to increase indefinitely.

Like most Western countries, Norway is facing an ageing population, due to low birth rates and increased life expectancy. Norwegian men and women have one of the longest life expectancies in the world, on average 82.5 years, which is number nine on the UN index for 2020. This causes fiscal challenges due to lower tax incomes and higher pension expenses. In 1970, there were two pensioners per ten in the working population. In 2060, this will have increased to four. Not only does this mean that taxes must rise to match the increase in pensions, as Norway has a pay-as-you-go system, but it also means that health budgets will increase. Norwegian health care is free, financed from the state budget, and most health services are public.

The Norwegian sick leave benefit covers 100 per cent of wages from day one, and the benefit extends to one year. This is the most generous statutory sick pay in the world. Over time, there has been an increase in the number of people diagnosed as disabled and who receive a disability benefit for life, two thirds of their former wage. As we saw in Chapter 12, we have a labour market that is highly productive and with high minimum wages. The Norwegian Model is not set up to include less productive workers in the labour market. High wages force companies to demand maximum efficiency: people might find that they cannot compete with better-qualified or more productive workers, and end up falling out of the labour market, going on benefits or a disability pension instead of taking a low-skilled or low-paid job. This has led to almost twenty-five per cent of the labour force, or 600,000–800,000 Norwegians, remaining outside working life.

As we have seen, the Norwegian Model's lack of flexibility also creates problems when faced with diversity, now visible as immigrants are struggling to get into the workforce. We also see a lack of balance between public and private responsibilities. The private sector is diminishing, with more and more people working in the public sector. According to polls, Norwegians are also more reluctant to take care of their own parents when they get old than people in other countries. And, of course, the welfare state is costly. When the number of workers falls compared to the number of people on welfare benefits and pensions in the years to come, fiscal challenges await.

Most importantly, however, we should remember that the Norwegian model is dynamic and able to change. As Norwegians get richer, we will probably see higher demands for shorter working days but also more demand for welfare, especially health care. That is only possible if the movement towards the market economy continues, as only a market economy can pay for higher levels of welfare. Norway is not a member of the European Union, but as a small country with an open economy, the need to be part of international trade and cooperation is always present. After the COVID-19 pandemic struck, questions that have not been asked in Norway for decades became highly relevant. How will Norway respond to questions of cooperation and globalization in the decades ahead?

In the years to come, Norway might not be able to rely on lucky circumstances. It is hard to foresee that *Les Trentes Glorieuses* will ever return. On the contrary, the 2008 financial crisis, Brexit, the 2016 election of Donald Trump, the COVID-19 pandemic, on top of global competition, climate change and a mounting migration pressure on Europe, have not represented luck for a small, open country like Norway, which has to rely heavily on international cooperation and trade to sustain welfare and wellbeing.

It is also likely that Norway will eventually become more similar to other European countries, especially if at some point it joins the EU. If Norway's success in the nineteenth and twentieth centuries was not just down to luck, but also due to Norwegian characteristics, then losing some of this exceptionality could change how well the country can handle future crises.

There are, however, some strengths that are likely to last in the decades to come. Norway ranks number one in the world on the global resilience index for 2020, published annually by FM Global. Published during the first wave of COVID-19 in May 2020, this index may tell us something about how countries will recover from admittedly the largest economic setback since the Second World War. Political stability and a sound business environment are among the factors that the index considers. Norway and Denmark (second on the ranking) have both had similar initial responses to the pandemic, and both countries seem to be able to handle the health care challenges, keeping deaths low one year after the outbreak of the pandemic. At the time of writing Norway has twelve deaths per 100,000, and a total of 650, whereas Sweden has 132 deaths per 100,000, and a total of more than 13,000. At this point it is too early to evaluate things economically. Both countries have spent considerable amounts to sustain businesses, and compared to many countries around the globe, both have a high likelihood of maintaining stability and resilience, mostly due to capable states and political responses, high levels of trust and competent leaders.

The Norwegian Sovereign Wealth Fund will still make sure that public finances are exceptionally good compared to other countries, even if Norway, like many Western economies, is facing an ageing population and a rise in pension obligation and health care services. Norway is still an oil-producing country and will probably continue to be so for many decades, even if the pressure from climate change continues. With some luck, Norway may be able to repeat its performance during the early nineteenth-century modernization and early twentieth-century industrialization: to use expertise to store carbon dioxide and to change energy production in a greener direction. In addition, energy-producing companies may also be able to engage in green energy. Norway still has its waterfalls, which are renewed with every rainfall.

It remains to be seen if our political system still will be able to seek compromises and find good solutions to difficult priorities that will have to be solved when public finances are more restrained. Norwegians' high level of trust, which has been a hallmark for centuries, has taken a long time to build but can be torn down if society is strained and populism takes hold.

Overall, Norway may have a fair chance of dealing with the economic pressures of demographic changes and the climate crisis, because a strong, cohesive society and culture have always served politics and economics well in the past. The greater threat to this reasoning would be the consequences if social cohesion is ripped apart. In other words, it will mostly come down to the Norwegians themselves, more so than external crises, to determine whether the Norwegian exception continues.

Yet as our title indicates, there remains a question mark as to whether Norway still merits the title The Norwegian Exception.

ACKNOWLEDGEMENTS

This book started as an idea to explain Norwegian society to a broader public. We want to thank Professor Torkel Brekke for suggesting Hurst Publishers. Thanks to this connection, we got acquainted with editor Michael Dwyer who encouraged us to go through with the idea.

We must also thank Fritt Ord and the director Knut Olav Åmås who gave us a grant for this project. Thanks to Hallvard Sandven who did the first editing and gave us valuable comments on the draft. We are also grateful to the excellent job that our editor at Hurst, Lara Weisweiller-Wu, has done. With her thorough comments and suggestions, this manuscript became much better.

Many people have written books that we have read, and they are listed in our bibliography.

We want to thank Professor of Economic History, Einar Lie, who gave us his draft for a book about the Norwegian Central Bank before it was published. We have both many colleagues and other projects that have been valuable to us, both at the University of Oslo and in the think tank Civita, too many to thank individually.

The work started before the COVID-19 pandemic, but thanks to Google Docs and Zoom, we have been able to proceed without too much difficulty. Thanks to both our families for support and

ACKNOWLEDGEMENTS

patience, and of course thanks to our dogs. We are both dog lovers, and they keep us company no matter how many lockdowns and COVID-19 restrictions.

NOTES

INTRODUCTION

1. All quotes are translated from Norwegian by the authors if not otherwise stated. The National Anthem, '*Ja vi elsker dette landet*', lyrics by Bjørnstierne Bjørnson, is translated from Wikipedia, available at https://en.wikipedia.org/wiki/Ja,_vi_elsker_dette_landet
2. 'Global Gender Gap Report 2020', World Economic Forum, 2020, available at http://www3.weforum.org/docs/WEF_GGGR_2020.pdf
3. 'Gender Inequality Index', United Nations Development Programme, 2020, available at http://hdr.undp.org/en/composite/GII
4. 'Social Environments for World Happiness', World Happiness Report, 20 March 2020, available at https://worldhappiness.report/ed/2020/social-environments-for-world-happiness/
5. 'Projected GDP Per Capita Ranking', Statistics Times, available at https://statisticstimes.com/economy/projected-world-gdp-capita-ranking.php
6. 'Findings and Insights', World Values Survey, available at https://www.worldvaluessurvey.org/WVSContents.jsp
7. 'Corruption Perceptions Index', Transparency International, 2020, available at https://www.transparency.org/en/cpi/2020/index/nzl
8. 'WJP Rule of Law Index 2020', World Justice Project, 2020, available at https://worldjusticeproject.org/our-work/research-and-data/wjp-rule-law-index-2020

9. Paul Stevens, Glada Lahn and Jaakko Kooroshy, 'The Resource Curse Revisited', Chatham House, 4 August 2015, available at https://www. chathamhouse.org/2015/08/resource-curse-revisited

1. THE 1814 EXPERIENCE

1. Claus Pavels, *Dagbøger* (entry dated 31 December 1814, p. 371), available at https://www.dokpro.uio.no/litteratur/pavels/frames.htm

2. CREATING A NATION

1. Quoted in Øystein Sørensen, *Kampen om Norges sjel, Norsk Idéhistorie* III, Oslo: Aschehoug, 2001, p. 142.
2. Quoted in Øystein Sørensen, 'Kampen om Norges sjel', 2001, p. 182.
3. Arne Garborg, *Den ny-norske Sprog- og Nationalitets-Bevægelse* (Kristiania: Cammermeyer, 1877), quoted in Øystein Sørensen, 'Kampen om Norges sjel', 2001, p. 349.

3. LIBERAL BUREAUCRACY, MODERN SOCIETY

1. Pål Thonstad, *Nasjonens velstand—Norsk økonomisk historie 1800–1940*, Bergen: Fagbokforlaget, 2018.
2. Jacob Aall, quoted in Francis Sejersted, *Demokratisk kapitalisme*, Oslo: Pax forlag, 2002.
3. Bredo Morgenstierne, 'Fattigondet og Socialismen', in *Statsøkonomisk Tidsskrift*, vol. 3, 1889.
4. The justification of the chair is written by Schweigaard, quoted in Mehlum, 'Samfunnsøkonomen Schweigaard', pp. 125–6. The quote is originally from Oskar Jaeger, *Socialøkonomien* in *Det Kongelige Fredriks Universitet 1811–1911*, Festskrift, Kristiania, 1911.
5. Johan Sverdrup in Stortingstidende 1869, quoted in Bergh and Hanisch, *Vitenskap og Politikk—Linjer i norsk sosialøkonomi gjennom 150 år*, Oslo: Aschehoug, 1984.
6. David Landes, interviewed by Francis Fukuyama, 'Wealth & Culture: What are the sources of economic success?', *The American Interest*,

1 September 2008, available at https://www.the-american-interest. com/2008/09/01/wealth-culture/ (accessed January 2011).

7. The two quotes from Anton M. Schweigaard are from Ola Mestad (ed.), *Anton Martin Schweigaard: professorpolitikeren*, Oslo: Akademisk publisering, 2009.

8. Einar Einarsen, *Gode og daarlige tider*, 1904, available at http://www. snl.no/.nbl_biografi/Einar_Einarsen/utdypning (accessed 29 July 2010).

9. This paragraph is greatly aided by the seminar at Vitenskapsakademiet in November 2019, and the numbers and statistics from Pål Thonstad, *Nasjonens velstand—Norsk økonomisk historie 1800–1940*, Bergen: Fagbokforlaget, 2018.

10. Quoted in Mathilde Fasting, *Torkel Aschehoug and Norwegian Historical Economic Thought*, London: Anthem Press, 2013.

11. Bo Stråth, 'The Normative Foundations of the Scandinavian Welfare States in Historical Perspective', in Nanna Kildal and Stein Kuhnle (eds.), *Normative Foundations of the Welfare State: The Nordic experience*, London: Routledge, 2005.

4. THE ROAD TOWARDS DEMOCRACY

1. Quoted in Carl Fougstad, *Det norske Storthing i 1833*, Kristiania: 1834, p. 9. Fougstad, a prominent civil servant, doesn't reveal the name of the commentator and clearly distances himself from the quoted view. See also Øystein Sørensen, *Anton Martin Schweigaards politiske tenkning*, Oslo: Historisk Institutt, Universitetet, 1986, p. 340.

5. THE 1905 MOMENT: HOW TO DISSOLVE A UNION
PEACEFULLY

1. A database containing the most relevant documents from 1905 is available at https://www.nb.no/baser/1905/dokumenter/database.php

2. Fridtjof Nansen, *Nansens røst vol 2: Artikler og taler 1897–1915*, Dybwad: Oslo, 1945, p. 349.

3. Bjørn Arne Steine, 'Folkeavstemningen om unionsoppløsning i 1905', Norgeshistorie, 25 November 2015, available at https://www.norgesh-

istorie.no/industrialisering-og-demokrati/1519-folkeavstemningen-om-unionsopplosning-1905.html

7. THE INTERWAR YEARS: AN EXPANDING POLITICAL SPECTRUM

1. All quotations from this debate are cited in Øystein Sørensen and Nik Brandal, *Det norske demokratiet og dets fiender 1918–2018*, Oslo: Dreyer, 2018, pp. 26–29.
2. Karl Kautsky, *Die Diktatur des Proletariats*, Vienna, 1918. An English version, *The Dictatorship of the Proletariat*, is available at https://www.marxists.org/archive/kautsky/1918/dictprole/index.htm
3. Quoted in Øystein Sørensen and Nik Brandal, 2018, p. 35.
4. Quoted in Carl Emil Vogt, *Fridtjof Nansen. Mannen og verden*, Oslo: Cappelen Damm, 2012, pp. 429–30.
5. Hans Fredrik Dahl, *Quisling: A Study in Treachery*, Cambridge: Cambridge University Press, 1999, p. 115.

8. THE WAR EXPERIENCE: 1940–45

1. "'Loven' og vi", *Fritt Folk*, 16 May 1940.
2. "'Loven" og vi', *Fritt Folk*, 16 May 1940.
3. Franklin D. Roosevelt, speech of 16 September 1942, available at 'Remarks on the Transfer of a Naval Vessel to Norway', The American Presidency Project, https://www.presidency.ucsb.edu/documents/remarks-the-transfer-naval-vessel-norway

9. THE POST-WAR DECADES: HEYDAY OF SOCIAL DEMOCRACY

1. Einar Lie, *Norsk økonomisk politikk etter 1905*, Oslo: Universitetsforlaget, 2012.
2. Contemporary History Forum (University of Oslo) FoSam interview with Ronald Bye, 28 November 2007, quoted in Mathilde Fasting, *Valgfrihet*, Oslo: Civita, 2013, also available at https://www.arkivverket.no/sok/_/attachment/inline/e833caf3-941f-43da-a753-7375d0f93bd8:

97d4e5db7ac02a7abd958f8cd2274784afd5c869/Intervju%20Ronald%20 Bye%2028.11.2007.pdf

3. Lange, Even, *Aschehougs Norgeshistorie: 1935–70: Samling om felles mål*, Oslo: Aschehoug, 2005.

4. Rune Slagstad, *De nasjonale strateger*, Oslo: Pax, 2001, p. 503

5. Wilhelm Keilhau, *Den norske pengehistorie*, Oslo: Aschehoug, 1952.

6. Rune Slagstad, 2001.

7. Fellesprogrammet, 'Arbeid for alle: De politiske partienes felles program', 1945.

8. Leif Arne Heløe, *Velferd på avveier?: Utviklingslinjer og dilemmaer i helse- og sosialpolitikken*, Oslo: Abstrakt forlag, 2010.

9. FoSam interview with Per Kleppe, 29 September 2005, available at https://www.arkivverket.no/sok/_/attachment/inline/f0143a0b-65fa-40a1-aa60-cd7e5ab00ad0:c20704d0a4ba6a0b5437c4437ca00d825bee8 46a/Per_Kleppe_intervju.pdf

10. THE NEW CONSENSUS OF THE 70s AND 80s

1. Nils August Andresen, 'Jakten på det norske', *Minerva* 4, 2013.

2. Gunnar Aakvaag, 'Frihet på norsk: den endimensjonale friheten', in Thomas Hylland Eriksen and Arne Johan Vetlesen (eds.), *Frihet*, Oslo: Universitetsforlaget, 2007.

3. Mathilde Fasting, *Valgfrihet*, Oslo: Civita, 2013.

4. Per Kristen Mydske, Dag Harald Claes and Amund Lie (eds.), *Nyliberalisme—ideer og politisk virkelighet*, Oslo: Universitetsforlaget, 2007.

5. Per Kristen Mydske, Dag Harald Claes and Amund Lie (eds.), 2007.

11. NORWAY AND THE WORLD: EUROPE AND OIL AT THE TURN OF THE MILLENNIUM

1. Paal J. Frisvold, *Mot Europa: Fortellingen om et nølende Norge*, Oslo: Origami dokumentar, 2014.

2. Jacques Delors, 'Statement on the broad lines of Commission policy', 17 January 1989, available at https://www.efta.int/media/publications/ efta-commemorative-publications/eea15.pdf

3. NOU no. 2, 2012, *Utenfor og innenfor: Norges avtaler med EU*, available at https://www.regjeringen.no/en/dokumenter/nou-2012–2/id669368/
4. Surveys from 2019 and 2020.
5. Einar Lie, *Norsk økonomisk politikk etter 1905*, Oslo: Universitetsforlaget, 2012.
6. Einar Lie, *Norges Bank 1816–2016*, Oxford: Oxford University Press, 2020.
7. Einar Lie, 2020, Chapter 14.

12. PEACEFUL COEXISTENCE OR POLARIZATION?
IMMIGRATION AND IDENTITY

1. Quoted in Øystein Sørensen, 'Ideologi og galskap—Anders Behring Breiviks totalitære mentalitet', in Øystein Sørensen, Bernt Hagtvet and Bjørn Arne Steine (eds.), *Høyreekstremisme. Ideer og bevegelser i Europa*, Oslo: Dreyer, 2012, pp. 24–25.
2. 'Number of Refugees to Europe Surges to Record 1.3 Million in 2015', Pew Research Center, 2 August 2016, available at https://www.pewresearch.org/global/2016/08/02/number-of-refugees-to-europe-surges-to-record-1-3-million-in-2015/

13. THE NORWEGIAN EXCEPTION?

1. Harald Eia and Ole-Martin Ihle, *Mysteriet Norge: Hvordan et fattigfolk i nord ble verdens rikeste, frieste og lykkeligste mennesker*, Oslo: Strawberry Publishing, 2020.
2. Nordisk Ministerråd, *Tillid—Det nordiske gull*, 15 June 2017, available at https://www.norden.org/da/publication/tillid-det-nordiske-guld
3. 'Norges viktigste næring', Regjeringen.no, available at https://www.regjeringen.no/no/tema/energi/olje-og-gass/verdiskaping/id2001331/ and 'Meld. St. 14 (2020–2021)', Regjeringen.no, available at https://www.regjeringen.no/no/dokumenter/meld.-st.-14–20202021/id2834218/?ch=3#kap3–5
4. Olav Korsnes, Marianne Nordli Hansen and Johs. Hjellbrekke (eds.) *Elite og klasse i et egalitært samfunn*, Oslo: Universitetsforlaget, 2014.

BIBLIOGRAPHY

Aakvaag, Gunnar, *Frihet: Et essay om å leve sitt eget liv*, Oslo: Universitetsforlaget, 2013.

Aarebrot, Frank and Kjetil Evjen, *Land, makt og følelser: Stats og nasjonsbygging*, Bergen: Fagbokforlaget, 2014.

Agøy, Nils Ivar, *Militæretaten og 'den indre fiende' fra 1905 til 1940: hemmelige sikkerhetsstyrker i Norge sett i et skandinavisk perspektiv*, Oslo: Universitetet i Oslo, 1994.

Akerhaug, Lars, *Norsk jihad: muslimske ekstremister blant oss*, Oslo: Kagge, 2013.

Amundsen, Kåre, *Norsk sosialøkonomisk historie 1814–1890*, Oslo: Universitetsforlaget, 1963.

Andenæs, Johs., *Det vanskelige oppgjøret*, Oslo: Universitetsforlaget, 1998.

Andresen, Nils August, 'Jakten på det norske', *Minerva* 4, 2013.

Bay, Ann-Helén, Aksel Hatland, Tale Hellevik and Charlotte Koren, *De norske trygdene. Framvekst, forvaltning og fordeling* (2nd edition), Oslo: Gyldendal Akademisk, 2010.

Bay, Ann-Helén, Axel West Pedersen and Jo Saglie (eds.), *Når velferd blir politikk*, Oslo: Abstrakt, 2009.

Berg Eriksen, Trond, Andreas Hompland and Eivind Tjønneland, 'Et lite land i Verden', *Norsk Idéhistorie* VI, Oslo: Aschehoug, 2003.

Berg Eriksen, Trond and Øystein Sørensen (eds.), 'Preface', *Norsk Idéhistorie*, 1, Oslo: Aschehoug, 2001.

Bergh, Trond, *LO's historie 1969–2009: Vol. III*, Oslo: Pax, 2009.

BIBLIOGRAPHY

Bergh, Trond and Tore J. Hanisch, *Vitenskap og Politikk—Linjer i norsk sosialøkonomi gjennom 150 år*, Oslo: Aschehoug, 1984.

Bergh, Trond et al., *Norge fra u-land til i-land: Vekst og utviklingslinjer, 1830–1980*, Oslo: Gyldendal, 2002.

Bergsgård, Arne, *Året 1814. Grunnlova*, Oslo: Aschehoug, 1942.

———, *Året 1814. Unionen*, Oslo: Aschehoug, 1945.

Bjørnson, Øyvind, *På klassekampens grunn (1900–1920), Arbeiderbevegelsens historie i Norge*, Oslo: Tiden norsk forlag, 1990.

Bondevik, Kjell Magne, *Et liv i spenning*, Oslo: Aschehoug, 2006.

Brandal, Nik., 'Ved utopiens slutt: Den vestlege maoismen', in Øystein Sørensen, Bernt Hagtvet and Nik. Brandal (eds.), *Venstreekstremisme*, Oslo: Dreyer, 2013.

Brandal, Nik., Øivind Bratberg and Dag Einar Thorsen, *The Nordic Model of Social Democracy*, Basingstoke: Palgrave MacMillan, 2013.

Brevig, Hans Olaf, *NS. Fra parti til sekt 1933–37*, Oslo: Pax, 1970.

Brevig, Hans Olaf and Ivo De Figueiredo, *Den norske fascismen: Nasjonal Samling 1933–1940*, Oslo: Pax, 2002.

Brundtland, Gro Harlem, *Mitt liv*, Oslo: Gyldendal, 1997.

Christiansen, Niels Finn et al, *The Nordic Model of Welfare: A Historical Reappraisal*, København: Museum Tusculanum Press, 2006.

Crepaz, Markus M. L., *Trust Beyond Borders: Immigration, the Welfare State, and Identity in Modern Societies*, Ann Arbor: The University of Michigan Press, 2008.

Dahl, Hans Fredrik, *Fra klassekamp til nasjonal samling: Arbeiderpartiet og det nasjonale spørsmål i 30-årene*, Oslo: Pax, 1969.

———, *Vidkun Quisling. En fører blir til*, Oslo: Aschehoug, 1991.

———, *Vidkun Quisling. En fører for fall*, Oslo: Aschehoug, 1992.

———, *Quisling: A Study in Treachery*, Cambridge: Cambridge University Press, 1999.

———, 'De store ideologienes tid', *Norsk Idéhistorie*, V, Oslo: Aschehoug, 2001.

Dahl, Hans Fredrik and Øystein Sørensen (eds.), *Et rettferdig oppgjør?: rettsoppgjøret i Norge etter 1945*, Oslo: Pax, 2004.

Danielsen, Rolf, *Høyres Historie: Borgerlig Oppdemmingspolitikk (1918–1940)*, Oslo: Cappelen, 1984.

BIBLIOGRAPHY

Doksheim, Marius and Kristin Clemet, *De nye seierherrene*, Oslo: Civita, 2012.

Dyrvik, Ståle and Ole Feldbæk, *Mellom brødre 1780–1830, Norges historie*, vol. 7, Oslo: Aschehoug, 1996.

Eia, Harald and Ole-Martin Ihle, *Mysteriet Norge: Hvordan et fattigfolk i nord ble verdens rikeste, frieste og lykkeligste mennesker*, Oslo: Strawberry Publishing, 2020.

Enstad, Nils Petter, *Sommeren som endret Norge*, Oslo: Civita, 2013.

Esping-Andersen, Gøsta, *The Three Worlds of Welfare Capitalism*, Princeton: Princeton University Press, 1990.

Falnes, Oscar, *National Romanticism in Norway*, New York: Columbia University Press, 1933.

Fasting, Mathilde, *Torkel Aschehoug and Norwegian Historical Economic Thought*, London: Anthem Press, 2013.

———, *Valgfrihet*, Oslo: Civita, 2013.

———, *Borgeren og fellesskapet*, Oslo: Civita, 2015.

Fasting, Mathilde, Marius Doksheim and Eirik Vatnøy, *Den norske velferden*, Oslo: Civita, 2011.

Frisvold, Paal J., *Mot Europa: Fortellingen om et nølende Norge*, Oslo: Origami dokumentar, 2014.

Frydenlund, Bård and Odd Arvid Storsveen (eds.), *Veivalg for Norden 1809–1813*, Oslo: Akadmika forlag, 2013.

Fuglum, Per, *Norge i støpeskjeen 1884–1919. Norges historie*, vol. 12, Oslo: Cappelen, 1978.

Fure, Eli (ed.), *Eidsvoll 1814. Hvordan Grunnloven ble til*, Oslo: Dreyer, 2013.

Gerhardsen, Einar, *Tillitsmannen: En håndbok for tillitsvalgte* (6th edition), Oslo: Tiden, 1931/1993.

———, *Tillitsmannen* (1st edition), Oslo: Arbeidernes Aktietrykkeri, 1938.

———, *Unge år: Erindringer fra århundreskiftet fram til 1940*, Oslo: Tiden, 1974.

Greve, Tim, *Fridtjof Nansen 1905–1930*, Oslo: Gyldendal, 1974.

Grimnes, Ole Kristian, *Norge under andre verdenskrig 1939–1945*, Oslo: Aschehoug, 2018.

BIBLIOGRAPHY

Grønlie, Tore, Rolf Danielsen et al., *Grunntrekk i norsk historie*, Oslo: Universitetsforlaget, 1991.

Grønlie, Tore and Yngve Flo, *Den nye staten: Tiden etter 1980*, Bergen: Fagbokforlaget, 2009.

Gunstad, Maria Flaten, *Rase og religion: Særtrekk ved Varg Vikernes' ideologi sammenlignet med den klassiske nazismen*, Oslo: Master thesis, Universitetet i Oslo, 2015.

Haave, Per, *Sterilisering av tatere 1934–1977. En historisk undersøkelse av lov og praksis*, Oslo: Norges forskningsråd, 2000.

Haffner, Vilhelm, *Stortinget og statsrådet 1915–1945*, Oslo: Aschehoug, 1949.

Hagemann, Gro, *Det moderne gjennombrudd 1870–1905. Norges historie*, vol. 9, Oslo: Aschehoug, 1997.

Halvorsen, Knut, *Velferd: Fra idé til politikk for et godt samfunn*, Oslo: Cappelen Damm, 2014.

Halvorsen, Terje, *NKP i krise: om 'oppgjøret med det annet sentrum' 1949–50*, Oslo: Gyldendal 1981.

———, *Mellom Moskva og Berlin: Norges kommunistiske parti under ikke-angrepspakten mellom Sovjet-Unionen og Tyskland 23. august 1929–22. juni 1941*, Oslo: Falken Forlag, 1996.

———, *Partiets salt: AUFs historie*, Oslo: Pax, 2003.

Hartveit, Karl Milton, *Djevelen Danser: Satanisme, Magi, Okkultisme*, Oslo: Gyldendal, 1993.

Hatland, Aksel, Stein Kuhnle and Tor Inge Romøren (eds.), *Den norske velferdsstaten* (3rd edition), Oslo: Gyldendal, 2003.

Haugland, Gine Marina, *Norske islamistiske grupperinger? En komparativ analyse av Islam Net og Profetens Ummah*, Oslo: Master thesis Universitetet i Oslo, 2016.

Hermansen, Tormod and Inger Marie Stigen, 'Ble det en bedre organisert stat?', *Norsk Administrativt Tidsskrift*, 3, 2013.

Hodne, Fritz, *Norges økonomiske historie 1815–1970*, Oslo: Cappelen, 1981.

Hodne, Fritz and Ola Honningdal Grytten, *Norsk økonomi i det 19. århundre*, Bergen: Fagbokforlaget, 2000.

———, *Norsk økonomi i det 20. århundre*, Bergen: Fagbokforlaget, 2000.

Hodne, Ørnulf, *Det nasjonale hos norske folklorister på 1800-tallet*, Oslo: NAVF, 1994.

BIBLIOGRAPHY

Jagland, Torbjørn, 'En fornyer av den sosialdemokratiske orden?', in Kristin Clemet and Harald Stanghelle (eds.), *Kåre Willoch: et debattskrift*, Oslo: Kagge, 2008.

Jensen, Peder, *Vitne til vanvidd*, Frederiksberg: Free Speech Library, 2015.

Johansen, Per Ole, 'Samfunnets pansrede neve', in *Statspoliti og overvåkning 1918–1941*, Oslo: Gyldendal, 1989.

Kautto, Mikko, 'The Nordic Countries', in Francis G. Castles et al., *The Oxford Handbook of the Welfare State*, Oxford: Oxford University Press, 2010.

Keilhau, Wilhelm, *Den norske pengehistorie*, Oslo: Aschehoug, 1952.

Kildal, Nanna and Stein Kuhnle (eds.), *Normative Foundations of the Welfare State: The Nordic experience*, London: Routledge, 2005.

Koht, Halvdan, *Johan Sverdrup*, vol. I–V, Kristiania: Aschehoug, 1918–25.

Kolmannskog, Haakon, *Ideologisk leiarskap i den norske ml-rørsla: det umogleges kunst 1965–1980*, Oslo: Master thesis Universitetet i Oslo, 2006.

Korsnes, Olav Marianne Nordli Hansen and Johs. Hjellbrekke (eds.), *Elite og klasse i et egalitært samfunn*, Oslo: Universitetsforlaget, 2014.

Kroglund, Nina Drolsum, *Hagelin: Quislings høyre hånd*, Oslo: Historie & kultur, 2016.

Kuhnle, Stein, 'Den skandinaviske velferdsmodellen?', in Anders Hovdum, Stein Kuhnle and Liv Stokke (eds.), *Visjoner om velferdssamfunnet*, Bergen: Alma Mater, 2000.

——, 'Den nordiske modellen', in Kristin Clemet and Harald Stanghelle (eds.), *Kåre Willoch: et debattskrift*, Oslo: Kagge, 2008.

Kuhnle, Stein and Liv Solheim, *Velferdsstaten: vekst og omstilling*, Oslo: Tano, 1991.

Kaartvedt, Alf et al., *Det norske Storting gjennom 150 år*, vol. 1, Oslo: Gyldendal, 1964.

——, *Kampen mot parlamentarisme 1880–1884*, Oslo: Universitetsforlaget, 1967.

——, *Høyres historie: Drømmen om borgerlig samling (1884–1918)*, Oslo: Cappelen, 1984.

Landes, David, *The Wealth and Poverty of Nations: Why Some Are So Rich and Some So Poor*, London: Abacus, 1998.

BIBLIOGRAPHY

Lange, Even, 'Samling om felles mål: 1935–70', in Aschehougs Norgeshistorie, 11, Oslo: Aschehoug, 2005.

Langslet, Lars Roar, *Konservatisme på norsk*, Oslo: Pax, 2011.

Larsen, Bård, *Idealistene*, Oslo: Civita, 2011.

Lie, Einar, *Norsk økonomisk politikk etter 1905*, Oslo: Universitetsforlaget, 2012.

————, *Norges Bank 1816–2016*, Oxford: Oxford University Press, 2020.

Lie, Einar, Egil Myklebust and Harald Norvik, *Staten som kapitalist: Rikdom og eierskap for det 21. århundre*, Oslo: Pax, 2014.

Lie, Einar and Hege Roll-Hansen, *Faktisk talt: Statistikkens historie i Norge*, Oslo: Universitetsforlaget, 2001.

Lie, Einar and Christian Venneslan, *Over evne: Finansdepartementet 1965–1992*, Oslo: Pax forlag, 2010.

Loock, Hans Dietrich, *Quisling, Rosenberg og Terboven: Den nasjonalsosialistiske revolusjon i Norge, dens forhistorie og forløp*, Oslo: Gyldendal, 1972.

Lorentzen, Håkon, *Fellesskapets fundament: Sivilsamfunnet og individualismen*, Oslo: Pax, 2004.

————, *Moraldannende kretsløp: Stat, samfunn og sivilt engasjement*, Oslo: Abstrakt/Civita, 2007.

Lorentzen, Håkon and Line Dugstad, *Den norske dugnaden: Historie, kultur og fellesskap*, Oslo: Høyskoleforlaget, 2011.

Lorenz, Einhart, *Det er ingen sak å få partiet lite. NKP 1923–1931*, Oslo: Pax forlag, 1983.

Lundestad, Geir, *America, Scandinavia and the Cold War 1945–49*, Oslo: Universitetsforlaget, 1980.

Lyng, John, *Brytningsår: Erindring 1923–1953*, Oslo: Cappelen, 1972.

Løvhaug, Johannes W., *Politikk som idékamp: Et intellektuelt gruppeportrett av Minerva-kretsen 1957–1972*, Oslo: Pax, 2007.

Maurseth, Per, *Fra Moskva-teser til Kristiania-forslag: Det norske Arbeiderparti og Komintern fra 1921 til februar 1923*, Oslo: Pax, 1972.

————, *Gjennom kriser til makt (1920–1935), Arbeiderbevegelsens historie i Norge*, vol. 3, Oslo: Tiden norsk forlag, 1987.

Mehlum, Halvor, 'Samfunnsøkonomen Schweigaard', in Ola Mestad (ed.), *Anton Martin Schweigaard: professorpolitikeren*, Oslo: Akademisk publisering, 2009.

BIBLIOGRAPHY

Mendelsohn, Oskar, *Jødenes historie i Norge*, vol. 1, Oslo: Universitetsforlaget, 1969.

————, *Jødenes historie i Norge*, vol. 2, Oslo: Universitetsforlaget, 1987.

Mestad, Ola (ed.), *Anton Martin Schweigaard: professorpolitikeren*, Oslo: Akademisk publisering, 2009.

Mestad, Ola and Dag Michaelsen (eds.), *Rett, nasjon, union*, Oslo: Universitetsforlaget, 2005.

Mjeldheim, Leiv, *Folkerørsla som vart parti*, Bergen: Universitetsforlaget, 1984.

Morgenstierne, Bredo, 'Fattigondet og Socialismen', in *Statsøkonomisk tidsskrift*, 1889.

Moynihan, Michael and Didrik Søderlind, *Lords of Chaos. The Bloody Rise of the Satanic Metal Underground*, Port Townshend: Feral House, 2003.

Mozaffari, Mehdi, *Islamisme. En orientalsk totalitarisme*, København: Informations Forlag, 2013.

Mydske, Per Kristen, Dag Harald Claes and Amund Lie (eds.), *Nyliberalisme—ideer og politisk virkelighet*, Oslo: Universitetsforlaget, 2007.

Myhre, Jan Eivind, *Norsk historie 1814–1905*, Oslo: Det norske samlaget, 2012.

Mykland, Knut, *Kampen om Norge 1784–1814. Norges historie*, vol. 9, Oslo: Cappelen, 1978.

Nerbøvik, Jostein, *Norsk historie 1860–1914*, Oslo: Det norske samlaget, 1999.

Nesser, Petter, *Islamist Terrorism in Europe*, London: Hurst Publishers, 2015.

Nissen, Bernt A., *Politikk for alle*, Oslo: J. W. Cappelens Forlag, 1949.

Nissen, Ingjald, *Psykopatenes diktatur*, Oslo: Aschehoug & Co, 1946.

Norland, Andreas, *Hårde tider. Fedrelandslaget i norsk politikk*, Oslo: Dreyer, 1973.

Notaker, Hallvard, *Høyres historie 1975–2001: Opprør og moderasjon*, Oslo: Universitetsforlaget, 2012.

Nøkleby, Berit, *Nyordning* (vol. 2) in *Norge i krig: Fremmedåk og frihetskamp 1940–45* (6th edition), Oslo: Aschehoug, 2007.

Ohman Nielsen, May–Brith, *Bondekamp og markedsmakt. Senterpartiets historie 1920–1959*, Oslo: Det norske Samlaget, 2001.

BIBLIOGRAPHY

Øisang, Ole, *Vi vil oss et land—arbeiderbevegelsen og det nasjonale spørsmål*, Oslo: Det norske arbeiderpartis forlag, 1937.

Olstad, Finn, *Einar Gerhardsen. En politisk biografi*, Oslo: Universitetsforlaget, 1999.

————, *Frihetens århundre. Norsk historie gjennom de siste hundre år*, Oslo: Pax, 2010.

Piketty, Thomas, *Capital in the Twenty-First Century*, Boston: Harvard University Press, 2013.

Preus, Lars, *Bakover mot det nye Norge: Ideologisk utvikling innen norsk nynazisme 1967–1985*, Oslo: Master thesis Universitetet i Oslo, 2014.

Ringdal, Nils Johan, *Gal mann til rett tid. NS-minister Sverre Riisnæs. En psykobiografi*, Oslo: Aschehoug, 1989.

Ringvej, Mona, *Marcus Thrane. Forbrytelse og straff*, Oslo: Pax, 2014.

Rogan, Bjarne (ed.), *Norge anno 1900. Kulturhistoriske glimt frå et århundreskifte*, Oslo: Pax, 1999.

Sandmo, Agnar, *Samfunnsøkonomi: En idéhistorie*, Oslo: Universitetsforlaget, 2006.

Sandvik, Pål Thonstad, *Nasjonens velstand—Norsk økonomisk historie 1800–1940*, Bergen: Fagbokforlaget, 2018.

Seip, Anne-Lise, *Om velferdsstatens fremvekst*, Oslo: Gyldendal, 1981.

————, *Sosialhjelpstaten blir til: norsk sosialpolitikk 1740–1920*, 2. ed. Oslo: Gyldendal, 1984.

————, *Veiene til Velferdsstaten: Norsk sosialpolitikk 1920–75*, Oslo: Gyldendal, 1994.

————, *Nasjonen bygges 1830–70. Norges historie vol. 8*, Oslo: Aschehoug, 1997.

Seip, Jens Arup, *Et regime foran undergangen*, Oslo: Gyldendal, 1965.

————, *Ole Jacob Broch og hans samtid*, Oslo: Gyldendal, 1971.

————, *Utsikt over Norges historie*, vol. 1, Oslo: Gyldendal, 1974.

————, *Utsikt over Norges historie*, vol. 2, Oslo: Gyldendal, 1981.

Seierstad, Åsne, *One of Us: The Story of Anders Breivik and the Massacre in Norway*, New York: Farrar, Straus and Giroux, 2015.

Sejersted, Francis, *Opposisjon og posisjon: Høyres historie 1945–1981*, Oslo: Pax, 2003, 1983.

————, *Demokrati og rettsstat*, Oslo: Pax, 2001.

BIBLIOGRAPHY

————, *Den vanskelige friheten*, Oslo: Pax forlag, 2001.

————, *Demokratisk kapitalisme*, Oslo: Pax forlag, 2002.

————, *Sosialdemokratiets tidsalder: Norge og Sverige i det 20. århundre*, Oslo: Pax forlag, 2005.

————, 'Frihetsrevolusjonen', *Nytt norsk tidsskrift*, 3, 2007.

Sjøli, Hans Petter, *Mao min Mao: Historien om AKPs vekst og fall*, Oslo: Cappelen, 2005.

Skirbekk, Gunnar, *Norsk og moderne*, Oslo: Res Publica, 2010.

Skirbekk, Helge and Harald Grimen, *Tillit i Norge*, Oslo: Res Publica, 2012.

Skodvin, Magne, *Striden om okkupasjonsstyret i Norge: Fram til 25. september 1940*, Oslo: Samlaget, 1956.

————, *Norsk historie 1940–1945*, Oslo: Samlaget, 1990.

Slagstad, Rune, *De nasjonale strateger*, Oslo: Pax, 2001.

Steen, Sverre, *Det frie Norge vol. I–V*, Oslo: Cappelen 1951–62.

Stenseth, Bodil, *En norsk elite. Nasjonsbyggerne på Lysaker 1890–1940*, Oslo: Aschehoug, 1993.

Storsveen, Odd Arvid, *Mig selv. En biografi om Henrik Wergeland*, Oslo: Cappelen, 2008.

Svendsen, Lars Fr. H., 'Helse, lykke og politikk', in *Minerva*, 2, 2008.

Sørensen, Øystein, *A. M. Schweigaards politiske tenkning*, Oslo: Universitetsforlaget, 1988.

————, *Hitler eller Quisling. Ideologiske brytninger i Nasjonal Samling 1940–45*, Oslo: Cappelen, 1989.

————, 'Liberalismens historie i Norge—noen hovedlinjer', in *Ideer om frihet* 1–2, 1991, available at http://www.ideeromfrihet.no/1991-7-sorensen.php

————, *Solkors og solidaritet: Høyreautoritær samfunnstenkning i Norge ca. 1930–1945*, Oslo: Cappelen, 1991.

————, *Nordic Paths to National Identity*, Oslo: NAVF, 1994.

————, *Bjørnstjerne Bjørnson og nasjonalismen*, Oslo: Cappelen, 1997.

————, *Kampen om Norges sjel, Norsk Idéhistorie*, III, Oslo: Aschehoug, 2001.

————, *Fra Marx til Quisling: Fem sosialisters vei til NS*, Oslo: Dreyer, 2012.

BIBLIOGRAPHY

———, 'Ideologi og galskap', in Øystein Sørensen, Bernt Hagtvet and Bjørn Arne Steine (eds.), *Høyreekstremisme. Ideer og bevegelser i Europa*, Oslo: Dreyer, 2012.

Sørensen, Øystein (ed.), *Jakten på det norske: Perspektiver på utviklingen av en norsk nasjonal identitet på 1800-tallet*, Oslo: Gyldendal, 2001.

Sørensen, Øystein and Nik. Brandal, *Det norske demokratiet og dets fiender 1918–2018*, Oslo: Dreyer, 2018.

Sørensen, Øystein and Torbjörn Nilsson (eds.), *1905—Nye perspektiver*, Oslo: Aschehoug, 2005.

Sørensen, Øystein and Bo Stråth (eds.), *The Cultural Construction of Norden*, Oslo: Universitetsforlaget, 1997.

Thonstad, Pål, Nasjonens velstand—Norsk økonomisk historie 1800–1940, Bergen: Fagbokforlaget, 2018.

Titlestad, Torgrim, *Peder Furubotn 1890–1938*, Oslo: Gyldendal, 1975.

Try, Hans, *To kulturer—en stat, Norges historie*, vol. 11, Oslo: Cappelen, 1979.

Tvedt, Terje (ed.), *(ml): en bok om maoismen i Norge*, Oslo: Ad Notam Gyldendal, 1989.

Vaale, Lars-Erik, *Dommen til døden: Dødsstraffen i Norge 1945–50*, Oslo: Pax, 2004.

Valaker, Tormod, *'Litt fascisme, Hr. Statsminister!'*, Oslo: Forum Aschehoug, 1999.

Vedung, Evert, *Unionsdebatten 1905*, Stockholm: Almqvist & Wiksell, 1971.

Vogt, Carl Emil, *Fridtjof Nansen. Mannen og verden*, Oslo: Cappelen Damm, 2012.

Willoch, Kåre, *Minner og meninger*, Oslo: Schibsted, 1988.

———, *Myter og virkelighet*, Oslo: Cappelen, 2002.

———, *Utfordringer*, Oslo: Cappelen, 2004.

———, *Erfaringer for fremtiden*, Oslo: Cappelen, 2010.

Witoszek, Nina, *The Origins of the 'Regime of Goodness': Remapping the Cultural History of Norway*, Oslo: Universitetsforlaget, 2011.

———, 'Fugitives from Utopia: The Scandinavian Enlightenment Reconsidered', in Øystein Sørensen and Bo Stråth (eds.), *The Cultural Construction of Norden*, Oslo: Scandinavian University Press, 1997.

BIBLIOGRAPHY

Wyller, Thomas Chr., *Nyordning og motstand: En framstilling og en analyse av organisasjonenes politiske funksjon under den tyske okkupasjonen 25.9.1940–25.9.1942*, Oslo: NAVF, 1958.

———, *Frigjøringspolitikk: Regjeringsskiftet sommeren 1945*, Oslo: Universitetsforlaget, 1963.

———, *Christian Michelsen: Politikeren*, Oslo: Dreyer, 1975.

INDEX

INDEX

INDEX

INDEX

INDEX

INDEX

INDEX

INDEX

INDEX

INDEX

INDEX